C0-CBU-081

How to Survive the E-Business Downturn

How to Survive the E-Business Downturn

COLIN BARROW

Cranfield School of Management

JOHN WILEY & SONS, LTD
Chichester • New York • Weinheim • Brisbane • Singapore • Toronto

658.84
B27h

Pubished in 2000 by
John Wiley & Sons Ltd,
Baffins Lane, Chichester,
West Sussex PO19 1UD, England

National 01243 779777
International (+44) 1243 779777
e-mail (for orders and customer service enquiries): cs-books@wiley.co.uk
Visit our Home Page on http://www.wiley.co.uk
or http://ww.wiley.com

Copyright © 2000 Colin Barrow

All Rights Reserved. No part of this publication may be reproduced, stored in a
retrieval system, or transmitted, in any form or by any means, electronic, mechanical,
photocopying, recording, scanning or otherwise, except under the terms of the
Copyright, Designs and Patents Act 1988 or under the terms of a licence issued by the
Copyright Licensing Agency, 90 Tottenham Court Road, London, W1P 9HE, UK,
without the permission in writing of the publisher or the copyright owner.

Colin Barrow has asserted his right under the Copyright, Designs and Patents Act
1988, to be identified as the author of this work.

UK

Other Wiley Editorial Offices

John Wiley & Sons, Inc., 605 Third Avenue,
New York, NY 10158-0012, USA

Wiley-VCH Verlag GmbH, Pappelallee 3,
D-69469 Weinheim, Germany

Jacaranda Wiley Ltd, 33 Park Road, Milton,
Queensland 4064, Australia

John Wiley & Sons (Asia) Pte Ltd, 2 Clementi Loop #02-01,
Jin Xing Distripark, Singapore 129809

John Wiley & Sons (Canada) Ltd, 22 Worcester Road,
Rexdale, Ontario M9W 1L1, Canada

British Library Cataloguing in Publication Data

A catalogue record for this book is available from the British Library

ISBN 0-471-49831-9

Typeset in 10 on 12pt Meridien by
Hewer Text Ltd, Edinburgh
Printed and bound in Great Britain by
Biddles Ltd, Guildford and King's Lynn

This book is printed on acid-free paper responsibly manufactured from sustainable
forestation, for which at least two trees are planted for each one used for paper
production.

Contents

University Libraries
Carnegie Mellon University
Pittsburgh, PA 15213-3890

Part V Abandon Ship

Introduction

This book does not debate or discuss the relevance of the Internet and the new economy, or whether or not it will dislodge the old economy. That debate seems rather superfluous. The Internet (or its replacement) is here to stay. The train and car replaced the horse as means of daily travel for the same reasons – cost and convenience. But mail order did not replace retail shops. They exist and compete together. The key question still to be answered is – will it make money.

While this book was being written, few Internet firms were making money and those that did were largely entrants from the old economy. Everyone in Internet-related businesses was expecting the great E-downturn. The National Association of Securities Dealers Automated Quotation (NASDAQ) system, a world barometer of E-virility, was swinging wildly up and down by double-digit percentages, an event on stockmarkets about as common as a total eclipse of the sun. Individual E-businesses have been experiencing extremely violent changes. In the first 2 months of the second quarter of 2000, Durlacher, the high-tech investment house, and QXL, the online auctioneer, had fallen in value by over 40%. There have been occasional shots of Viagra, usually in the form of yet another claim that the business world was in for a once-off re-rating, the economic cycle had finally been killed and growth was here forever, revived the ailing patient. But then, the fact that a significant proportion of the value of the world's stockmarkets comprised companies that had never made a buck, let alone paid a dividend, brought the whole E-edifice closer to the brink, yet again. Even the few Internet firms that were making serious money were experiencing vertigo. Cisco Systems, renowned as the being in the relatively secure business of selling jeans to the gold miners, rather than doing any panning themselves, saw their shares fall 27%, wiping $146 billion off the company's value. At its peak in March 2000, Cisco was trading at 213 times earnings for the previous 12 months, more than any company in Wall Street's history and 10–15 times the multiples a decent old-economy stock might expect.

As you can see from the chart below, Cisco would have to outgrow Microsoft's historic growth rate by a wide margin to be really worth its recent share price. The chances of that must be close to zero in a market that is maturing fast and overflowing with new entrants. To see how difficult it is to maintain profit growth in a mature market you only have to look at GE, a star of the 'old economy's' record. IBM's growth performance is a salutary reminder of what can happen to a great company if it stumbles.

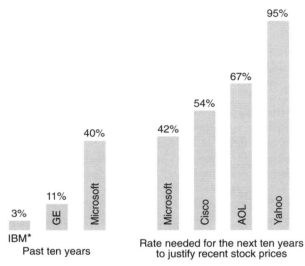

Figure 1 Compound growth in operating profits needed to justify recent share price (Source: Company records   *Over past four years IBM's compound growth has been 9%)

Whether or not that downturn has actually happened by the time you are reading this book is to some extent academic. If it hasn't yet, it surely will, in a few months or years. And if you are under 60, the chances are that you will see at least two downturns brought about by economic factors, and maybe even another burst of new technology growth brought about by the next printing press, steam engine, electricity, telephone, radio, television, bio-technology and, of course, the Internet.

What is much more likely is that you will experience a very personal E-downturn. The Internet billionaires you read about in the papers are rather less common than lottery winners. The

E-world is more volatile than the old world and failure is much more common than success.

So you are going to need the tools to keep your business on track in turbulent times, to revive it when things go wrong, and to help you see when and how to exit gracefully and perhaps even richly when harvest time arrives. But will the old old management tools be of much use in the new new economy? Are E-businesses really so different that those tools won't work?

However little you believe the 'new paradigm', there really are some big differences between Internet firms and other types of business.

Compressed Timescales

Timescales are usually compressed for E-businesses. In a few short years they go through all the stages of growth (and decline) that an old economy firm takes decades to experience. This can have the unpleasant side effects an overdose of growth hormones might have on a child. E-businesses may get bigger, but often they don't grow up.

Loads of Money

Money is another big difference. Internet firms get much more of it and they get it much more quickly than their old-economy counterparts. But just like anyone getting too much too soon, they run through it quickly and are back for more. 'Burn rate' has replaced 'overtrading' in the E-business vocabulary. The latter has long been viewed as a sign of imprudence in the old economy. The new word, however, has a ring of masculinity about it, although it is every bit as dangerous. Internet firms have another money difference from their more mundane old business siblings. Their value is based on multiples of whatever high number they can think of. Subscribers, site hits, sales and even cash consumption have been used as proxies for the price:earnings ratio used by more worldly firms. How long this will last is anyone's guess. Amazon.com, probably the bell-wether for this sector, in its fifth year of trading and something of an old man in the world of E-tailors, was still burning cash at a rate of millions a day, with profits still on some distant horizon. Although even they have recognized that one day they will have to make money for the people that have given them money. Their accounts are now cast to show that book sales, though now a modest part of their empire, are sort of making a profit. But the whole is still a less than zero sum game.

An Imperative to Grow

Old-economy companies might spend 3–5% of sales income on new technology each year. In Internet companies, the spend in this area will be several orders of magnitude greater. For these firms, website technologies do not remain stable as a percentage of sales, they vary massively. Servers, software licences and staff all have to upgrade to the next level of capacity at much more frequent intervals than in other firms. Schwab, a case explored later, shows just how big and fast this expenditure to keep up can be. And even then they had serious network failures, as they grew.

This high expenditure, relative to other costs, creates a series of step functions. eBay is a good example. Their cost of technology varied between 15% and 35% of sales up to 1999, and this is despite the sharp fall in cost of some areas of computer hardware that seems to be ongoing in the industry (to put this in context, Amazon.com, as we shall see later, spent $61 million out of revenues of $401 million on 'technology and content' in the fourth quarter of 1999, which equates to 15%).

The pattern of expenditure in Internet companies is similar to that in any capital-intensive business, but the amplitude is more violent. Typically, the technology infrastructure of Internet companies will always be upgraded to take account of anticipated demand. This creates a temporary excess capacity, so the company has to scramble for more customers and more products and services to sell to them. This pushes up marketing costs. eBay spent 13% of net revenues in the first quarter of 2000 on product development against just 5.1% in the same period in 1999. Marketing, product development and technology costs spiral upward together. This pattern of costs will generate losses in the short run, and perhaps even periodically in the long run, when particularly high bursts of expenditure on new technology are called for. These spurts can also be triggered by a flood of new market entrants with better technology than the people who set up last year. As with any business with high fixed costs, the pressure to grow sales to cover fixed costs is enormous. If you add that pressure to the natural demands of the stockmarket for growth at almost any cost, you end up with a highly volatile cocktail.

The whole edifice can only be supported by growth in sales. The game is a bit like playing pontoon for ever higher stakes. If you don't raise your bid, you can't stay in the game, and if you get seen now, the picture may not look great.

Claims that the Internet really only supports very large or very small companies bring little that is new to the debate. Life has always been tough for mid-sized companies, whatever their sector. But add stockmarket finance to the equation and you most surely bring to bear a factor that is notoriously unforgiving of slow growth or, worse still, of decline.

But it's Not That Different

But after these differences, there is much about the Internet firm that looks very much the same as every other firm. All businesses have some similar elements. Someone sells and someone buys. The deal is not consummated until the goods change hands and the cash clears. E-businesses have had rather more problems with these areas of business than have old-economy firms. Despite re-branding 'delivery' and calling it by new-economy-sounding names, such as 'logistics' and 'fulfilment', companies such as E-Toys greeted the new millennium with the same old problem. They failed to deliver thousands of toys in time for a critical, and not to be repeated that year, date. However, there is a fair chance that as long as their managers confine their reading to the more arcane computer press, that won't worry them, because just like old-economy companies did for years, (although less so now) they don't listen to their customers anyway. A recent survey on the state of the Internet in Europe revealed that 14% of companies selling on the Web take more than 5 days to reply to their customer's e-mails and 30% never reply.

Fraud is as prevalent in Internet payment systems as it is everywhere else, maybe more so. And whole sections of the E-economy are being held to ransom by old-style bandits, overcharging and monopolizing the supply of key raw materials. Telephone charges and browsers are just the most obvious examples.

Mismanagement

E-management teams are generally younger, and indeed, there generally are management teams, which is a fairly rare event for start-up firms. But the myth, started by Apple's founder, Steve Jobs, that great people don't need managing, is beguiling but ill-conceived. Just because people in E-businesses are often better educated, share a common language (Web talk) and want the same thing – lots of money quickly – it doesn't follow that they will do what you want, when you want and in the way you want. E-staff need leading, managing and motivating just as all staff do. But many Internet firms are founded and led by people with little or no experience of managing anything, yet alone a business that takes on board several hundred employees within 2 years of starting up. Money is often used as a substitute for management in the misguided belief that a common greed is sufficient to achieve a commonality of purpose. But as a motivator, money has the shortest shelf-life of all and perhaps the least predictable of outcomes. Employees can pursue the same elusive goal of personal wealth by moving to another firm. E-workers are just as disloyal, disorganized and disgruntled as anyone else's workers can be, and perhaps even more so. Although many cash-strapped Internet firms may find it hard to believe, their fundamental problems lie elsewhere. More usually, it's the management processes that are flawed.

Doubtful Business Models

There are some common elements to many of the larger Internet business and to some extent to them all. Being first to market, building a brand, and a global one at that, and buying up companies along the way to accelerate the growth process, all feature high in the strategic purpose of E-businesses.

Gaining 'first mover advantage' are words used like a mantra to justify high expenditure and headlong expansion. This principle is one of the most enduring in business theory and practice. Entrepreneurs and established giants are always in a race to be first. Research from the 1980s shows that market pioneers have enduring advantages in distribution, product-line breadth, product quality and, especially, that market share underscores this principle.

It's the centrepiece of battles such as those being waged between Amazon and Barnes & Noble. Beguiling though the theory of first mover advantage is, it is probably wrong. A thorough review of the research studies that supported this theory was published in the *Sloan Management Review* (1996), and the findings were found to be flawed (the authors of this paper also drew on many other studies which lent support to their views). Amongst the many errors in the earlier research, the authors of the *Sloan* paper revealed that the questions used to gather much of the data were at best ambiguous, and perhaps dangerously so. For example, the phrase 'one of the pioneers in first developing such products or services' was used as a proxy for 'first to market'. In fact, the only compelling evidence from all the research was that nearly half of all firms pursuing a first-to-market strategy were fated to fail, whilst those following fairly close behind were three times as likely to succeed.

The next strand in the Internet growth strategy is aggressive acquisition. It is the cornerstone of the strategy of Cisco and a host of other E-business firms. Cisco's top management claims such expertise in the acquisition process as to have a steady stream of management consultants visiting them to learn how it should be done.

But once again the jury is out on acquisition strategy as a route to creating shareholder value. A review of the literature by the author 2 years ago (see Table I.1) does not support the view that growth by acquisition is a winning strategy for anyone other than the share-holders of the company being acquired. On average they make a positive gain, whilst the buyers mostly lose value. The drivers of acquisitions are the desire for growth by investment analysts, the chance to make millions in fees, whatever the outcome, by corporate finance departments, and the egos of CEOs in acquiring firms, who see the acquisition process as a proxy for gladiatorial combat.

There is evidence that some conditions are more favourable than others for the creation of shareholder value via a strategy involving acquisitions. For example, cash deals, cross-border acquisitions and deals where either the management of the company being acquired own few shares, or there are few outside directors, all bode well for the creation of shareholder value for the acquirer. Deals in which the size disparity is too great, or the move away from the corporate culture is too great, are less likely to deliver extra value.

Few E-business acquisitions meet many of these conditions. Whilst investors are content to value Internet firms on multiples of sales rather than profits, any acquisition will be seen as beneficial. But when sanity returns and profit again becomes the measure of economic worth, most of these 'growth by acquisition' strategies will be unmasked and found to have been extravagant failures. For a detailed analysis of the doubtful value of growth by acquisition strategies, see Barrow (1998a)

The third strand pursued by many Internet firms is the desire to build a brand, usually a global brand, and so accrue to themselves the advantages of price premium and customer loyalty. But creating a brand is not easily done overnight, neither can it be done without

Research	Create value	Do not create much or any value
Hogarty (1970)		✓
Halpern (1973)	✓	
Mendelker (1974)	✓	
Dodd and Ruback (1978)		✓
Firth (1979, 1980)		✓
Asquith et al. (1983)		✓
Eberling and Doorley (1983)	✓	
Halpern (1983)	✓	
Jensen and Ruback (1983)	✓	
Lubatkin (1983)	✓	
Malatesta (1983)		✓
Roll (1986)		✓
Porter (1987)		✓
Weidenbaum and Vogt (1987, 1988)		✓
Bradley et al. (1988)		✓
Alberts and Varaiya (1989)		✓
Franks and Harris (1989)		✓
Jarrell and Poulsen (1989)		✓
Ravenscraft and Scherer (1989)		✓
Carper (1990)		✓
Loderer and Martin (1990)		✓
Pettway et al. (1990)		✓
Datta, Pinches and Narayanan (1992)		✓
Gregory and Westheider (1992)		✓
Gould, Campbell and Alexander (1994)		✓
Anslinger and Copeland (1996)	✓	
Cotter, Shivdasani and Zenner (1997)	✓	
Gibbs (1997)	✓	

Table I.1 Do mergers and acquisitions create *extra* value for the acquiring company's shareholders?

a clear understanding of both the market segment being served and the image to be created. Simply spending large sums of money or having hundreds of thousands of subscribers does not constitute a brand. The benefits conferred on teenagers drinking 'the real thing' rather than a substitute product, such as Virgin Cola, are crystal clear to members of that age group, as Virgin's sales figures clearly demonstrate. How the Amazon brand is supposed to operate is far from clear. Once a book or CD reaches the end user, its 'consumption' is invisible to the outside world. And Lastminute. com's proposition seems the antithesis of a true brand, where people are being invited to buy cheap(er) services, such as hotel rooms and holidays that are surplus to the provider's level of demand. It's hard to see how consumers will feel in any way 'special' using such a service, which in any event is also invisible.

This is not to say that Internet firms can't create brands, successfully acquire other companies, enter new markets, launch new products and services successfully and become profitable. However, to achieve these results requires the use of conventional management and control processes, quickly. There is evidence that shareholder patience is wearing thin waiting for profits to arrive, rather than world domination.

To use a Darwinian expression, 'we forget that though food may be now superabundant, it is not so at all seasons of each recurring year'. Venture capital providers who have stumped up much of the 'food' for the E-economy have done so in the expectation of a benevolent initial public offering (IPO) market allowing them a quick exit from their investments, even before profits have been generated. American Venture Capitalists (VCs) average returns of 147% in 1999, compared with a long-run average over the preceding decade of around 20%, are entirely dependent on the public's unlimited capacity to absorb unprofitable IPOs. Once this stops, the food chain is broken and business-as-usual conditions return. Business-as-usual means Internet firms will have to place a premium on sound business and marketing strategy, good management, reliable business controls and making returns on investment, rather than on over-sophisticated technology and an unrestricted flow of cash to finance overruns and extravagant mistakes.

This book shows how you can use proven management tools and concepts, adapted in ways that best suit E-businesses. The tools are brought into sharp focus by using some 40 case studies and numerous examples showing how Internet firms have overcome problems, reversed decline and prospered. These are techniques that you can easily use yourself. Not even batteries are needed here.

The case studies cover some industry classics, IBM, Amazon.com, Cisco, Netscape and Schwab included. Some newcomers such as eBay, E*Trade and Lastminute.com are also covered, as are others, such as PeaPod (USA), Boo.com (UK), Spray (Sweden) and Monex (Japan) to cover the three continents dominated by Internet fever. Over 100 Internet and new economy firms have been drawn on to show processes in action. Some of the case examples are longer, and whilst they can and do serve to illustrate many aspect of managing a business, they are positioned in the text close to the topic concerned.

The book contains numerous action plans and self-evaluation checklists to help you apply the processes to your business and so move forward quickly and with confidence to achieve profitable growth.

Part I

One Step Forward, Two Steps Back

Left to chance alone, ventures follow only one natural law – the law of gravity. Gravity comes in many forms – economic downturns, technological change or just plain mismanagement.

Developing a sound strategy and keeping it constantly under review is the only way a business can consistently defy gravity. The single most important reason why over half of all new Internet firms, including those who have IPO'd, won't see their fifth birthday is that they never learn that lesson.

So how can you get out of the 'serendipity cycle' that sweeps new firms in and out like a particularly vicious tide? Well, a snazzy business model with a well-blurred title, such as 'Solution Branding', 'Dynamic Pricing', 'Value Bundling' or 'Cybermediation', may play a much smaller part in your survival plan than you think.

Like all firms, E-businesses go through distinctive phases during which changes in strategy and structure that have to be gone through if the business is going to arrest decline and move on to the next stage of growth. Management processes and systems that work well at one stage may be fairly useless later on.

The business needs a clear mission, vision, objectives and a business plan. No rocket science in that. A survey of 475 global firms published by Bain, the US management consultants, confirmed that 74% had mission and vision statements (even more in the USA), and used the process to revitalize and direct growth.

But what is distinctive about Internet firms is that things happen faster in the E-economy and the margin for error is small. So the guiding principles need to be clear to all key players in the firm, so that the friction caused in moving from one stage of growth to another is not so great as to burn the organization up.

E-crisis Management 1

All business growth and development calls for change. The problem for business is that change is not always incremental. Children do not grow seamlessly from being babies to adulthood. They pass through phases: infancy, adolescence, teenage and so on. Businesses also move through phases if they are to grow successfully. Each of these phases is punctuated by a 'crisis', a word that derives from the Chinese and translates loosely as 'dangerous opportunity'. Researchers such as Greiner (1972) and Churchill and Lewis (1983) have identified each distinctive phase in a firm's growth pattern, and provided an insight into the changes in organizational structure, strategy and behaviour that are needed to move successfully onto the next phase of growth (Figure 1.1). The ability to recognize the phases of growth and to manage the transition through them successfully is probably the single most important task of the business founder.

Typically, a business starts out by taking on any customers it can get, operating informally with little management and few controls. The founder, who usually provides all the ideas, all the drive, makes all the decisions and signs the cheques, becomes overloaded with administrative detail and operational problems. Unless the founder can change the organizational structure, any further growth will leave the business more vulnerable. The crises of leadership, autonomy and control loom large.

Over time, the successful owner-manager tackles these crises: finds a clear focus, builds a first-class team, delegates key tasks, appraises performance, institutes control and reporting systems and ensures that progress towards objectives is monitored and rewarded. The firm itself consistently delivers good results. Another Microsoft or Cisco Systems has been born.

There is no set time that each of these growth phases should last. An old economy company may take anything from 3 to 10 years to pass through each phase. IBM, for example, took over 70 years to hit the buffers of Phase 4 growth. But for new economies, the luxury of this marathon approach has been supplanted by a series of stressful sprints.

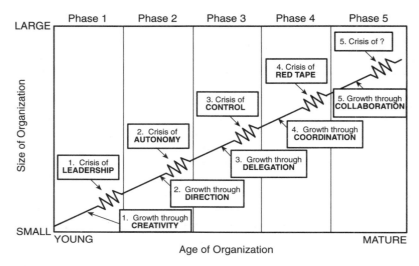

Figure 1.1 The organizational phases of growth. Reproduced with permission from Greiner (1972)

Each phase of growth calls for a different approach to managing the business. Sometimes strong leadership is required, at others a more consultative approach is appropriate. Some phases call for more systems and procedures, some for more cooperation between staff. Unfortunately, most founders try to run their business in much the same way, as it gets bigger, as they did when it was small. They end up with a big small company, rather than the small big company that is required if successful growth is to be achieved. They believe the problems of growth can be solved by taking on another salesperson, a few hundred square metres of space or another large shot of venture capital. This approach is rather like suggesting that the transition from infancy to adulthood could be accomplished by nothing more significant than providing larger clothes. For larger clothes substitute faster burn rate, and you could easily be forgiven for thinking that the only thing that prevents an Internet business realizing its potential is cash. That's certainly the view taken by many Internet prima donnas.

Let us now look more closely at each of these five phases, and see how some E-business founders have fared in approaching their crises.

Phase 1. Growth through Creativity

Any business starting up does so because somebody (you!) has a good idea about providing a product or service for which they believe there is demand. If the idea is successful, then the business can grow or evolve with equal success. The founder of the company is at the heart of everything. The emphasis is on informal systems, perhaps even no systems at all. Anything that generates sales, perhaps even of things the firm is not particularly good at or even set out to do, is considered a great idea. One Internet company that exhibited some of the symptoms of doing too much of too many things too soon is Boo.com. Their backers, including Bernard Arnault of LVMH, the luxury goods group, and Goldman Sachs, were reported to be keen to minimize losses from the £80 million of start-up finance they gave Boo's two founders, and less than enthusiastic about coming in for another financing round until the direction was more clear.

Boo.com

Founded in 1999 by a trio of Swedish entrepreneurs, Ernst Malmsten, Kajsa Leander and Patrik Hedelin, Boo.com was the first truly global Internet retailer of fashion and sportswear, or rather *it* wanted to be.

Described by *Elle* magazine as the 'literary rock stars of Europe', Kajsa and Ernst went into partnership in the early 1990s, orchestrating a series of cultural projects initially in their native Sweden and later around the world. In 1996 they set up Leander Malmsten, a publishing house with the specific aim of introducing up-and-coming authors to the Swedish market. With signature dust jackets and an innovative stable of authors, Leander Malmsten soon built up a reputation as Scandinavia's premium publishing boutique.

Following this early success, in August 1997 Kajsa and Ernst set up the Internet bookstore bokus.com. A phenomenal hit, bokus.com exceeded all expectations, rapidly becoming the world's third largest on-line bookstore after Amazon and Barnes & Noble. In February 1996, Patrik Hedelin was retained as financial advisor to bokus.com. Shortly thereafter, Patrik negotiated the sale of the company to Swedish Cooperative KF, one of the largest retail and media companies in Scandinavia.

It was at this point that Boo.com was born. The vision was clear. In the words of one of Boo's founders, to become the world's leading on-line retailer of fashion and sportswear. The vehicle – a cutting edge website and a team of dynamic individuals, handpicked from the worlds of fashion, new media, marketing, business, technology and finance. The outcome – an awesome virtual shopping experience that we believe surpasses anything that currently exists on the Web. The retail site is complimented by *boom*, an interactive on-line magazine that brings together street life, fashion, sport, art and technology from around the world.

Within hardly a year of starting up, Boo had to acknowledge they had bitten off rather more than they could chew. One in five of the workforce had lost their jobs by May 2000. The Boo management team had to admit they had made mistakes. 'We have always been very ambitious and wanted to do everything in one go. We have been over-optimistic in some areas'.

Boo sought to become a global brand right from the start, launching simultaneously across Europe and the USA. They also wanted to create one of the more sophisticated Internet sites. Although Boo had attained considerable recognition, it was not always for the right reasons. The launch of their website was delayed by 6 months, costs overran and the main sportswear makers were reluctant to come on board.

Ernst Malmsten, Chief Executive, and Kajsa Leander, the Co-founder and former fashion model, took to the platform at a First Tuesday event in April 2000. Mr Malmsten said he would start with 'the hot issue' right away. He said, 'Boo has never revealed any financial information and has been seen as very secretive. This has fuelled speculation about targets, burn rate and our valuation'. To scotch some of this speculation, Mr Malmsten pulled a piece of folded paper from his pocket. Reading from a 'Post it note', he read out Boo.com's sales figures from Monday. They revealed that the gross order value of goods sold that day, net of the new 40% discount, was $83 063 (£50 648). These came from 1078 orders. Visitors viewing the site amounted to 36 381. The conversion rate was 2.96%.

In spite of this attempt at transparency, during the questioning – or the 'interactive mode', as the First Tuesday host dubbed it – one person asked whether the figure was representative of Boo's underlying sales. The numbers were stuck during the first week of Boo's sale – a period when revenues would be expected to be significantly higher than during normal trading. Boo did not comment. The figures were the first they had published since the company was set up. The company has never confirmed how much investment it has attracted from investors, which include Bernard Arnault, chairman of LVMH, the luxury goods group, and Goldman Sachs.

Boo also took the opportunity to fend off criticism about job cuts and management changes. *'We made internal reorganizations like any company does. To say it is the end of the industry is crazy', said Ms Leander. 'In a maturing business, this is natural'.*

Even the slimmed-down workforce is regarded as extremely high for an Internet start-up. For example, finance director Dean Hawkins quit to join Dutch broadband firm Chello just a few weeks after joining from Adidas. His predecessor and one of Boo's founders, Patrick Hedelin, has returned to Sweden and no longer played an active role in the company.

Others in the sportswear world claim the Boo team underestimated the industry expertise they needed. They were projecting very aggressive return rates for goods of 10%, when the mail order average is nearer 30% for sportswear and footwear.

Internet watchers said that, even scaled 'down' to 400 people, they were way too big. QXL, the pan-European auction house, only has 120 employees. The burn rate on these staffing levels, with rent ad site development on top, could exceed $6 million a month.

In May 2000, Boo's backers finally pulled the plug on an expensive £80 million mistake. Despite backers with sector experience, such as Benetton,

the company had only a vision and no strategy or real idea how that should
be implemented.

For those companies who do not make it through to the next
phase of growth, a cycle of one step forward and two steps back will
probably begin, or else a gentle decline will set in. The end of this
first growth phase is signalled by a *crisis of leadership*. Many old-
economy businesses can linger long at this stage, but E-economy
firms are snuffed out when the next round of cash is not forth-
coming. As one industry watcher said at the time, of Boo's prospects,
'Lots of turtles are hatched, but not many make it to the water'.
Unlike Boo, most Internet early failures are silent affairs, as the case
below illustrates.

Violet.com

Violet.com, an online retailer with a hip boutique-style website, was nothing if
not low-key when it announced in late April 2000 that it was shutting down.
On 26 April, the company told customers it was cutting off access to its on-
line catalogue: 'Though we are closing our doors, we hope you'll continue to
seek out unique and interesting items that bring inspiration to the things you
do every day.'

The San Francisco-based company said that orders submitted before the
previous afternoon would be filled, but nothing later. Executives didn't
respond to calls or e-mails enquiring about the cause of the shutdown. As
closures go, it was about as quiet as it gets. Which, in the usually publicity-
hungry dot-com industry, is often the way companies like to handle their
unsuccessful experiments.

'They either get combined into some company, or change their name, or
just slip into the night', according to Kirk Walden, Director of Venture Capital
Research at Price Waterhouse Coopers. Although Internet companies make
every effort possible to draw attention when they're starting out, shutting
down is another matter. As a result, Walden claims, there is a dearth of
statistics demonstrating exactly how many promising Internet start-ups aren't
making it to maturity. Furthermore, there is little incentive on the part of the
venture community or start-ups themselves to draw a lot of attention when
things go awry. Even though venture capitalists recognize that only a small
percentage of their investments are going to be home runs, identifying the
ones that went completely belly-up is a tough thing to get people to admit
to.

The silence surrounding start-up failures is so pervasive that one Internet
entrepreneur has devoted a website to building a community where veterans
of failed ventures can congregate for community and support. 'In the
business community, we tend to sweep those things under the rug', said
Nicholas Hall, founder of a site called *Startupfailure.com*. After all, Hall says,
most entrepreneurial ventures don't make it anyway. Of the small minority of
companies that actually secure venture funding, he said, 60% go bankrupt.
In addition, 40% of new businesses fail within the first 5 years of operation.

Phase 2.   Growth through Direction

A strong leader is required to pull the company through the crisis that follows the first phase of growth, a leader who is able to make tough decisions about priorities and provide the clear, single-minded direction and sense of purpose needed to move the business forward. The 'anything-goes-as-long-as-it-gets-sales' mentality needs to be replaced by a top-down, strongly directional and impersonal style of management. Costs centres, budgets, salary systems and efficient recruitment systems need to be put in place.

Now, ideas the pioneer founder used to carry in his head have to be formalized. Policies need to be evolved, teams built up and key people appointed, with specific roles to play and objectives to achieve. The personal management style of the founder becomes secondary to making the business efficient.

Games Workshop

Shares in Games Workshop fell 13% after the maker of fantasy games and figures said that restructuring costs over the next 2 years would be about £5 million. The company, which is both manufacturer and retailer, said it wanted to streamline its operations to tackle mismatches between sales and production. It said stronger central coordination was needed. The shares lost 62½ p to 470 p.

Games Workshop's sales units in each in each country are largely autonomous when it comes to ordering stock, forecasting demand and establishing spending commitments. 'We need to simplify our organization and simplify the supply chain,' said Chris Prentice, Chief Executive. He said that many changes were an acceleration of programmes already under way; 'It's become more urgent and the structural inadequacies had started to inhibit our sales growth'. Jeremy Hilditch, an analyst at Williams de Broë, said: 'When it was floated it was a very entrepreneurial, hands-on management operation. As it's grown and got into more overseas markets, they've found they have not had the depth or breadth of management to handle the transition to the larger company.' Pre-tax profits in the 6 months to November 28 were down 27% at £3.8 million (£5.21 million) after £1.86 million of restructuring costs; turnover was £39.1 million (£35.5 million) (preceding year's figures in brackets).

For Games Workshop, it was unfortunate that changes already under way had to come to a head so rapidly, requiring more radical measures. The company claims that the changes will deliver annualized benefits to operating profits of £2–2.5 million at the end of the second year. But this depends on whether senior management can nurture an expanding business. More experienced staff from outside are long-needed and hopefully the restructuring will completely transform a company that has in the past been guided by enthusiasm for the product into one guided by business acumen. On the plus side, on-line sales more than doubled in the period.

This heavy emphasis on management is often ill-suited to the easy style of the E-entrepreneur, and he or she has to make way for imported top management. This was the case with Benjamin Cohen, founder of Logic Works, a New Jersey software house. Cohen built the company in just 4 years into a $40 million success story, and the company was even named one of *Business Week*'s top growth companies, with Cohen's picture on the front cover. After getting off to a hot start in year four, the company found itself in trouble. Costs soared way beyond revenues and the company looked like stalling. Whilst a brilliant technician, Cohen guessed he was not the person to move the business forward. Gregory Peters, the CFO, became acting CEO and Cohen became chairman with no day-to-day responsibilities. Logic Works had grown so much, so quickly, that it outgrew its founder.

Lastminute.com, whose share price collapsed by 60% within a month of their IPO, found themselves in a similar situation. They had to introduce a new tier of senior management to run the day-to-day business almost immediately, after their float, to steady the nerves of their investors if for nothing else.

Often, the skills needed to create a company in a basement just aren't the same as those needed to build it into an industry giant.

The end of Phase 2 is signalled by discontent from management team at heavy-handed leadership.

Phase 3. Growth through Delegation

Eventually, as the company grows and matures, this directive top-down management style starts to become counter-productive. Others working in the organization acquire more expertise about their particular sphere of operations than the boss. Not surprisingly, they want a greater say in the strategy of the business. Such subordinates either struggle for power so that they can be heard, or become demotivated and leave.

E-businesses can be particularly vulnerable at this stage, if too much pressure is put on them from outside investors who have finally lost patience. The company's founder will need to be ready, not only for another change in style him- or herself, but perhaps also to help the company's financiers see that what appears like a retrograde step, in giving managers freedom to act, is necessary if the company is to move forward, not lose key staff and perhaps gain a new competitor as well. This is the *crisis of autonomy*, and if it is not recognized and managed, it will absorb so much energy and time that it will drag the company down.

The solution to the crisis of autonomy is to recognize that more responsibility has to be delegated to more people in the company. The trouble is that most founders hang on to too many jobs in their firms, mostly out of a belief that nobody else can do the job as well as them. The reasons for this argument are legion and include the often-expressed: 'It takes more time to explain the job than to do it myself'; 'A mistake would be too costly'; 'They lack the experience'; and so on. There is probably an element of truth in all of these arguments, but until you learn how to *delegate decisions* rather than simply *dumping tasks*, your organization will never reach full maturity.

Whittman Hart Inc.

Whittman Hart Inc., an information technology (IT) consulting company in Chicago, had for the past 7 years grown revenues at a more than 40% annual rate. But it was the next year's projections of $120 million that scared Whittman executives. 'Growth companies tend to lack foresight', says Stan Martin, Senior Partner and Vice President of Marketing and Business Development at Whittman. 'We didn't want to be like that as we got bigger and became a $100 million company'.

So Whittman decided to implement processes of communication and strategy. The goal: to standardize the way the company goes to market, services customers and communicates internally. 'We're no longer a 400-person company (it now has 1400 employees),' Martin says, 'So we need to ensure that there are formal procedures in place. That's the only way we can continue to grow'.

The company also strengthened its management team, and gave managers responsibility for developing their own plans and objectives. Now strategy meetings were scheduled once a week so reps could plan out their sales approaches with their managers and each other. The objective was two-fold: give salespeople a strategy to call on customers, and improve communication internally. As for the planning aspect, salespeople quickly noticed a positive effect. 'We used to just try and sell as much as possible, without doing any market planning', says one Whittman sales rep. 'It was difficult when we were with big clients and we hadn't come up with a strategy for the call. Now we come to customers much more prepared because we've actually taken the time to map out a plan. Also, clients appreciate it more, and it makes our work more interesting and challenging'.

Martin believes the most important aspect of his new process is that salespeople don't sell alone. Whittman has 50 salespeople and 400 other employees who are involved in business development, meaning they touch the customer at some point. They're part of the sales process. Salespeople used to approach clients on their own, informing prospects about services the company provides. Now they can take people from departments such as research, technology or marketing on sales calls with them.

The process put Whittman on pace to hit its aggressive goals again, and Martin says it has improved the company internally. 'People from different departments communicate more, so everybody knows what others are doing', he says. 'Now that we have a uniform process, we can continue to grow and we'll always know that this is the way we do business. It will allow us to go to the next level'.

Problems can arise at this stage. First, a number of the managers you appointed earlier on will simply not be up to the task of accepting their new responsibilities. Not all people who can take direction can take part in a bottom-up planning process that is dependent on high-quality inputs. So this means you are back in the recruiting game. You may be wise at this stage to stop relying on personal contacts or direct press advertising, as the majority of small firms do, and go for executive search through a consultancy using sound selection techniques. You probably thought this too expensive at Phase 1 and possibly so at Phase 2, but by now you will have made enough mistakes in recruitment to know that it is a profession in its own right, and requires knowledge and skills you may not have. Furthermore, the indirect costs of getting the wrong people more than outweigh the cost of paying for an expert. One owner-manager was a little startled, to say the least, when he discovered that doing the recruitment himself cost him over six times as much as using an agency, if he counted in the cost of his time and the cost of getting it wrong.

Recruiting and motivating management teams are not easy tasks. When Apple thought they were going to be a big company and go head to head with IBM, Steve Jobs went out and hired in professional managers. Most were a dismal disappointment, who could neither fit in to nor change the company's mistaken growth strategy. Apple got it wrong and, in Job's own words, they had hired a bunch of 'bozos'. Had they hired someone of a similar name with just one vowel transformed (Bezos), their future might well have been different!

But even with good management teams in place, further problems can occur. Once managers you can delegate to are in place, they will make their own decisions as well as the ones you delegate to them. In time, the organization will become increasingly fragmented and uncoordinated. This often becomes apparent in fairly dramatic ways, such as loss of profits, margin erosion, unplanned development and a lack of an overall strategy that everyone can commit to. Another crisis looms: the *crisis of control*.

Phase 4.   Growth through Coordination

During this phase, the crisis of control is overcome by achieving the best of both the delegation and the direction phases. Decision making (and power) is still delegated, but in a systematic and regulated way, with accountability becoming a byword for the first time. Staff functions begin to appear in the firm. At this point the organization begins to put in place strategic planning of some sort, to combine bottom-up and top-down planning methods. Systems and policies are developed to regulate the behaviour of managers at all levels. Communication is vital and a corporate culture takes shape, giving new employees a feel for the way things are done in the company. This growth phase usually ends in the *crisis of red tape*, where the clutter of rules and regulations that bind the company together results in missed opportunities. Bureaucracy rules and development and initiative are stifled. This crisis can be overcome, or even circumvented, by introducing innovative, non-bureaucratic planning procedures or by subdividing the business into manageable units with their own separate missions and management. This is fine as long as you do not return these units to Phase 1-type growth in a desperate bid to release creativity.

IBM, who successfully overcame the other crisis stages in its growth, nearly floundered at this stage. After growing to dominate the computer world, in much the same way as Microsoft has, and facing similar accusing voices, the company stumbled and nearly fell. The outside view of the company was encapsulated in the phrase used at that time to describe their staff – 'Button down shirt, button-down mind'.

Nicola Becket, founder and chief executive of NSB and winner of the Veuve Clicquot 2000 Business Woman of the Year Award, worked in IBM just before its profits slide began. She claims that IBM was incredibly arrogant in the 1970s: 'We believed we were the best'. The trouble with having that belief is that change is difficult to implement from within, with an 'It ain't broke, so why fix it' mentality.

Phase 5.   Growth through Collaboration

The way to circumvent red tape is to inculcate an attitude of collaboration throughout the organization. This calls for much-simplified and integrated information systems and an emphasis on team-orientated activity – and of course a greater willingness to listen to the market, import new ideas and methods and accept change. E-businesses are not the only ones to run into problems after a long period of success. Old economy firms, such as Marks and Spencer, have come unstuck in later phases of growth. Phase 5 can last for decades, as was the case with IBM (see below), or have a fairly short duration. It can be followed by yet another crisis, which takes a firm back one or more phases. As the exact nature of this crisis is variable, it is characterized by a question mark in Figures 1.1 and 1.2.

A further emphasis at this stage of growth is on management education and personal development. This activity is viewed as a luxury in a new venture, and as a good investment in a mature one.

First, tempting though it will be, do not try to skip phases. Each phase results in certain strengths and learning experiences that are essential for success in subsequent phases. When one entrepreneur was introduced to this way of looking at growth, the scales fell from his eyes. He had tried to delegate authority and involve his key managers in developing strategy almost from the time he launched the business. As a result, there was not a clear enough set of goals for them to aim for and they left one after another. The organization nearly failed too. This was as a direct result of trying to move too quickly from Phase 1 to Phase 3, skipping Phase 2.

At the end of this chapter there is a checklist that will help pinpoint where your company is now, in terms of the phases of growth.

The IBM case which follows is an interesting example of a firm which has been through these phases, not without setbacks, but so far successfully. Taking Microsoft, AOL and Cisco out of the equation, IBM's net income of some $8 billion probably exceeds the sum of the rest of the Internet industry, a fact not yet represented in its share price.

Interestingly enough, IBM breaks its own history up into five phases (the early years, 1890–1938; the era of innovation, 1939–1963; a new family, 1964–1980; the PC era, 1981–1992; and a new IBM, 1993–present), which in some ways could be seen as a proxy for the phases described above. It is also worth noting how much shorter each of IBM's major growth phases lasted: 48, 24, 16, 11 and 7 years, respectively.

IBM

Phase 1 – The Early Years, 1890–1938

IBM was incorporated in the state of New York on 15 June 1911 as the Computing-Tabulating-Recording Company. But its origins can be traced back to 1890, during the height of the Industrial Revolution, when the USA was experiencing waves of immigration. The US Census Bureau knew that its traditional methods of counting would not be adequate for measuring the population, so it sponsored a contest to find a more efficient means of tabulating census data.

The winner was Herman Hollerith, a German immigrant and Census Bureau statistician, whose Punch Card Tabulating Machine used an electric current to sense holes in punch cards and keep a running total of data. Capitalizing on his success, Hollerith formed the Tabulating Machine Co. in 1896.

In 1911, Charles R. Flint, a noted trust organizer, engineered the merger of Hollerith's company with two others, Computing Scale Co. of America and International Time Recording Co. The combined Computing-Tabulating-Recording Co., or C-T-R, manufactured and sold machinery ranging from commercial scales and industrial time recorders to meat and cheese slicers and, of course, tabulators and punch cards. Based in New York City, the company had 1300 employees and offices and plants in Endicott and Binghamton, NY.; Dayton, OH; Detroit, MI; Washington, DC and Toronto, Canada. Flint turned for help, to manage what was rapidly becoming a large and complex business, to the former No. 2 executive at the National Cash Register Co., Thomas J. Watson. In 1914, Watson, age 40, joined the company as general manager.

The son of Scottish immigrants, Watson had been a top salesman at NCR, but left after clashing with its autocratic leader, John Henry Patterson. However, Watson did adopt some of Patterson's more effective business tactics: generous sales incentives, an insistence on well-groomed, dark-suited salesmen, and an evangelical fervour for instilling company pride and loyalty in every worker. Watson boosted company spirit with employee sports teams, family outings and a company band. He preached a positive outlook, and his favourite slogan, 'THINK', became a mantra for C-T-R's employees.

Within 11 months of joining C-T-R, Watson became its president. The company focused on providing large-scale, custom-built tabulating solutions for businesses, leaving the market for small office products to others. Its name was changed to International Business Machines Corp., or IBM. Phase 1 of IBM's growth was firmly behind it.

Phase 2 – The Era of Innovation, 1939–1963

Despite being called the Era of Innovation, in practical terms there was rather less innovation than now, for example. When World War II began, all IBM facilities were put at the disposal of the government. They took their first step towards computing in 1944 with the Harvard-developed 'Automatic Sequence Controlled Calculator', the first machine that could make long computations automatically. It weighed in at 5 tons. In 1952 the IBM 701, using vacuum tubes, was introduced and by 1959 the transistor replaced valves.

Thomas Watson passed the title of President on to his son, Thomas Watson Jr, in 1956, just 6 months before his death. The new president re-focused the business again, seeing the company's future in tabulators rather than scales and meat slicers. He pushed IBM to meet the challenge, leading the company's transformation from a medium-sized maker of tabulating equipment and typewriters, amongst other things, to a global business. Along the way, management systems and processes were tightened up, and a complex, and at times unwieldy, hierarchy came into being.

Phase 3 – A New Family, 1964–1980

On 7 April 1964, IBM introduced the System/360, the first large 'family' of computers to use interchangeable software and peripheral equipment. Rather than purchase a new system when the need and budget grew, customers could now simply upgrade parts of their hardware. It was a bold departure from the monolithic, one-size-fits-all mainframe. *Fortune* magazine dubbed it 'IBM's 5 billion gamble'.

System/360 offered a choice of five processors and 19 combinations of power, speed and memory. A user could operate the same magnetic tape and disk products as another user with a processor 100 times more powerful. The 360 was arguably the first pervasive, partially open, information technology architecture. In the late 1960s, once the System/360 became the dominant mainframe solution, IBM began to unbundle component pricing and selectively open the system, in part because of government pressure. Published standards permitted competitors and component suppliers to produce a wide range of IBM-compatible products and programmes that were interchangeable with, and sometimes superior to, IBM's own. By licensing its MVS operating system to Amdahl, for example, IBM made it possible for Fujitsu, Amdahl's partner, to produce clones of the IBM mainframe. Much of what was not licensed away voluntarily was acquired anyway by the Japanese through massive intellectual property theft.

Hundreds of new companies selling IBM-compatible mainframe products and software placed intense competitive pressure on IBM. But they also ensured that the IBM standard would always be pervasive throughout the mainframe computing world. As a result, even today IBM controls some two-thirds of the IBM-compatible mainframe market and an even higher share of its profits, not only for central processing units, but also for disk drives, systems software, and aftermarket products like expanded memory. Because they have no choice but to maintain compatibility with the IBM standard, competitors must wait to reverse-engineer IBM products after they are introduced. Typically, by the time competitive products are on the market, IBM is well down the learning curve or already moving on to the next generation. And as the owner of the dominant architecture, IBM can subtly and precisely raise the hurdles whenever a particular competitor begins to pose a threat. For over 20 years, in generation after generation, IBM has played this game brilliantly and won every time.

Phase 4 – The PC Era, 1981–1992

IBM came into this era having settled one anti-trust action, and fighting another. That dragged on for 13 years until the US Justice Department concluded it was 'without merit' and dropped it in 1982. IBM's competitors filed 20 anti-trust actions during the 1970s. None succeeded. By these standards, Microsoft's battles have only just begun.

IBM badly fumbled desktop computing, handing over the two most critical PC architectural control points – the systems software and the microprocessor – to Microsoft and Intel. Since any clone maker could acquire the operating system software from Microsoft and the microprocessor from Intel, making PCs became a brutal commodity business. As a high-cost manufacturer, IBM now holds only about 15% of the market it created.

Despite, or perhaps because of, its efforts in research, which produced few Nobel Prize winners in physics, the company plunged into a disastrous series of losses and its very survival was frequently called into question. John Akers became CEO in 1985 and focused on streamlining operations and re-deploying resources, typical Phase 4 strengthening strategies. The arrogance that pervaded in the 1970s was replaced with a greater ability to listen to markets and customers.

Phase 5 – A New IBM, 1993–Present

Louis V. Gerstner Jr arrived as IBM's chairman and CEO on 1 April 1993. For the first time in the company's history, IBM had found a leader from outside its ranks. Gerstner had been chairman and CEO of RJR Nabisco for 4 years, and had previously spent 11 years as a top executive at American Express.

Gerstner brought with him a customer-orieniated sensibility and the strategic thinking expertise that he had honed through years as a management consultant at McKinsey & Co. Soon after he arrived, he had to take dramatic action to stabilize the company. These steps included rebuilding IBM's product line, continuing to shrink the workforce and making significant cost reductions.

Despite mounting pressure to split IBM into separate, independent companies, Gerstner decided to keep the company together. He recognized that one of IBM's enduring strengths was its ability to provide integrated solutions for customers – someone to represent more than piece parts or components. Splitting the company would have destroyed a unique IBM advantage. He decided that an IBM that engendered collaboration between its units, rather than competing as separate businesses, was the best way forward.

IBM's business has recovered from a near-basket case to a triumphant success in just a decade or so. The early 1990s saw profits return, and by the end of the century the company was once again a leader, if not *the* leader, in the IT world (Table 1.1).

	1999	1998	1997	1996
Revenue	$87 548	$81 667	$78 508	$75 947
Net income	7 712	6 328	6 093	5 429
Investment in plant, rental machines and other property	5 959	6 520	6 793	5 883
Return on stockholders' equity	30.0%	32.6%	29.7%	24.8%
At end of year:				
Total assets	$87 495	$86 100	$81 499	$81 132
Working capital	3 577	5 533	6 911	6 695
Total debt	28 354	29 413	26 926	22 829
Stockholders' equity	20 511	19 433	19 816	21 628

Table 1.1 IBM's 5-year comparison of selected financial data (in millions of dollars, except per share amounts)

Action Checklist: Which Phase of Growth Are You at Now?

❑ The Organizational Development Diagnostic Questionnaire consists of 60 descriptive statements. Your task is to work through this list and to identify those statements you believe to be accurate in describing your company. It would be useful to get others in your company to do the same.

❑ Each time you come to an apt description, you should tick it on the questionnaire. When you have looked through all 60 statements, please transfer the ticks to the score sheet (Figure 1.2) recording your choice by putting a tick in the box carrying the same number.

❑ Add up your ticks and total them at the bottom. Around which vertical columns do your scores group? This would appear to be your diagnosis of your company's present stage of development. What are the inherent challenges you face?

Organizational Development Diagnostic Questionnaire (from Barrow, C., Brown, R. and Clarke, C., 1997)

1. ❑ The organization structure is very informal.
2. ❑ Top management are finding themselves overloaded, with many unwanted management responsibilities.
3. ❑ Management are most concerned about efficiency of operations.

4. ❏ Staff lower down in the organization possess more knowledge about, for example, markets, products, services, technology and trends than top management.

5. ❏ The main management focus is on expansion of markets.

6. ❏ Top management feel they are losing control of the business.

7. ❏ The main management focus is coordination and consolidation.

8. ❏ There is a lack of confidence between head office and the field.

9. ❏ The main focus of management is on problem solving and innovation.

10. ❏ There is an over-emphasis on teamwork.

11. ❏ The top management style is very individualistic and entrepreneurial.

12. ❏ Top management takes too long in responding to queries and requests.

13. ❏ The organizational structure is centralized and functional, i.e. based on specialisms.

14. ❏ There is not enough freedom to act delegated to those capable of doing so.

15. ❏ The organizational structure is decentralized and individuals have a high level of autonomy.

16. ❏ Many people at lower levels have too much freedom to run their own show.

17. ❏ Units that were once decentralized have been merged back into product groups.

18. ❏ Line managers resent heavy top management direction.

19. ❏ The organizational structure is a matrix of task or project teams.

20. ❏ There is a dependency on group-think to the extent that some managers are losing the confidence to make individual decisions.

21. ❏ Meeting sales targets is all that matters here.

22. ❏ Top management does not provide enough direction.

23. ❏ Top management style tends to be directive.

24. ❏ Management tends to be over-directive and could easily delegate more.

25. ❏ The top management style is delegative.

26. ❏ The organization has probably become too decentralized, breeding parochial attitudes.

27. ❏ The top management style is to be a watchdog, pouncing on anyone getting out of line.

28. ❏ We seem to have lost the ability to respond to new situations or solve problems quickly.

29. ❑ The top management style is highly consultative, meeting frequently on problem issues.
30. ❑ We spend more time looking inside the business and tend to overlook what is happening in the outside world.
31. ❑ Long hours are rewarded by modest salaries but with the promise of ownership benefits in the future.
32. ❑ We never see the boss any more.
33. ❑ The main control systems seem to be concerned with standards and costs.
34. ❑ Flexibility suffers because those who could take decisions have to wait for top management to agree.
35. ❑ The main control seems to be profit contribution reporting and cash burn rates.
36. ❑ Power seems to have shifted away from top management.
37. ❑ Each service product group is an investment centre with extensive planning controls.
38. ❑ Everyone is criticizing the bureaucratic systems that have evolved.
39. ❑ The main control system is for work groups to evaluate their own performance through real-time information systems integrated into daily work.
40. ❑ There is too much personal feedback about behaviour at meetings, etc.
41. ❑ The management focus is mainly on operations and selling.
42. ❑ Top management are very harassed – conflicts between them are growing.
43. ❑ The main way managers are rewarded is by salary and merit increases.
44. ❑ People are demotivated (even leaving) because they do not have enough personal autonomy in their jobs.
45. ❑ The way managers are rewarded is by individual bonuses.
46. ❑ More coordination of operations is needed if things are to improve.
47. ❑ The way managers are rewarded is through profit sharing and stock options.
48. ❑ Fun and excitement seem to be lacking in the company.
49. ❑ Rewards are geared more to team performance than to individual achievement.
50. ❑ The constant high expectation of creativity in the organization is stressful.
51. ❑ Top management are close to customers and have a good understanding of what the market requires.

52. ❑ Top managers do not seem able to introduce the new business techniques that are necessary.
53. ❑ To get on in this company, it's best not to question decisions made by your seniors.
54. ❑ Staff have their performance appraisals from bosses who have little understanding about the subordinate's job and work problems.
55. ❑ People are told what is expected of them and then allowed to get on with their jobs as they see fit. It is management by exception.
56. ❑ Senior managers are continually checking up to make sure that jobs are completed – they tend to overdo this.
57. ❑ There are many 'head office' personnel who initiate company work programmes to review and control line managers.
58. ❑ Too many people are working to the book.
59. ❑ Interpersonal conflicts are brought into the open and, on the whole, managed in a constructive way.
60. ❑ Trying to be always spontaneous and open in relationships at work is proving stressful.

Phase 1 Growth through creativity	1 Crisis of leadership	Phase 2 Growth through direction	2 Crisis of autonomy	Phase 3 Growth through delegation	3 Crisis of control	Phase 4 Growth through coordination	4 Crisis of red tape	Phase 5 Growth through collaboration	5 Crisis of ?
1	2	3	4	5	6	7	8	9	10
11	12	13	14	15	16	17	18	19	20
21	22	23	24	25	26	27	28	29	30
31	32	33	34	35	36	37	38	39	40
41	42	43	44	45	46	47	48	49	50
51	52	53	54	55	56	57	58	59	60

Figure 1.2 Score Sheet for Organizational Development Diagnostic Questionnaire

Mission Impossible　　　2

Most dot-coms have a mission statement, if only because the business plan writer package they used to put their proposition to financiers included a template with that title. But many have no idea what a mission really is and what it does for the strategic effectiveness of the business. Missions are often thought to be more an incantation than an action statement.

Three missions of E-businesses are shown below:

'IBM

At IBM we strive to lead the world in the creation, development and manufacture of the industry's most advanced information technologies, including computer systems, software, networking systems, storage devices and microelectronics. We translate these advanced technologies into value for our customers through our professional solutions and services business worldwide.'

'NASDAQ

To facilitate capital formation in the public and private sector by developing, operating and regulating the most liquid, efficient and fair securities market for the ultimate benefit and protection of the investor.'

'iSky

iSky provides a complete outsourced customer loyalty management solution to both electronic businesses and traditional companies seeking to enhance their customers' on-line and off-line experience before, during and after a purchase. Our customer loyalty management services use interactive one-to-one communications, enhanced by real-time, personalized data collection and management, to find, win, keep and enhance profitable customer relationships. We offer our clients a customized, fully integrated, Web-enabled solution for interacting with their customers through a variety of media, including real-time, text chat, e-mail, voice over Internet protocol, telephone and facsimile.'

iSky was a company that had to pull its IPO at lunchtime on that day in April 2000 when the NASDAQ plunged several hundred points. To be absolutely fair to them, the statement above was included in their IPO filing documentation under the heading, 'Our Business', but I suspect many people would read it as a mission statement.

'eComplaints

- To be a credible, constructive consumer advocate through the use of both a public and private monitored forum.
- To re-insert the customer into a position of influence in companies.
- To help interested companies improve their customer service process, improve their problem resolution success rates, and to help salvage individual customer relationships in a timely manner by acting as an impartial third party.
- To provide leverage to the wronged consumer and provide information to potential consumers before they purchase a product or service in order to reduce their own risk.
- To offer complaint information and analysis as a trusted and credible source to interested third parties.'

The mission statement for a company founded 20 years ago, with a turnover in the low millions and a respectable profit, unlike almost every other E-tailor, is given below.

'Blooming Marvellous (Mission Statement, 1980)

We make clothes for mothers-to-be that will make them feel they can still be fashionably dressed and get them to them in the most efficient manner.'

They have only added a line to that statement since 1980, to incorporate their entry into the babywear and nursery products sectors. The heart of their proposition is that fashionable women like to be fashionably dressed even (especially!) when they are pregnant. Most of their competitors concentrated on comfort and economy. They saw clothes for mothers-to-be as having a pretty short shelf-life and so unlikely to command a premium price. These company founders had found, from their own experience, a segment of consumers that did not have economy high on the list. They wanted to feel just as good about the way they looked when pregnant as when not.

The Blooming Marvellous mission was evolved long before the Internet was even thought of, yet they had no difficulty in absorbing it into the core of what they did, without changing a single word. Even though they are now themselves an Internet company, deriving great benefits from it, they have still not used words such as those in technology-based companies' mission statements. Perhaps seeing the Internet as a business tool rather than a nerds' paradise is what saved Judy Lever and Vivienne Pringle, the company founders, from the obscure mumbo jumbo that stands in for mission statements in most other Internet firms.

Some Useful Rules

A mission is a direction statement, intended to focus your attention on the essentials that encapsulate your specific competence(s) in relation to the market/customers you plan to serve. First, the mission should be narrow enough to give direction and guidance to everyone in the business. This concentration is the key to business success, because it is only by focusing on specific needs that a small business can differentiate itself from its larger competitors. Nothing kills off a business faster than trying to do too many different things too soon. Second, the mission should open up a large enough market to allow the business to grow and realize its potential.

Figure 2.1 The mission pyramid

But you can always do as Lever and Pringle did and add a bit on later.

Ultimately, there has to be something unique about your business that makes people want to buy from you. That uniqueness may be contained in the product or service, but it is more likely to be woven into the fabric of the way you do business. Try telephoning any three car hire firms, hotels, plumbers, or walking into three restaurants, print shops or exhaust fitting centres. The chances are that it will not be their products but their people and systems that make them stand out. You will get the same experience visiting different websites or using Internet order systems. In summary, the mission statement should explain what business you are in or plan to enter. It should include some or all of the following:

- Market/customer needs: who are we satisfying/delighting?
- With what product/service will we meet those needs?
- What are our capabilities, both particular skills and knowledge, and resources?
- What market opportunities are there for our product or service, and what threats are there from competitors (and others)?
- What do we enjoy doing most?
- What do we want to achieve both now and in the future?

Above all, mission statements should be realistic, achievable and brief. You almost certainly don't need long weekends in country hotels with flip charts and management consultants. If you can't distil the essence of what you plan to do in a sentence or two that read like the Blooming Marvellous mission, then you had better get the next stage of finance lined up fast.

The Missing Mission

So what happens if you don't have a mission? Does nothing get done? Worse than nothing, everything gets done, including a whole lot of things neither the founder nor the backers wanted or expected. Following a visit to a very busy company that was losing money hand over fist, it became clear to the consultant that no-one had any idea what the business was supposed to be doing. As fast as one team took on business, another was turning the same type of business away because they thought the firm was 'not in that business'. In the consultant's report he used this quote, which he said was representative of most of the 26 face-to-face interviews he had conducted with the management team:

'We have lost our way. That is, if we ever knew it.'

The best imagery to describe what is going on in rudderless firms with no clear mission is that of resultant forces (Figure 2.2). In the left-hand side of the figure everyone is pulling hard but in different directions, and they are getting absolutely nowhere. Try telling anyone in this organization that they are not working hard enough and they will laugh at you. The staff will be launching new services, upgrading websites, and offering clients customized, fully integrated, Web-enabled solutions by the dozen. The cash burn rate may be, probably will be, astronomic, but nothing much is really happening as everyone is pulling in different directions. The right-hand part of Figure 2.2 represents what the mission sets out to do in getting everyone pulling together but in the *same* direction. Sure, that may have to change over time, but then everyone will still be pulling the same way and the company will move forward, rather than stand still or decline.

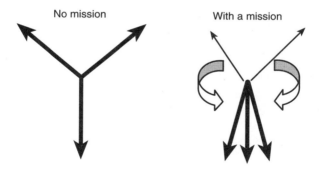

Figure 2.2 Let's all pull together

After the PeaPod case below there is an Action Checklist to help you see how effective your mission is likely to be in helping you achieve profitable growth.

PeaPod, Inc

Three companies (among others) in the USA are currently pioneering on-line grocery shopping: PeaPod, Streamline, and NetGrocer. All three offer the informational benefits of ordering groceries on-line. Standard items can be entered by default. Unusual items are easy to search for. Budgeting is transparent. The user can be prompted with the family's regular brand preferences. Sellers can present special offers and customized discounts. Nutritional and recipe information can be cross-referenced. In the not-too-distant future, a smart refrigerator could do some of the ordering unprompted.

PeaPod Inc., the Skokie, Illinois, company, has been trying to turn a profit selling groceries on-line for more than 11 years now. Founded by Andrew Parkinson, a former Procter & Gamble manager of such high-profile brands as Pringles, Duncan Hines and Parkay, along with his younger brother Thomas, a software designer, PeaPod began delivering groceries in the Chicago area and then expanded to San Francisco, Houston, Dallas, Austin, Boston, Atlanta and other regions filled with high-tech, high-income, time-crunched people. By its 11-year anniversary in 2000 (see Table 2.1), more than 100 000 households were ordering through the service, and PeaPod was posting annual revenue of close to $100 million. Yet its quarterly operating loss more than doubled to nearly $13 million.

| | Quarter ended March 31 | |
	2000	1999
Statement of operations		
Net sales	24 914	18 008
Cost of sales	19 216	14 366
Gross profit	5 698	3 642
Operating expenses		
Fulfilment operations	8 931	4 872
General and administrative	2 039	1 573
Marketing and advertising	1 340	1 238
System development and maintenance	1 189	723
Depreciation and amortization	664	474
Pre-opening expenses	–	280
Non-recurring expenses	4 118	–
Total operating expenses	18 281	9 160
Operating loss	(12 583)	(5 518)

Table 2.1   PeaPod Inc. first quarter, 2000. Financial summary (unaudited) (in thousands of dollars, except per-share and operating data)

PeaPod built the country's most well-known on-line grocery brand through local advertising, attracting press coverage, and sending out America Online-type mass mailings of millions of free sign-up diskettes to potential customers in its target metropolitan areas. Its tag line ('America's Internet Grocer') and its slogan ('Smart Shopping for Busy People') seem to say exactly what it is and does. Yet despite its name recognition, its market value and overall financial performance have been immensely disappointing. *Barron's*, in 1997, honoured PeaPod with the distinction of being the worst-performing Web-related initial public offering (IPO) of the year.

PeaPod is not the one making money from buying the food wholesale and selling it retail. In each local market, consumers transmit their orders over the Web, then PeaPod personnel gather the food from local supermarket shelves, which are three times more expensive to stock and maintain as central warehouses located in industrial areas. The company has begun building such warehouses, enabling PeaPod to pick and pack up to five times faster. But that reduces its costs only somewhat, and doesn't change the fact that PeaPod is ultimately just a delivery boy for the big supermarket chains. It makes its money charging subscription fees (usually $4.95 per month) and per-delivery charges (typically $5 per order). As PeaPod has grown, signing up more and more households in more markets, this business model has become a near-perfect paradox. The more successful they are, the more money they lose. In a recent 4-year period, net losses have increased every year, to a terrifying total of more than $50 million, with nearly $18 million of that occurring in the half year to 31 March 2000.

Industry watchers say that PeaPod seems to have lost sight of what its main mission should be: providing the ultimate life-simplifying solution to its customers. Since it has been struggling to find a way to make money from delivering groceries, it has turned much of its attention back to the makers of the products it sells, rather than keeping focused on the people it's serving. Every click, every purchase, every on-line move a consumer makes on the PeaPod service is captured into databases. The information is sold back to the P&Gs, Krafts and Unilevers of the world.

It is still not clear that the difference in informational functionality between a notepad and a computer screen is really the reason why many would choose to use one of these on-line shopping services. The reason, if any, is physical: avoiding the trip to the store, the queuing and the stress involved in shopping in a supermarket – to say nothing of the time it all takes. And the real question is how big a premium, if any, the homemaker will be willing to pay to avoid the burden of physical shopping.

PeaPod purchases directly from wholesalers and speciality providers. This results in higher costs for consumers, as PeaPod cannot get the volume discounts of large chains, and delivery costs are added on to each order. Apart from the nutritional cross-references or the capacity to connect to the smart refrigerator, there is little value outside of delivery convenience. For a segment of busy and affluent families, the service is worth some premium. But clearly not enough to make a profit. PeaPod's gross margin of 23% hardly indicates a truly innovative service, valued by the market. One can't but think that if there were real pent-up demand, it would probably have been realized before the Internet, rather than because of it.

PeaPod's latest CEO, William Malloy, left suddenly in March 2000, leaving a further round of financing in jeopardy, and a number of angry recent purchasers of their stock reaching for their lawyers (according to the 10-Q report files on 3 May 2000).

Checklist: Mission Statements

❑   Write down your company's mission statement – from memory.
❑   Ask your newest recruit, whatever job he or she does, to write down the company mission statement.

❏   Ask your longest-serving employee to do the same.
❏   Now compare the three. Do they look anything like each other?
❏   How long ago did you write your mission statement?
❏   Does it still accurately reflect what you do?
❏   Would this mission statement stand out in a crowd?
❏   Could a 14 year-old understand it? (This is the standard of the average tabloid reader.)
❏   Does your mission statement provide a clear guide to action?
❏   Does it tell you what businesses you are not in?

Shaping the Vision   3

Visions are not the same as mission statements. Missions can be thought of as providing direction for the medium term along a line that most people can follow. A vision is about stretching the organization beyond its present grasp. Few now can see how the vision can be achieved, but can see that it would be great if it could be.

Microsoft's vision of a computer in every home, formed when few offices had one, is one example of a vision that has nearly been reached. As a mission statement 15 years ago, it might have raised a wry smile. After all, it was only a few decades before then that IBM had estimated the entire world demand for its computers as seven!

NASDAQ's vision is

'To build the world's first truly global securities market . . . a world-wide market of markets built on a world-wide network of networks . . . linking pools of liquidity and connecting investors from all over the world . . . assuring the best possible price for securities at the lowest possible costs.'

It certainly points to beyond the horizon envisaged by the mission quote earlier.

Building Commitment

The vision, just like the mission, needs to be developed with the people in the business and their commitment to it must be gained. If the feeling is that the vision is not relevant, or at any rate only to the top team and the management consultant who sold them on it, then a real corporate advantage is being squandered. It is only when everyone knows and shares the long-term goal of the business that it is likely to be achieved. The long term happens so much sooner today, and all parts of the organization are connected to each other, to the market and the industry, in such a complex series of relationships, that the top team can't hope to achieve anything much without everyone's input. Rather in the way that markets work better with perfect information, businesses work better when everyone knows and believes in the goal.

ICL

The ICL experience is interesting because it illustrates that having a clear management vision and absolute determination is not enough unless you get others on board as well. ICL barely survived one major recession. After a large rescue deal put together by the government and the City, it had to demonstrate very different ways of doing things around here. At the start of their culture change process, there was intense communication, and Robb Wilmot, as CEO, was heavily involved. He issued mission statements, he put together a video, he stood on the top of the ICL organization with his loudspeaker, he preached the new message on every opportunity and . . . people nodded, but ICL realized nothing much was changing. Wilmot knew that things had to change and he found it immensely frustrating that he could not get the organization to move fast enough. To get change in behaviour, the vision and values must be stated, restated, reinforced and communicated *ad nauseam*. Wilmot had somehow to get his people as familiar with the reasons for change as he was. He put 2000 of his managers through a core programme, variously known as 'mind expansion' and 'the sheep dip'. It started top-down and ran for 3 years. The programme lasted 5½–6 days. The objective was to get people to realize that things had to change. The event is now viewed as a watershed. People realized that there was a real external threat. The world did not owe them a living. People came away saying, 'I understand the problem', and the programme created a common language for ICL. Part of this common language was summed up in a brochure distributed by Wilmot, called *The ICL Way*. It summed up the ICL philosophy in seven commitments:

- Commitment to change.
- Commitment to customers.
- Commitment to excellence.
- Commitment to team-work.
- Commitment to achievement.
- Commitment to people Development.
- Commitment to creating a productivity show-case.

The initial reaction was disbelief and cynicism, but later *The ICL Way* became so accepted that it went out with the offer document to every new recruit.

Living the Vision, through Values

Motley Fool claims to be America's biggest financial website, founded by Tom Gardner and his younger brother, David. For many investors, the Gardner brothers' views have clout. Since it was set up in 1994, the Motley Fool portfolio has acquired almost legendary status amongst American investors. The British site was launched in May 1998, Germany in April 2000, and then in Japan, France and Italy. Gardner claims that four guiding values have contributed to their success as their business and employee numbers have grown. The principles are: not to make money by luring customers in through on-line stockbroking; dealing only in simple truths; educating people to ensure that making money can be easily understood; and having fun. Last year they raised $26 million from investors to fund growth.

Having a vision is the easy bit. Living it is what really delivers the payback. Charles Schwab, the billionaire founder of Schwab, is so certain of the value of vision that he insists that examples of Schwab's vision and values are communicated to all new employees. In that way they can know and understand, from the outset, what sort of a business they are joining, and get guidance on how to behave. One example of the Schwab way is in the case below.

Schwab

Charles (Chuck) Schwab was an early convert to the idea of Web-based share trading. He founded what is now America's largest discount brokerage 25 years ago on the back of an innovative idea. When the US Government scrapped fixed commissions in 1975, he offered investors discounts of up to 80%, if they knew what they wanted to buy or sell.

Once Charles Schwab saw that secure Web trading could become a reality, the company moved quickly. On 7 October 1995 four people met at the first brainstorming session to evaluate the Web development. The party included Vincent Phillips, Vice-President of Web Systems; James Chong, now Vice-President and Chief Architect of the IT Group; Ken Richmond, Project Director of Sentry Middleware; and Cynthia Alley, Director of Electronic Brokerage Product Development. The group decided that its members lacked the resources to conduct an internal Web development project itself. As a result, the group decided to outsource the task. In late November of that same year, Schwab recruited a senior executive who was familiar with Web business. Gideon Sasson had been Vice-President of Information Services at IBM, and was responsible for IBM's proposed Web business and e-mail services. Sasson was hired as Schwab's Executive Vice-President of Electronic Brokerage in the last week of November 1995 – before such a business existed.

Soon after Sasson began work at Schwab, he received a call from Chuck Schwab saying that he wanted to launch Web trading in 60 days – on Valentine's Day. The Schwab team managed to convince Chuck Schwab that it would take another 30 days to deliver a Web trading system.

The project was called 'Cupid' for the original Valentine's Day launch. In the meantime, the bids to develop the Website came back from IBM, MCI,

Sun Microsystems and three smaller vendors. Most required 9–12 months and cost more than $2 million. Schwab did not have the time. As a result, the company decided to build the system internally. The team succeeded in building the system in 3 months for a cost of less than $1 million, as opposed to the 9–12 months and the $2 million that outsourcers had asked.

Rapid growth forced Schwab's systems staff to add servers on a daily basis, at times going from three in April 1996 to 50 in May 1998. Adding 47 Web servers required expansion to the network infrastructure. Schwab went from two Cisco 7500 routers to eight 7500 routers between April 1996 and May 1998.

By May 1998, Schwab's global network used 550 Cisco route and several unspecified Catalyst 5500 switches. Metropolitan AT high-speed communications services linked Schwab's most important urban regional offices.

Schwab, however, suffered setbacks due to the failure of its systems to cope with the tremendous increase in trading volume. According to *Information Week,* in early 1999, Schwab's trading system failed twice due to problems with its mainframe computers. Despite the problems, Schwab persisted with its mainframe-based E-commerce architecture. In fact, in the second quarter of 1999, Schwab began a migration from batch processing to real-time processing of trades on its mainframe computers, and completely redesigned its website, to add new services and technology for active traders. By May 1999, Schwab added two mainframes in the three IBM and three Hitachi mainframes in its primary data centre. It also increased the scale of its Web system from 88 IBM RS/6000 Web servers to 154.

By May 2000 the company was handling $1.7 million trades each week, accounting for $25 billion in transactions. Eight out of 10 of their trades are now on-line. Schwab currently has more than 160 000 customers with $1 million – plus portfolios – hopefully not made up exclusively of Internet stocks.

In 1999 the company overtook its rival, Merrill Lynch, in market capitalization, at $32 billion, vs. $31 billion. Three years ago the company was valued at just over $10 billion (Figure 3.1).

At Schwab a lot of time is spent in gathering stories of their values in action. The most compelling stories are videotaped and used in orientation and other events of the company. One such story goes like this:

'After the market crash in 1987, there were a few individuals who owed the firm large sums of money. Generally, these customers had been trading on margin and got caught in the downdraft. The task of collecting these large balances fell to Jim Losi, one of the senior vice-presidents. His first call was on a family in Southern California who had lost more than their net worth. All that they had left was an account with Schwab and the family home overlooking the Pacific Ocean. The client knew that he owed Schwab the money, and told Jim that he couldn't pay it. Both he and his wife were in their late 60s and neither was in very good health. Jim talked to him for a long time, and finally struck an agreement that Schwab would take the equity in the house to settle the debt. By agreement, the customer and his wife could live in the house until they no longer needed it, at which time it would revert to Schwab. We also agreed that they could keep the account as a necessary adjunct to their retirement funds. Jim felt like he was out on a limb when he made this deal. After all, we are not in the real estate business. Nonetheless, the debt would eventually get paid, and Jim's empathy and sense of fairness would not allow him to put this couple out of their family home.'

This would have been a good story of Schwab's values if it had stopped there. But there was more:

'A couple of years after the settlement, the husband of the couple died and his wife continued to live in the house. But in 1993, there was a fire in that part of the Southern California coast, and the former client's house burned to the ground. Schwab could have taken the insurance money at that point. Appropriately, an entirely different Schwab employee assessed the situation in exactly the same way that Jim had. We helped the woman negotiate a settlement with the insurance company, rebuilt the house, and she moved back into it. She lived in it until she died in 1998, and then the debt was finally settled.'

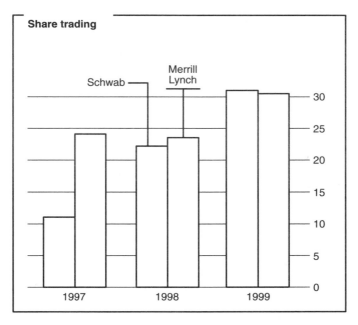

Figure 3.1 Schwab pulls ahead (year end, $ billion)

Action Checklist: Whose Vision Is It Anyway?

❑   Write down your vision statement.
❑   How did you arrive at the vision statement?

❑ Get your team to draw – yes, draw – their idea of the vision of the company. (One company founder received a picture of a flock of geese on the wing. The message was that the company should ultimately comprise individuals who knew the common goals, took turns in leading and adjusted their structure to the task in hand. Geese fly in a wedge, for instance, but land in waves.)

❑ How big is the gap between where you are now and where your vision is taking you?

❑ What are the major milestones between now and achieving your vision?

❑ How can you ensure that your vision and values are shared more effectively by everyone in the business?

❑ What internal factors look like working against you in terms of achieving your vision, and how could you overcome them?

❑ What external factors look like working against you in terms of achieving your vision, and how could you overcome them?

❑ What factors are working in your favour in terms of achieving your vision, and how could you use them more effectively?

❑ Now re-write your vision statement and prepare a statement of company values.

Shooting for the Stars 4

Objectives give some idea of how big you want the business to be, and the role that people in business will play in helping achieve that goal. Here are two examples of the prime objectives that E-entrepreneurs have claimed, both very different in style and content. The second example includes a mission statement as well.

Baltimore Technology

Fran Rooney bought a tiny Irish software company from an academic at Trinity College Dublin for less than £400 000 and built it into a FTSE 100 company in under 4 years. The company is losing money, employs fewer than 800 people across the world, and is valued at £2.5 billion.

Rooney has always gone in for goals. At 29 he decided that by 40 he wanted to be heading a company. At 45 he wanted to pay off his mortgage and by 50 he wanted to be in a position to retire. He is running a bit ahead of himself, as at 43 he is worth about £68 million. From Day One he wanted Baltimore to be a global company, even when they only employed six people. He only employs dynamic self-starters who share his ambitious targets for the company.

Adventure Works Travel

Adventure Works Travel has as its mission to be the leading provider of hassle-free European Adventure Holidays to the 25–35 year-old young professionals market, initially operating within a 25 mile catchment area, but quickly starting to sell its services worldwide, via the Internet. Sale of travel services is the fastest-growing category of business to consumer activity on the Internet. In 2000, the value of this market is an estimated £2700 million.

'The emphasis will be on providing a complete specialist service, based on having a detailed knowledge of the holiday destination and adventure activities being offered. Our market research shows that the major criticism our type of client has of existing travel agencies is that they know nothing about their products – 'They just open the catalogue and read', to quote one of the many disappointed adventure holiday takers. Also, by using our experience in the Adventure Works clothing shop, we will be able to both advise and signpost our clients to sources of the type of travel equipment they will need to get the very best out of their holiday experience.

Our financial objectives are to earn at least £180 000 post-tax profit in the next year, up from £80 000 last year. We intend to make £300 000 in 2 years' time. Our profit margin on sales by year 3 will be a respectable 10%, up from the present 7%. We also intend that the business should be fun. The present staff are passionate about adventure holidays, and we intend to maintain their enthusiasm by constant product and skill training. We will only recruit new people who share our vision.'

Table 4.1 gives the main areas in which prime business objectives are usually set. We will look at the areas in a little more detail in a later section. Suffice it to say here that what gets measured, gets done. So, if site hits per day are the first market-measurable event, just as sales calls per week are in many businesses, then you need objectives for that.

Criteria	Areas
• Measurable	• Profit
• Challenging	• Margins
• Achievable	• Return on capital
• Accepted	• Value-added per employee
• Allocated	• Volume/value and market share
• Timescaled	

Table 4.1 Objectives

Have Targets that Stretch

The objectives need to be challenging but achievable too, which is something of a contradiction in terms. Problems start to arise as soon as 'professional' managers come aboard. They, and probably you, tend to take objectives and the ensuing budgets very seriously. They have to be hit, so it makes sense to pitch on the conservative side.

But in the E-world, goals have to be attainable only with break-through thinking and performance. The question is not. 'How can I grow the business by 20% a year?', but 'How can I grow it by 20% a month?' But if goals are set too aggressively, people leave. Even, perhaps especially, great performers will balk if the hurdle is put too high.

A way to get the best of both worlds is to have a performance band rather than just one number. The reward for achieving a really great result should be equally massive. If this high goal is missed slightly, the manager should be rewarded as if the goal had been set slightly lower. This technique has an impressive pedigree in the E-business world. Charles Schwab claims that by using it he gets what he calls an 'inspiration dividend'. His team set higher goals than they might otherwise have set, and even when they miss them, the year-on-year improvements are stunning.

Business Plans

The business plan is the natural place for the mission and objectives to appear. A business plan is a *selling* document that conveys the excitement and promise of your business to any potential backer or stakeholder. That audience can include outsiders, such as the bank, venture capitalists or even current and prospective new employees, who need to be confident that there is a future in the business for themselves. The plan needs to be prepared and written by those working in the business and who are vital to its implementation. This job advertisement, which appeared on a new dot-com businesses website, seems to slightly miss this point:

> '*Onlinewakeup.com seeks a Business Development Executive – Philadelphia (but relocation is not necessary)*
>
> Onlinewakeup.com Inc (*www.onlinewakeup.com*) is seeking a self-motivated individual who is looking to join a start-up Internet company, as our *Head of Business Development.* We're working on a great concept that we feel can be huge. We have the technology and we just need someone with a proven track record who can write a strong business plan and run all the business affairs of the company. Compensation includes salary plus an equity share in the company, since you'll be joining us on the ground floor. Please e-mail questions or resumé to *jason@onlinewakeup.com* – or call him at 877–822–3233 anytime. We're based in Huntingdon Valley, PA (right outside of Philadelphia), but relocation is not necessary for this position'.

No start-up or growing business should be without a *current* business plan that has been thoroughly reviewed within the past 6 months. It is not unusual for Internet firms to put their business plan away until it needs dusting down for the next round of financing. The planning horizon should be at least 3 years. It takes this long to implement anything of strategic merit. The first year of the business plan will form the framework for the *operating budget*. This is the line-by-line profit-and-loss-style description of how you plan to execute your strategy.

Live4Now.com

Serena Doshi was working as an accountant at Schroder's until a moment of serendipity in November 1999 changed her life. 'I called out for an engineer to fix my printer', said the 27 year-old from London's Fulham. 'This chap showed up and when we started talking, we just hit it off'. The young chap in question was 21 year-old Ewan MacLeod. Their business, Live4Now.com, a lifestyle site for 18–35 year-olds, raised £250 000 in seed capital, and was valued at £20 million early in 2000.

But whilst the founders got on in a flash, their business plan took a bit more working on. In order to make their idea credible to prospective backers, Doshi spent 6 months working until 9 pm at Schroder's, then coming home and working until 3 am on the business plan. Doshi's 4 years at Arthur Andersen came in handy here.

Some Pointers on Putting Together the Business Plan

- *What do you plan to do and why do people want your product or service (very badly, if it's to be a venture capital deal)?* You need to spell out exactly what it is you do, for whom and why that matters:

   'Our website makes ordering office supplies for small businesses simple. It saves the average customer 5 hours a week browsing catalogues and £5000 a year through bank discounts, not otherwise available to firms this size. We have surveyed 200 local small firms who rate efficient purchasing as a key priority.'

  This statement has the ring of practical authority about it.

   'We will provide a complete outsourced customer loyalty management solution to both electronic businesses and traditional companies seeking to enhance their customers' on-line and off-line experience before, during and after a purchase.'

  This statement sounds as though it has been lifted intact from an MBA project.

- *Believable projections.* Future charts always look like a hockey stick. That's fine, if you can explain exactly what drives growth, how you capture sales and what the link is between activity and results. This is a conversion percentages game – X% of site visitors will buy Y amount of product. But more than believable, the initial projections have to be achievable. Missing targets is one thing venture capitalists (VCs) do not like. It will make further financing rounds hard, if not impossible, if you fall behind schedule, miss launch dates, get figures lower than forecast, and so forth. Whatever else happens, make the targets for the first couple of months more than achievable. Nothing builds confidence more or faster than a goal exceeded.

- *How big is the market?*   VCs are generally only interested in Big Markets.   Jim Clarke's Healtheon venture was focused on the $1.5 trillion per year health market. About a third of that was wasted on paperwork. Healtheon's proposition was that the Internet was ideal as a means of bringing all parties to any healthcare transaction together – doctors, patients, health authorities and pharmacists – without paper. Healtheon would take a slice of these savings.

    Amazon.com started up in the $25 billion book market. AOL and Yahoo! are in the $200 billion advertising business.

    Small percentages of these markets may be hard to achieve – but if it works, at least they are worth achieving. Going for 10% of a market measured in millions rather than billions may come to the same number, but it won't be as interesting. Remember, in 2000, E-business amounted to less than 1% of business done. Amazon only claimed 3% of the book market, and that was after 5 years and countless millions of investment capital being pumped in.

- *Who are you and who are the team?*   You need to demonstrate a track record of accomplishments in past jobs or past companies. People are now amazed that Boo.com's team were given £80 million, with barely a business plan, yet alone a great idea. But Boo's ace in the hole was that two of their founders had started up and sold out a successful Internet book business a year previously.

- *Non-executive directors.*   A useful addition to a young team, but they need to have relevant experience or be able to open doors and do deals. They need to be interested in you and your business and able to offer insights into how things really work in your industry.

- *How much money do you need and why?* You need to explain precisely what you need the money for and when it will be needed – build website, hire CFO, advertising budget, product development and so forth. Despite the hype in the press, no-one is just chucking money at Internet businesses. And in any event the market is maturing. The days when VCs knew nothing about the technology are long gone. They wear T-shirts when making house calls and would feel at home with any group of IT engineers.

- *What's the deal?* You have to spell out what share of the company you propose to offer up in return for the cash. A 'term sheet' needs to be prepared showing exactly what the deal is, which needs some legal input to put together. This will be the starting point for negotiation – so start low.

- *Financial forecasts.* You need projected cash flows, profit-and-loss accounts and balance sheets for at least 3 years out. No one believes them after Year One, but the thinking behind them is what's important.

  Looking longer ahead in the Internet world is difficult. Netscape went from a browser company to enterprise software maker to Web portal in less than 3 years, and sold soon after that.

  The profit margins will be key numbers in your projections, alongside sales forecasts. These will be probed by any VC. Amazon makes 25% gross margins on books. If your plan suggests 55%, you had better have a convincing reason.

- *What are the big steps on the way?* You need to show where you are now, where you plan to go and what the major milestones on the way are. For each milestone, explain what is involved and how you will overcome it.

- *Executive summary.* This may be all the VC reads. In a nutshell, the executive summary pulls together the key elements of your proposition – how big the market is, why everyone needs your product or service, and why you are the team to do it. In truth, few business ideas are unique. People and teams with the unique talent, drive, passion and energy, with business savvy, are what's really in short supply. That you have these attributes in abundance has to come through in both the plan and the executive summary.

- *The recipient.* Clearly, a business plan will be more effective if it is written with the reader in mind. This will involve some research into the particular interests, foibles and idiosyncrasies of those readers. Bankers are more interested in hearing about certainties and steady growth, whilst VCs are also interested in dreams of great things to come. Business angels like to know how their particular skills and talents can be deployed in the business.

  It is a good idea to carry out your reader research before the final editing of your business plan, as you should incorporate something of this knowledge into the way it is presented. You may find that slightly different versions of the 'deal on offer' have to be made for different audiences. This makes the reader feel the proposal has been addressed to them, rather than just being the recipient of a 'Dear Sir/Madam' type of missive. However, the fundamentals of the plan will remain constant.

- *Packaging.* Every product is enhanced by appropriate packaging and a business plan is no exception. Most experts prefer a simple spiral binding with a clear plastic cover front and back. This makes it easy for the reader to move from section to section, and it ensures that the document will survive the frequent handling that every successful business plan is likely to get. A letter quality printer, using a 12-point typeface, double spacing and wide margins, will result in a pleasing and easy-to-read plan.

  Talking with others in the venture capital industry, it was something of a surprise to learn that one in three business plans don't meet these basic criteria.

- *Layout and content.* There is no such thing as a universal business plan format. That being said, experience has taught us that certain styles have been more successful than others. Following these guidelines will result in an effective business plan which covers most requirements. Not every subheading will be relevant, but the general format is robust.

  First, the cover should show the name of your business, its address, phone, fax, e-mail number and Web address, together with the date on which this version of the plan was prepared. It should confirm that this is the business's current view on its position and financing needs.

  Second, the title page, immediately behind the front cover, should repeat the above information and also give the founder's name, address and phone number. A home phone number can be helpful particularly for investors, who often work irregular hours too.

- *Writing and editing.* The first draft of the business plan may have several authors and it can be written ignoring the niceties of grammar and style. Now would be a good time to talk over the proposal with your legal adviser to keep you on the straight and narrow, and with a friendly banker or VC. This can give you an insider's view as to the strengths and weaknesses of your proposal.

  When the first draft has been revised, then comes the task of editing. Here grammar, spelling and a consistent style do matter. The end result must be a crisp, correct, clear and complete plan, no more than 20 pages long. If you are not an expert writer, you may need help with editing. Your local librarian or college may be able to help here.

- *The presentation.* Anyone backing a business does so primarily because he or she believes in the management. Backers know from experience that things rarely go to plan, so they must be confident that the team involved can respond effectively to changing conditions. You can be sure that any financier you are presenting to will have read dozens of similar plans and will be well rehearsed. They may even have taken the trouble to find out something of your business and financial history.

  Keep these points in mind when preparing:

  1. Rehearse your presentation beforehand, having found out how much time you have. Allow at least as much time for questions as you take in your talk.
  2. Use visual aids and if possible bring and demonstrate your product or service. A video or computer-generated model is better than nothing.
  3. Explain your strategy in a business-like manner, demonstrating your grasp of the competitive market forces at work. Listen to comments and criticisms carefully, avoiding a defensive attitude when you respond.
  4. Make your replies to questions brief and to the point. If they want more information they can ask. This approach allows time for the many different questions that must be asked either now or later, before an investment can proceed.
  5. Your goal is to create empathy between yourself and your listeners. While you may not be able to change your per-

sonality, you could take a few tips on presentation skills. Eye
contact, tone of speech, enthusiasm and body language all
have a part to play in making a presentation go well.

6. Wearing a suit is never likely to upset anyone. Shorts and
sandals could just set the wrong tone! Serious money calls
for serious people and the Internet world is growing up.

• *Be prepared.* You need to have every aspect of your business
plan in your head and know your way around the plan back-
wards, forwards and sideways. You never know when the
chance to present may occur: It's as well to have a 5, 10 and
20 minute presentation ready to run at a moment's notice.

For a full and comprehensive methodology for putting together a
business plan for an entrepreneurial venture, see the book by
Barrow et al. (1998) which, together with another book by Barrow
(1998d), is incorporated in the *Microsoft Business Planner*: this self-
write software package is bundled with Office 2000.

JavaSoft/Hotmail

In September 1988, Sabeer Bhatia arrived at Los Angeles International
Airport. He had won the transfer scholarship to Cal Tech by being the only
applicant in the entire world (there are usually about 150 who give it a try) in
1988 to get a passing score on the notorious Cal Tech Transfer Exam.
Sabeer had scored 62 out of 100. The next-highest score was 42.

Sabeer intended to get his degrees and then to go home to work,
probably as an engineer for some very large Indian company. He was
following the modest path of life, as set by his parents. His mother was an
accountant at the Central Bank of India for her entire career, and his father
spent 10 years as a captain in the Indian Army. But as a graduate student
at Stanford, Sabeer was drawn to the basement of Terman auditorium. There
the speakers were entrepreneurs like Scott McNealy, Steve Wozniak and
Marc Andressen. Their fundamental message was always the same – you
can do it too. Sabeer knew that famous people always say such things.
They want to be inspirational. But Sabeer's impression of these successful
entrepreneurs was that they really were fairly ordinary smart guys, not much
different from him and his classmates.

When he graduated, Sabeer did not want to go home. So, along with Jack
Smith, he took a job at Apple Computers. Sabeer could have worked at
Apple for 20 or 30 years. But he got swept up in the decade's fever – you
haven't lived until you've gone solo.

Sabeer met a man named Farouk Arjani. Arjani had been a pioneer in the
word processing business in the 1970s, and had since become a special
limited partner of Sequoia Ventures. The two hit it off well, and Arjani
became Sabeer's mentor. What really set Sabeer apart from the hundreds of
entrepreneurs for Arjani was the size of his dream. Even before he had a

product, before he had any money behind him, he had become completely convinced that he was going to build a major company that would be worth hundreds of millions of dollars.

In mid-1995, Sabeer began taking around a two-page executive summary business plan for a Net-based personal database called JavaSoft. When Jack Smith, by now a partner in the venture, albeit a reluctant one, and Sabeer came up with the Hotmail idea. In December, JavaSoft became, in effect, the front for Hotmail. Sabeer knew that Hotmail was such an explosive concept, he didn't want a less-than-ethical VC to reject him, then turn around and copy his idea. He kept showing JavaSoft, and showed Hotmail only to those VCs he had gained respect for:

'It was fine that they were rejecting JavaSoft. But in so doing, I got to see how their minds worked. If they rejected JavaSoft for stupid reasons, then I said "thank you" and left. If they rejected it for the right reasons, then I showed them Hotmail.'

Sabeer's presented his business plan to Steve Jurvetson of Draper Fisher Jurvetson. Jurvetson remembers:

'Sabeer's revenue estimates showed that he was going to grow the company faster than any in history. Most entrepreneurs have that trait, but they also are concerned with looking like a fool. Sabeer's projections were dismissed outright, but Sabeer's passionate belief was unchanged, and he was right. He grew the subscriber base faster than any company in the history of the world.'

One might have presumed that, since Sabeer had been rejected by 20 previous VCs and was virtually a nobody, he would be grateful to accept Draper, Fisher, Jurvetson's $300 000 on their terms. The VC made the perfectly reasonable offer of retaining 30% ownership on a $1 million valuation. Sabeer held out for double that valuation – their cut, 15%. Their negotiations got nowhere, so Sabeer shrugged, stood up, and walked out of the door. His only other available option was a $100 000 'friends and family' round that had been arranged as a back-up – not nearly enough money. If they had gone along that route, Hotmail wouldn't exist today.

Draper and Jurvetson relented; they called back the next day to accept their 15%.

It took enormous confidence to do what Sabeer did: first, to hide his real idea, and second, to hold out for the valuation he thought the company deserved. Both are extremely rare. But Sabeer gives the credit to the culture of the Valley itself.

'Only in Silicon Valley could two 27 year-old guys get $300 000 from men they had just met. Two 27 year-old guys who had no experience with consumer products, who had never started a company, who had never managed anybody, who had no experience even in software – Jack and I were hardware engineers. All we had was the idea. We didn't demo proof-of-concept software or a prototype, or even a graphic printed on a piece of paper. I just sketched on Steve Jurvetson's whiteboard. Nowhere in the world could this happen but here.'

On New Year's Eve, 1997, Sabeer sold Hotmail to Microsoft in exchange for 2 769 148 of their shares. At that time those shares were worth $400 million. It was barely 9 years since Sabeer had stepped off his flight from Bangalore, India, with $250 in his pocket, the limit allowed by Indian customs officials.

Action Checklist: Objectives and Plan

❑ Does everyone in the business have some measurable objectives that impact directly on the fundamental performance of the business?

❑ What happens if people meet, exceed or miss those objectives?

❑ How are those objectives arrived at?

❑ How frequently are objectives and targets revised and reviewed?

❑ Why have you chosen that time period?

❑ How do you know that people are committed to achieving their targets?

❑ Do you have a current business plan? That is one that was written or substantially revised over the last 6 months?

❑ Did you and your team write it?

❑ What time period does it cover?

❑ If you have you recently presented your business plan to financiers, what would you do differently the next time?

Protecting the Crown Jewels 5

Having gone to so much trouble to develop a business model incorporating your mission, vision, objectives and culture, and be all set for meteoric growth, it would be an awful pity to have someone come along and steal it before you made a dime. Even when times are hard, this is probably not an area to include in any cost-cutting exercise. But in the Internet world, where all the value is in the anticipation of profits from day one, the intellectual property may be all that's, really worth saving.

Since the 1998 US Supreme Court decision *State Street Bank vs. Signature Financial Group*, a sort of business-method patent frenzy has swept over Internet companies (Figure 5.1), resulting in not only a rise in the number of computer-related business-method patents issued, but also in a rise in lawsuits for patent infringement. By the end of 1999, DoubleClick was at the forefront of the lawsuit brigade, suing Internet and networks competitors, such as Sabela (since acquired by 24/7 Media) and LA-based L90.

In a retaliatory move, 24/7 Media announced, in May 2000, that it had filed a suit against DoubleClick for allegedly infringing its own

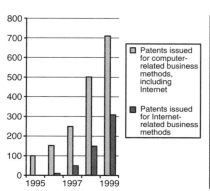

Companies	Subject
Amazon.com vs. Barnesand Noble.com	"One-click" checkout
Broadvision vs. Art Technology Group	Personalization
DoubleClick vs. L90	Ad monitoring and tracking
NetMoneyIN vs. Cybersource, Elliance	Third party payment systems
Novadign vs. Marimba	Updating applications
Priceline.com vs. Expedia.com (Microsoft)	Reverse auctions for travel
Response Reward Systems, planetU, e-centives, CoolSavings.com	Coupons and promotions
Trilogy Software vs. CarsDirect.com	Selecting options on cars

Figure 5.1 Internet business methods, patents and lawsuits
(Sources: US Patent and Trademark Office, company reports)

patent (US Patent No. 6026368, 'On-Line Interactive System and Method for Providing Content and Advertising Information to a Targeted Set of Viewers'). 24/7 Media is seeking monetary damages and has requested an injunction barring DoubleClick from further infringement of the patent.

CoolSavings.com

CoolSavings, launched in 1995 by Steve Golden, provides a comprehensive suite of E-marketing services to both online and offline advertisers, focused on building one-to-one customer relationships. By leveraging the established CoolSavings brand and its widely recognized pig icon, advertisers can deliver, target and track a broad range of incentives, including printed and electronic coupons, personalized e-mail, rebates, samples, sales notices, gift certificates, contests and banner advertisements, to promote their products or services. These incentives are delivered to targeted segments of the company's 'membership' base who have registered their demographic profiles on Coolsavings.com and have given their permission to receive personalized savings opportunities. CoolSavings's incentives may be redeemed on-line or in traditional bricks-and-mortar stores. As of 1 March 2000, CoolSavings had over 6 million registered members, representing nearly 4.7 million households. The company analyses the database of member registration and shopping preference data with sophisticated data analysis, targeting and tracking technology that allows advertisers to execute effective promotional campaigns, while maintaining a strict consumer privacy policy. As members redeem the incentives offered, the company gathers extensive shopping behaviour and preference information. This information further enriches the member database, providing advertisers with a higher degree of targeting. In 1999, advertisers included leading brands, such as Barnes & Noble, BigStart, CDNow, First USA, JC Penney, Kids'R'Us, MCI WorldCom, MotherNature.com, NetGrocer, petsmart.com, Service Merchandise, SmarterKids.com and US News & World Report.

Before launching their website, even before raising their first million dollars, the founders of CoolSavings.com Inc. in 1995 sought a potentially more valuable asset for a young Internet company: a US Patent. Shortly after receiving the patent in June 1998, CoolSavings put it to use. It sued nine other companies, also in the business of distributing coupons and promotions via the Internet, for infringement.

Those lawsuits quickly became the opening salvos in a multifront war. Three rivals of CoolSavings acquired patents of their own and countersued. And Henry Von Kohorn, an 86 year-old man in Florida, joined the fray, claiming he had invented electronic distribution of coupons in the 1980s. Mr Von Kohorn sued five market contenders, including CoolSavings.

CoolSavings.com had considerable foresight when they filed their patents. But suing is a long and painful process, with unforeseeable outcomes. Three of the companies CoolSavings has sued for patent infringement have settled. One of them, emaildirect Inc of Aliso Viejo, California, claims to have obtained a license from CoolSavings that 'didn't cost us anything'. Others are fighting back. Brightstreet.com Inc. of Mountain View, California, which makes software to create promotions and coupons, filed papers with the Patent Office challenging CoolSavings's patent, claiming it had developed some of the same ideas first.

In at least two cases, CoolSavings sued not just its rivals in the coupon business, but companies that do business with them. As part of a July 1999 settlement with CoolSavings, the female-orientated website, iVillage Inc. of New York, agreed to stop doing business with a subsidiary of Catalina Marketing. A suit is pending against Brodbeck Enterprises Inc., which operates the Dick's Supermarkets chain in Wisconsin and offers coupons through PlanetU Inc. of San Francisco, another Internet promotions site.

CoolSavings.com are just the tip of what looks like a very large iceberg as rivals rush to the US Patent and Trademark Office to certify their latest innovations. Those smart, or lucky, enough to have obtained patents for which they applied 4 or 5 years ago increasingly wield them as weapons to prohibit others from employing the same technology.

The disputes involve the biggest names in electronic commerce. Amazon.com, the Seattle-based on-line retailer, for instance, has won a court order barring New York rival Barnes & Noble from using its patented 'one-click' checkout system, which allows a shopper to place an order with a single tap of the mouse, instead of re-entering billing information. Priceline.com, the Stamford, Connecticut, Internet discount retailer, wants to stop Microsoft Corp.'s Expedia unit from using 'reverse auctions', in which buyers name their price and sellers decide whether to take the bid, to fill airplane seats and hotel rooms.

Statistics suggest many more legal battles lie ahead. The Patent and Trademark Office in Arlington, Virginia, issued a single patent in 1995 for what it now calls 'Internet-related business methods'. Last year, the total grew to 301. The number of applications is doubling annually; it takes 2–3 years, on average, to obtain a patent.

Patents and the Internet are a particularly volatile mix. Because it's much cheaper and easier to copy Internet technology than to build a pharmaceutical plant, for example, the legal protections of a patent can be that much more important in cyberspace. And because readily available capital has led to a flowering of Web companies built around a single idea – such as Priceline's reverse auctions – an entrepreneur is apt to guard that idea with singular jealousy. All the action is not confined to the USA. In May 2000, the UK courts made their first award on Internet trademarks. Mandata, a computer company, included the trademark of its competitor, Road Tech Computer Systems, in its 'metatags' (key word used to flag down search engines) and in hidden text in the first pages of its website. This ingenious technique for diverting traffic from their rival's site resulted in an award of £80 000 in costs and damages against Mandata. As the first decision of an UK court, it provides clarification, on this matter at least, for everyone doing business on the Internet.

Further tension to intellectual property protection arises as most of the software developed before the mid–1980s was not patented, making it difficult for examiners to determine whether an idea is truly novel.

Assignment Checklist: Protecting the Crown Jewels

❑ Do you have any patents on your business model?
❑ Do your competitors have patents on theirs?
❑ Is there anyone else out there in the long grass (see the Cool-Savings.com case) who could have some rights over parts of our business model?
❑ If you do have patents, who actually has them – you, an employee, the company?
❑ Have rights to the patents been assigned to anyone?
❑ Patents are not the only area of intellectual property that can protect your business. Trademarks – do we have any and are they registered?
❑ Design and drawings also can be protected. Do these form any part of our business proposition?
❑ Copyright covers words, literature, brochures, etc. – do we have anything we should protect (slogans?)?

Part II

Upgrading Marketing

Understanding customers is the key to growing the business. Many E-businesses never meet their customers face to face. They may never even speak on the telephone. Nevertheless, they have to develop techniques to understand what will inspire them to buy, or what might push them away. The evidence on how great E-businesses are at listening to and understanding customers is not exactly heartening. A recent survey on the state of the Internet in Europe revealed that 14% of companies selling on the Web take more than 5 days to reply to their customer's e-mails and 30% never reply. Another 12% do not publish an e-mail address or any way to make contact except via the site itself.

Perhaps the problem starts for some Internet firms with the way in which their proposition gets developed in the first place. As many if not most E-entrepreneurs, in the first wave at any rate, were computer- and Internet-literate, many started with a snazzy piece of software or a product or service concept and then started looking for customers that might want it. Often they don't even 'look' for customers, but just dump the 'product' onto a website and wait . . . and wait . . . and wait.

Industry experts believe that PeaPod and their many competitors may be wasting their time, and millions of investors' money, pursuing a market that either does not exist, or is too small to be worth gearing up for. The immortal words of Yahoo!'s founder, 'There are lots of companies on the Net, but not many businesses' has an uncomfortable ring of truth about it.

That's not to suggest that Internet or new-economy firms are unique in frequently having 'room for improvement' in their marketing skills. Books have been, and surely will continue to be filled with marketing disasters listing products and services that no-one really wants or, if they do want them, won't pay an economic price. But what is particularly dangerous, for investors and E-entrepreneurs alike, is the quasi-scientific jargon of the business models, which engenders the erroneous belief that just because someone is clever, they could be smart at business. The second problem arises from the vast amounts of money needed so early in the business process. This puts great pressure on young Internet firms in particular, to ignore the fundamental marketing processes and, as they say, 'cut to the chase'.

Boo.com, according to industry watchers commenting before their failure, spent too much money on everything but serious market research. Great businesses arise from market needs, rarely, however exciting, from technology alone. Another gem from the US Patent Office revealed that less than 0.5% of all patents filed had ever been successfully commercially exploited.

Bookham Technology is a stunning example of an entrepreneur recognizing a business opportunity for an E-business, then doggedly setting out to create and acquire the technology that would allow him to realize his dream. The personal billion pounds he made when the firm floated on NASDAQ and the London Stock Exchanges, in May 2000, was perhaps a well-deserved reward.

Bookham Technology

We saw the market opportunity and then went looking for the technology. That is the right way to do it.

Bookham Technologies, founded by Andrew Rickman in 1988, could well have been an example of a high-tech start-up in search of a market. With an honours degree in mechanical engineering from Imperial College, London, and a PhD from the University of Surrey, Rickman certainly had the makings of a boffin. But an MBA from Cranfield leveraged his fervour for technology as an end in itself. He says:

'Back in 1988 I came across the forerunners of the Internet and it struck me at the time that optical fibre was going to become a very important part of the Internet because it was the best way of transmitting lots and lots of information.'

Rickman is part academic, part new-economy entrepreneur and part traditional businessman. He spurns the dressed-down uniform of the E-world for a sober suit, white shirt and tie, and is at his most animated explaining at a blackboard how data travels down optical cables.

Communication via optical fibres, rather than copper wires, uses light instead of electrical signals to carry and process information and is ideally suited to the heavy data traffic of the Internet age. Fibre-optic cables have been used for at least 10 years but the optical components at each end of the cables were expensive, involving the hand assembly of tiny lasers, filters and lenses.

This was the problem that Rickman set out to solve. He says:

'Our vision at the beginning of the business was to find a way of integrating all of the functions needed in optical components on to a chip in the same way that the electronics industry has done.'

This simplification would allow automated volume manufacture, bringing down cost and allowing the growth in the use of the Internet. 'The only thing that is likely to prevent the continued exponential growth in the use of the Internet is that cost reduction in use does not come down fast enough', he says.

The business started in a room above the garage of his home, with his wife as company secretary. But the idea did not stem from academic research work that Rickman, who holds a doctorate in integrated optics from Surrey University and an MBA from Cranfield, had carried out. Instead Rickman designed the business model to meet a market need, rather than to exploit an existing technology. He says:

'I had briefly worked in the venture capital community and at the outset of Bookham formulated a model for the ideal technology company. We saw the market opportunity and then went looking for the technology. That is the right way to do it.'

Once the initial scientific breakthroughs had been made, the company raised private equity finance, totalling $110 million over several rounds, and had backing from 3i, Cisco, Intel and others. He says:

'It was a very long road to travel with substantial challenges, but now we are producing tens of thousands of components, scaling up in a way that has not been seen in the UK.'

Bookham, like Cisco, is a supplier of 'picks and shovels' to the Internet market. In May 2000 they employed 400 people and had annual sales of about £10 million. In true dot-com fashion, the company is not profitable – yet. The company listed on the London Stock Exchange and the NASDAQ in May 2000, and was valued at £5 billion. This made Rickman an entrant to the growing list of European E-billionaires.

Flying Blind

6

E-entrepreneurs are fond of talking about the leap of faith required by their investors, when very often all they are doing is taking a leap in the dark. In effect the formative months and years are just one enormous market research experiment – is there anyone out there who wants what we've got?

A study by The University of Southern California in April 2000 surveyed 4500 senior managers in 'knowledge industries'. The study included in its conclusions that although companies were making large investments in technology and hiring in top talent, eight out of 10 said that they lacked adequate knowledge about what competitors were doing.

But is this ignorance about the market place really necessary? In growing a business, you need to ensure that there are enough customers out there with sufficient money to spend on your products or services to enable you to meet your objectives. You must also see who else will be competing against you for their business and how you will be better or different. There is absolutely no chance of achieving profitable growth without superior market knowledge.

One fact no Internet E-tailor should be unaware of is how deeply dissatisfied most people are with their on-line experience. A recent study by Boston Consulting Group (BCG) found that 65% of all virtual shopping carts are abandoned. When did you last see a real shopping cart abandoned, except outside a block of flats where someone has dumped it after a particularly heavy shopping trip?

Procter and Gamble test marketed the home dry cleaning product Dryel on 150 000 households for more than 3 years before introducing the product in 1999. Contrast this with how Drugstore.com tested the waters. Before its launch in February 1999, the on-line company spent less than a week surveying only about 100 people. For many on-line companies, market research was reduced to slapping up a web-site and hoping for the best. Now that the party is over, it seems likely that new Internet firms will have to hasten a bit more slowly and follow some of the old rules of marketing. It may be that they have to speed things up but, with so many Internet firms, being first to market has translated into little less than being first out of it. All Boo.com had to show for $135 million investment when the business failed was a bid from the Bright Station company (formerly Dialog) for $400 000 for the technology.

There is much evidence that the successful E-business firms take marketing very seriously and use superior knowledge to create superior growth.

What Do We Need to Know?

The areas to research include:

- Your *customers*: who will buy more of your existing goods and services and who will buy your new goods and services? How many such customers are there? What particular customer needs will you meet?

- Your *competitors*: who will you be competing with in these new product/market areas? What are their strengths and weaknesses?

- Your *product* or *service*: how should it be tailored to meet customer needs and to give you an edge in the market?

- The *price* you should charge: what would be seen as giving value for money and so encourage both customer loyalty and referral?

We will look again at these areas in a little more depth later.

The example below is one showing how a new dot-com has used market research to position a new proposition on the Internet.

Virgin.com

Virgin.com, which went live in May 2000, in typical Virgin style, claimed it could cut 22% off the purchase price of new cars sold in Britain. They planned to do this by sourcing from European dealers, who sell at considerably lower prices than are available in the UK. Virgin, up to this point, was offering nothing very new. Lots of old-economy firms, including a ferry company (P&O Stena) and the Consumers' Association, were in the same business at least a year earlier. The uniqueness of Virgin's offer lay in its research into the requirements of female buyers. They claim that not only do female car buyers like the directness of the Internet, which cuts out the interface with high-pressure salesmen in car showrooms, but they also appreciate the demystifying software, which reduces car buying to a simple process using simple terms. Virgin don't aim to be the cheapest in the market, but they do expect the mainstay of their offering to be the service package that comes with each car, which includes warranty, delivery and servicing.

- The *advertising* and *promotional* material needed to reach your market: what newspapers, journals and so forth do your potential customers read and what websites do they visit? The first wave of Internet ventures burnt cash at a staggering rate, advertising for customers. Super Bowl advertisements or blanketing the market with free disks may create huge short-term growth, but there is little evidence that the 'clients' won by indiscriminate blunderbuss advertising works well. Certainly, few people using such techniques make any money. Unglamorous as it is, analysing data on what messages actually influence people to buy, rather than just to click, holds the key to identifying where and how to promote your products and services.

  If you plan to use the Internet to advertise on, it would make sense to check out the site. The site may publish a fair amount of gobbledegook about the site scoring 'hits' that often run into millions. But that doesn't mean they have millions of visitors. You can increase the hit rate by the simple expedient of adding the number of pages each viewer must download to view the page.

  Another mildly meaningless measure of the advertising value of a site is the notion of a 'subscriber'. Anyone visiting a website and passing over their e-mail address has become part of that company's share price! It is rather like suggesting that anyone passing a shop and glancing in the window will turn into hard cash tomorrow.

  Any real analysis of website use starts with 'page impression'. Measured by software on the website, this tells you how many times an individual page has been viewed. The Audit Bureau of Circulations (ABC), which started its life measuring newspaper response, has now turned its attention to auditing websites (*www.abce.org.uk*)

- Your *location*: where do you need to be to reach your customers most easily, at minimum cost? This could of course include your search engine strategy, but equally importantly it may help answer the question, do you need a physical location at all.

  Many of the old economy entrants to the E-economy have kept the 'mortar' as well as acquiring 'clicks'. When Tesco's Chief Executive, Terry Leahy, announced the separation of its E-commerce business in May 2000, one great strength he claimed for the new business, Tesco.com, was that 'Customers know and trust Tesco, and that gives us a real competitive edge'. That trust stemmed from customers being able to physically see what the company stands for. Using software produced by the leading UK Internet software company, Tesco plans to offer My Web, an

intelligent Internet tool that reacts to customers' shopping habits, suggesting different sites related to subjects or products they
are interested in. In that way they hope to build a similar level of
trust, but over the Internet. Tesco uses its local stores for 'pick
and pack' and delivers locally using smaller vehicles. They claim
to have sales of £125 million in 2 years. The PeaPod business
model has taken them 11 years and their sales are barely half
that level. Tesco.com offers more than 20 000 products on-line,
many times more than their largest store. They claim that 50%
of turnover is new, little of it is low value added bottled water,
and that they are not merely cannibalizing sales from stores.

Your research needs to be:

- *Systematic* – The research needs to be a planned and continuous
  process.

- *Objective* – The information should not be biased by either the
  researcher or the research process.

- *Useful* – Research should produce information to help make
  decisions on specific issues.

How Can We Find That Out?

Market research is conducted in seven stages.

Stage 1.   Formulate the Problem

Before embarking on market research, you should first set clear and
precise objectives, rather than just setting out to find interesting
general information about the market. It is often helpful to set your
objectives in the form of a problem. For example, you may pose as
your problem, 'How can we retain our existing customers for
longer?' or 'How can we get customers to give us a greater share
of their business?'.

Stage 2.   Determine the Information Needs

If you want to improve customer loyalty, then you will need will need
to know why customers are leaving. Is it because their tastes are
changing or are they buying much the same products, but from a
competitor? If they are buying from a competitor, you will want to find
out why, and more importantly what you can do to win them back.

Stage 3.   Where Can You Get the Information?

Market research conjures up images of people with clipboards
accosting you in the street – and you might well have to do that.
But much of the information you need will already have been
published, so some of your work can be done from the comfort of a
chair in a good library or at the click of a mouse. This type of
research is called 'desk research' and it is well worth doing first.

Desk Research

There is increasingly a great deal of secondary data available in
published form, either on the Net, on CD-RoM or in hard copy. It is
also accessible through the business sections of public libraries,
government bodies, trade associations and professional associations.
Using websites such as Sleuth.com, you can find out some basic data
on most businesses, and even find out how many other people are
watching the same firms (Table 6.1).

Don't overlook some inexpensive low-tech sources of market
research information. These include: journals, newsletters newspapers, advertisements for jobs and products, customers, competitors,
friends and contacts, public records, suppliers, employees and their
families and friends. Job interviews are one popular way for Internet
firms to find out exactly what is going on in certain areas of the market.

Most of the basic information to 'solve' market research problems
can be found via desk research. Virgin.com could have, and perhaps
did, draw on published data on the Internet to tell them all they
needed to know about the number of females who buy or could be
tempted to buy cars.

Top 10 companies being watched	Top 10 stakeouts requested this week
1. America Online Inc. (*AOL*)	1. America Online Inc. (*AOL*)
2. Infonautics Inc. (*INFO*)	2. Infonautics Inc. (*INFO*)
3. Microsoft Corporation (*MSFT*)	3. Yahoo! Inc. (*YHOO*)
4. Yahoo! Inc. (*YHOO*)	4. Microsoft Corporation (*MSFT*)
5. Dell Computer Corporation (*DELL*)	5. Cisco Systems Inc. (*CSCO*)
6. Cisco Systems Inc. (*CSCO*)	6. Lucent Technologies Inc. (*LU*)
7. Lucent Technologies Inc. (*LU*)	7. Dell Computer Corporation (*DELL*)
8. Amazon.com Inc. (*AMZN*)	8. Amazon.com Inc. (*AMZN*)
9. Intel Corporation (*INTC*)	9. QUALCOMM Inc. (*QCOM*)
10. Compaq Computer Corp. (*CPQ*)	10. IBM (*IBM*)

Table 6.1 Top ten companies being watched on Sleuth's website on
16 May 2000

Field Research

If no one has answered your questions, then you are into field research to collect specific information yourself or with outside help. The customer loyalty and referral problems above are examples where field research will almost certainly be called for.

Stage 4. Decide the Budget

Market research will not be free, even if you do it yourself. At the very least, there will be your time. There may well be the cost of journals, phone calls, letters and field visits to plan for. At the top of the scale could be the costs of employing a professional market research firm.

Starting at this end of the scale, a business-to-business survey comprising 200 interviews with executives responsible for office equipment purchasing decisions cost one company £11 280. Twenty in-depth interviews with consumers who are regular users of certain banking services cost £7552. Using the Internet for Web surveys is another possibility, but that can impose too much of your agenda onto the recipient and turn them away from you.

Doing the research in-house may save costs but may limit the objectivity of the research. Also, as time is usually the most scarce commodity for E-entrepreneurs, it will probably make more sense to get an outside agency to do the work. Another argument for getting professional research is that it may carry more clout with investors.

Whatever the cost of research, you need to access its value to you when you are setting your budget. So, if getting it wrong will cost £10 000 000, then £50 000 spent on market research may be a good investment.

Stage 5. Select the Research Technique

For a growing independent business, two forms of field research are most prevalent.

Observation

In observational studies, the subject is not interacted with. So a basic 'footfall' study could be confined to counting the number of people walking down a particular street in each hour of the day. This may provide information on both volume of people and peaks and troughs. One company collects licence registration plate numbers at shopping centre car parks. These are fed into a computer to show where the shopping centre's customers live. A direct mail campaign aimed at these groups increased sales by 40%.

Survey

This covers a multitude of techniques involving contact with people. The most popular forms of interview are:

- *Personal (face-to-face) interview*, which accounts for about 55% of all survey activity. This is popular with consumer markets. Steve Bennett, who founded Jungle.com with backing from the venture capital firm 3i, markets an enhanced Web shopping experience using a 'product advisory wizard', which asks customers questions and then helps them decide which computer to buy. Bennett's last business was the Software Warehouse. He started that in 1989 with the help of a Government Enterprise Allowance Grant of £40 per week. He has sold his 31-outlet business via a management buy-out to his management to concentrate on the Internet. But he does miss some things about traditional shops. 'I could go and stand on the shop floor', he claims, 'and once a quarter I would go and work as an assistant. All the research in the world won't give you a gut feel'. Interviews can give you the nearest thing there is to a gut feel, and you don't need a shop to be able to talk to customers.

- *Telephone surveys* account for about 32%. of all surveys. Hewlett-Packard (HP) is a business that has an enviable track record of delivering high-quality products. During the early days of its computer printer business development, its market research team noticed that Epson, a Japanese competitor, could create a very broad product line by making small variations in the same basic platform. HP, on the other hand, had a history of creating an entirely new platform for each new product version. HP engineers were unenthusiastic about the marketing team's recommendation that they make modifications to existing platforms. It was only after the product manager forced engineers to conduct a telephone poll of customers, which showed that customers wanted to buy a product that was a slight variation of an existing HP platform, that they reluctantly agreed. HP was then able to get to market faster with 'new' products and capture a larger share of the growing printer market.

- *Test, discussion and focus groups*, 7%.

- *Post*, 6%. Popular for industrial markets.

- *Web surveys* are growing in popularity. One useful spin-off is that the data can be harnessed to analysis software for a quick turn-around. In the fast-changing Internet world, saving a few days or weeks might be the difference between life and death.

Personal interviews and postal surveys are clearly less expensive than getting together panels of interested parties or using expensive telephone time. Telephone interviewing requires a very positive attitude, courtesy, an ability not to talk too quickly, and listening whilst sticking to a rigid questionnaire. Low response rates on postal surveys (less than 5% is not uncommon) can be improved by an accompanying letter, explaining the purpose of the questionnaire and why respondents should reply; by offering small rewards for completed questionnaires; by sending reminders; and by providing a free reply-paid envelope.

There are six simple rules to guide the survey process, which apply to all surveys, however administered:

1. Keep the number of questions to a minimum. More than a dozen will call for a dedicated respondent with a powerful reason to provide your answers.
2. Keep the questions simple and preferably multiple-choice, i.e. yes, no, don't know, don't care.
3. Avoid ambiguity by using precise rather than vague words, and look for facts rather than opinions, i.e. prefer, 'Do you take the paper every day?', to 'Do you take the paper regularly?'.
4. Test out the questionnaire on a small representative sample to iron out bugs before going live.
5. Have a cut-out question early on to eliminate unsuitable re-spondents, e.g. those who could never use the product.
6. Have an identifying question to show a cross-section of respon-dents. This could cover demographics by asking about age, sex, education, income and job title, for example.

Stage 6. Sample Design

It is rarely possible or even desirable to include every possible person in a survey. Imagine trying to talk to *all* pet owners if you were planning to launch petfeed.com. Instead you would select a sample of people, who represent the whole population being surveyed. You need to take care and ensure you have included the Innovator and

Early Adopter segments in your research sample. These will be discussed later, but they are particularly important to Internet firms, whose entire first year's sales could be confined to these groups.

Sampling saves time and money and can be more accurate than surveying an entire population. Talking to all pet owners may take months. By the time you have completed your survey the first people questioned may have changed their opinion, or the whole environment may have changed in some material way.

There are two methods of sampling, each with variants:

- *Probability sampling.* This is done to statistical rules, with each member of the sample population having a known chance of being selected. In *simple* random sampling, a selection is made from the whole of a population, using a method that ensures randomness. This could be achieved by picking names out of a hat or by using random number tables. In the *stratified* random sampling technique, the total population is divided into subgroups, each of which is treated as a simple random sample. This would be used if certain subgroups of the population could be expected to behave differently, but were all-important to the study. It is often not possible or practical to get a list of the whole of a population, for example a city, but parts of it can easily be obtained. Area postcodes within the city will be easier to obtain and use. An area or cluster sample is chosen simply by taking a random sample of the postcodes on the list. These are then the people to include in the survey.

- *Non-probability sampling.* This is used when probability sampling is not possible, as when no list of the population exists or when the population is not stable over time, e.g. an airport booking hall. *Convenience* sampling includes such methods as calling for volunteers on the street interviews and using students as guinea-pigs in an experiment. In *judgement* sampling, researchers select people or groups of people that they believe will result in a group that is representative of the population as a whole. *Quota* sampling is a refinement of judgement sampling, in which the people sampled represent the overall population in some important respect. For example, if we know that 60% of pet owners are women, then we might construct our sample with that proportion of women in it.

The accuracy of your survey will increase with the sample size, as Table 6.2 shows. For most basic research, a growing business will find the lower sample sizes accurate enough, given the uncertainty surrounding the whole area of entering new markets and launching new products.

Size of random sample	95% of surveys are right within percentage shown below
250	6.2
500	4.4
750	3.6
1000	3.1
2000	2.2
6000	1.2

Table 6.2 Accuracy of a survey

Stage 7. Process and Analyse the Data

If you have wisely chosen a multiple-choice format, it will be relatively easy to count up the number of responses to any question. The difficulty arises when cross-tabulation is required. Suppose, in the pet food sample above, we asked people about their sex, age, income and type of pet. Our data would contain valuable information that could only be gleaned by calculating the totals for many different subgroups – affluent women cat owners and middle-aged male dog owners, for example. Here we need a spreadsheet-type model to do the sums for us. Fortunately, such models are now readily available. For a more detailed review of market research processes in entrepreneurial firms, see Barrow (1998c) and Barrow and Brown (1997).

Action Checklist: Are We Flying Blind?

❑ How much do you know about your customers?
  ❑ Their age, sex
  ❑ Buying habits and preference
  ❑ What other related products and services they also buy
  ❑ Which of your competitors they also use
  ❑ What share of their business you have now
❑ How much do you know about your competitors?
  ❑ Who are they?
  ❑ What are their sales, profits, price?
  ❑ How do they promote their services and products?
  ❑ Do your customers rate them more or less highly than your offerings?
❑ What big gaps have these (and other questions) thrown up in your knowledge of the market?
❑ How can you plug those gaps?

Cutting up the Cake 7

Henry Ford is reputed to have used the slogan, 'You can have any colour you like, as long as it's black'. In Volkswagen recently a cheer was heard when two identical cars came off the production line on the same day. This illustrates the change in marketing emphasis from mass marketing to market segmentation – the strategy of subdividing the market.

Targeted, almost one-to-one marketing has been made possible by just-in-time manufacturing processes and sophisticated marketing databases. But above all it is customers who increasingly want products and services tailored to their needs and will pay for the privilege.

SevenCycles.com

An interesting example of individualizing products is SevenCycles, founded in 1997 near Cambridge, Boston (Massachusetts, USA). The 12-person company was founded with the goal of building a unique bicycle for each rider. The name came from the fact that the founders all cycle every day of the week.

This is SevenCycles' proposition:

SevenCycles exists because you have asked for more from your cycling. We understand, for we too are devoted cyclists. We are a team of skilled craftspeople – designers, engineers, machinists, welders and service professionals – whose love for cycling fuels a single-minded desire to build the world's finest bicycle frames and accessories.

We want to create the best bicycle you have ever ridden, using an uncompromising approach to design, materials choice, workmanship and service. That is an aspiration we have fulfilled for thousands of serious cyclists in 50 states and in more than 12 countries. Now it's your turn. Let us build the bike you have always dreamed of.

Most people thought Rob Vandermark, SevenCycles's CEO, crazy when he and his co-founders started the business. The rest of America has passed its bicycle manufacture to China and Taiwan, to lower the cost of manufacturing.

The factory's main raw materials are lightweight titanium rods, which are delivered through the front door and taken back to three workstations, or 'jigs', manned by people in jeans and special glasses, busily measuring, cutting, fitting and polishing the silvery rods under bright fluorescent lights.

Each bike comes to the customer with a card signed by whoever worked on it, complete with a short bio. These craftspeople are starting to develop a following. 'Customers from all over the world will request that Matt must make their frame', Vandermark says, 'or that it just must be welded by Tim'.

For each order, 60 pieces of data are entered, including the customer's length of arms, thighs, inseams and shoulders, the measurements of the previous bike, riding habits, plans for the new bike, colour preferences, whether he or she experiences back or neck pain, and how he or she would like the bike to handle, choosing specific gradations of agility and rigidity. Without the Web and other simple software tools, the company would have a tough time managing all that information.

Only when such orders come in does SevenCycles's staff jump into gear, choosing specific sizes, weights and frame assemblies in response to the order data. 'Most companies will estimate demand and build batches of different sizes', says Vandermark, who previously spent 10 years working for a mass-production bike maker that lost money nearly every year. 'We make them all one at a time and this year we made money'.

However, the company, doesn't sell direct. Even if a customer submits an order over the Web without visiting a local bike shop, as a growing percentage do, they must take their delivery through an authorized dealer. After SevenCycles's first year in business, nearly 100 dealers around the world had officially signed up, and new customers who submit their orders through the Web are constantly recommending new dealers in their area. If customers don't live near a SevenCycles dealer, they can just enter in the name of any local bike shop, and SevenCycles will arrange delivery through that store.

The company can make and ship a bike in as little as 2 weeks from when the order is placed. Since titanium rods do not depreciate nearly as fast as computer parts, the company can afford to carry some inventory – usually less than 30 days' worth. But SevenCycles usually receives payment for its products before having to pay for the parts that are used to build them.

The market that SevenCycles serves is high-end. Its products typically retail for $2000 and up, with the average price around $4500. One recent custom order came to $12 000 because the buyer requested that the frame come in several pieces. This way it could come apart easily for packing in an airplane's overhead storage bin. 'We're really aiming at the racers, the serious enthusiasts, and other customers with money', Vandermark says.

All told, SevenCycles eked out a small profit in its first full year in business.

Market Segmentation

This is the name given to the process whereby customers and potential customers are organized into clusters of similar types. SevenCycles see the market for their type of products cut up in a number of ways. One way of looking at the market is by income group. Clearly their bicycles are more expensive than you might find in any retail outlet. However their customers are also cycling enthusiasts who would perceive more value in having a bike that does exactly what they want, and whilst not affluent might stretch to afford it. It follows that the whole marketing strategy for Seven-Cycles will be different from a mass market cycle makers. As well as the price, the promotional messages and the product itself will be different for each of these segments of the bicycle market.

How to Segment Markets.

The following are some of the ways by which markets can be segmented:

Demographic Segmentation

This groups customers together by such variables as age, sex, interest, education and income. Some Internet companies have made their whole proposition age-focused. Live4Now.com is only interested in those aged 18–35, although in practice they find it useful to segment this down further. Dan Thompson, the founder of 365 Corporation, started his business on the back of his belief, shared presumably by the stockmarket, who valued the firm at £285 million when it floated in December 1999, that people have passion centres. Thompson, an Oxford graduate and chartered accountant, had previously founded and run his own computer games and software company, Renegade Software. At 35 he sold it to Time Warner for £5 million, netting about £1 million himself. The first service to be offered was Football365, which provides personalized football content and news aimed at people who are passionate about football. The company is following the sector's tradition by having accelerating losses, £14.6 million in the year to March 2000, up from £1.2 million the preceding year, and is on the acquisition trail.

There is something of the flavour of SevenCycles about the target market segments. Passionate enough about cycling to answer 60 questions on a Web questionnaire, wait 3 weeks and then drive miles to pick up a bicycle a bit like the one you could have taken away from a shop the same day. Whilst Thompson believes his passion segment is right and that the Internet is a 'fantastic medium for making money', 365 was not making money in 1999.

Returning to the issue of age, one of the reasons advanced for

Merrill Lynch's relatively slow and late entry to Internet share trading is that their client base was of a generation that is not comfortable trading on-line.

Psychographic Segmentation

This divides individual consumers into social groups such as Yuppy (young, upwardly mobile, professional), Bumps (borrowed-to-the-hilt upwardly mobile professional show-offs), and Jollies (jet-setting oldies with lots of loot). These categories try to show how social behaviour influences buyer behaviour. Forrester Research, the Internet research house, has made rather a lot, perhaps even more than the subject deserves, of this type of segmentation. In a recent book by the company's vice-president of research, a 'secret' was shared with the readers. 'When it comes to determining whether consumers will or will not go on the Internet, how much they'll spend and what they'll buy, demographic factors such as age, race and gender don't matter anywhere near as much as the consumer's *attitudes towards technology*'. Forrester uses this concept, together with their research, to produce technographics market segments as an aid to understanding people's behaviour as digital consumers.

They have used two dimensions, 'technology optimists' and 'technology pessimists', alongside income and what they call 'primary motivation' – career, family and entertainment – to divide up the whole market (Figure 7.1). Each segment is given a new name, 'Techno-strivers', 'Digital Hopefuls' and so forth, followed by a chapter of explanation on how to identify them, see if they are likely

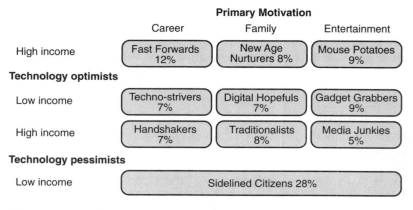

Figure 7.1 Consumer technographics segments in the USA.
Reproduced by permission from Modahl (2000)

to be right for your product or service, and some pointers on what marketing strategies might get a favourable response from each group.

Benefit Segmentation

This recognizes that different people can get different satisfaction from the same product or service. Lastminute.com claims two quite distinctive benefits for their users. First, they aim to offer people bargains which appeal because of price and value. But lately the company has been laying more emphasis on the benefit of immediacy. The theory is rather akin to the impulse-buy products placed at check-out tills that you never thought of buying until you bumped into them on your way out. Whether 10 days on a beach in Goa or a trip to Istanbul is the type of thing people pop in their baskets before turning off their computer screens, time will tell.

Geographic Segmentation

These arise when different locations have different needs. For example, an inner city location may be a heavy user of motorcycle despatch services but a light user of gardening products. But both locations can 'consume' both products if properly presented. An inner city store might sell potatoes in 1 kg bags, recognizing that its customers are likely to be on foot. An out-of-town shopping centre will sell the same product in 20 kg sacks, knowing that their customers will have cars. Internet companies have been slow to extend their reach beyond their own back yard, which is surprising considering the supposed global reach of the service. Microsoft exports only 20% of its total sales beyond American borders and less than 16% of AOL's subscribers live outside the USA. That figure for AOL greatly overstates the company's true export performance. In reality, AOL does virtually no business with overseas subscribers. Rather, it serves them through affiliate relationships. Few of the recent batch of Internet IPOs have registered much overseas activity in their filing details. By way of contrast, the Japanese liquid crystal display industry exports more than 70% of its entire output.

Industrial Segmentation

This groups together commercial customers according to a combination of their geographic location, principal business activity, relative size, frequency of product use, buying policies and a range of other factors. Logical Holdings is an E-business solutions and service company that is about to float on the London Stock Exchange and TechMARK index. The anticipated price is over £1.5 billion which would make it one of the UK's biggest IT companies. Logical was formed from about 30 acquisitions, all made in the past 3 years, and has sales of £800 million, employing 2000 people worldwide. The company is headed by Rikke Helms, formerly head of IBM's E-Commerce Solutions portfolio. Her company has split the market into three: small, medium-sized and big, tailoring their services specifically for each.

Multivariant Segmentation

This is useful where more than one variable is used. This can give a more precise picture of a market than using just one factor. These are some useful rules to help decide if a market segment is worth trying to sell into:

- *Measurability.* Can you estimate how many customers are in the segment? Are there enough to make it worth offering something 'different' for?

- *Accessibility.* Can you communicate with these customers, preferably in a way that reaches them alone? For example, you could reach the over-50s through advertising in a specialist 'older' people's magazine, with reasonable confidence that young people would not read it. So if you were trying to promote Scrabble with tiles 50% larger, you might prefer young people did not hear about it. If they did it might give the product an old-fashioned feel.

- *Open to profitable development.* The customers must have money to spend on the benefits you propose offering.

Innovators Unlock Markets

Even once you have target market segments to aim at, your growth may not come through as fast as you were hoping. Let's suppose you have identified the market for your Internet Flower service. Initially your market has been constrained to affluent men within 5 miles of your base because of initial difficulties with delivery. So, if market research shows that there are 100 000 people that meet the profile of your ideal customer and they have regular access to the Internet, the market open for exploitation at the outset may be as low as 2500, i.e. 2.5% of the total (Figure 7.2).

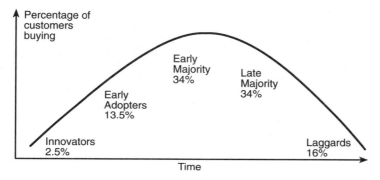

Figure 7.2 Product/service adoption cycle

Only the Innovators, generally the more adventurous types who try out new things early on, are likely to buy initially. The Early Adopters will only start buying when the service has the seal of approval from the Innovators, and so on down the chain, until you reach the Laggards. The Forrester segmentation model, referred to in Figure 7.2, seems to be implying that for Internet markets, the Laggard population, (for 'Laggard' read 'Sidelined Citizens') is larger than for old-economy markets. This is in part because not everyone has access to the Internet every time they want to buy, and in part because a group of people have been left behind by this particular technology. We need to bear in mind that a group of people have been left behind by *every* new technology. Some people would never use the telephone, take a train or watch TV, so what's so new about this technology? However, anything that brings a greater degree of conservatism into Internet sales projections has to be welcomed.

One further issue that has a profound effect on marketing strategy is that Innovators, Early Adopters and all the other subsegments don't necessarily read the same magazines or respond to the same images and messages. So they need to be marketed to in very different ways. This makes the blitz approach to market penetration taken by PeaPod.com and others look a bit suspect. Blitz marketing with a single message may work in stimulating a mature market, but how much use will it be in a market that is still looking for the signal of approval from further up the chain?

Intuit-Quicken.com

In 1983, Intuit founders Scott Cook and Tom Proulx embarked on a quest to revolutionize the way individuals and small businesses manage their finances.

Quicken®, the company's first product, introduced in 1984, struck a chord with consumers and has since become synonymous with personal finance. Quicken's success fuelled the creation of Intuit's other businesses, beginning with QuickBooks® small business accounting software in 1992, and continuing with TurboTax® personal tax software (through acquisition of ChipSoft in 1993). To enhance the value of these products, Intuit created a financial supplies business, selling paper cheques, forms and envelopes to software customers. In 1995, the company pioneered the notion of E-finance by adding on-line banking and bill payment to Quicken.

However, Intuit's entry onto the Web nearly didn't happen – at least not in 1996. In late 1995, Intuit entered a 'period of reflection' to reconsider 'who we were and what we were about'. They had just had a bruising experience after the collapse of the proposed merger with Microsoft and needed to take stock of their direction.

One of Intuit's strengths was to take customer research very seriously indeed. They asked customers what they wanted and went out and tried to supply it. In 1996, following the period of reflection, Intuit's management decided to explore the Web. They asked their customers if they would put their personal financial information on a website.

The answer was a resounding 'No'. No ifs, or buts – just no. Yet today their website has over 1.5 million personal financial portfolios on it. So did market research fail Intuit? Probably not. It looks as though their customer base had a fairly normal new product adopter base. If only 2.5% (the Innovators) said, 'Yes, we'll put our finances on the Web', the remaining 97.5% probably said 'No', in various ways. Yet introducing new Web products quickly caught on, once the Innovators bought in.

Income statement summary	July 1999	July 1998	July 1997	July 1996
Total revenues	847 568	592 736	598 925	538 608
Cost of sales	209 143	123 443	138 770	137 869
Other expenses	618 539	505 875	460 195	406 515
Loss provision	0	3 380	3 308	4 728
Interest expenses	18 252	432	652	305
Income pre-tax	617 349	−19 823	9 809	1 870

Table 7.1   Four year financial survey (in thousands of US$)

Customers Are Not Always Consumers

There are very often two or more people to understand in the marketing process. Often the person buying is not the person consuming. Gifts are an obvious product that fits this description, but there are others too. Business travel, for example. Depending on the amount of influence in the buying process each of these parties has, it may be necessary to incorporate both parties into your segmentation process.

Action Checklist: Market Segmentation

❑ How do you currently segment your market?
❑ Are you satisfied with that process? If not, re-segment.
❑ What are the size, growth rate and the competitive position in each of your main market segments?
❑ Which of these segments are you not currently in and why?
❑ Which segments offer the best scope for extending your market?
❑ Do you market differently in respect of price, promotion and so forth, in the different segments?
❑ Do you know the characteristics of the Innovators in each of your main market segments?

What Are We Good At?   8

SWOT Analysis

A strengths, weaknesses, opportunities and threats (SWOT) analysis is a way of consolidating everything we know about our competitive market position before we move on to make choices about our future marketing strategy. According to the *Journal of Marketing Management*, it is one of the most-used techniques when business people are formulating marketing strategy; 54% claim to carry out SWOTs regularly and only 7% have tried using it and given up.

Whilst it may be a most-used technique, it is also a most-abused one. The most common mistake is to try to carry out the analysis on the business as a whole. It has to be carried out on each important market segment separately. As customer needs in each segment are different, it follows that we have to do different things in each segment, to satisfy those needs. We may be up against different competitors in each segment, so our strengths and weaknesses will be particular to that competitive environment. For example, for national family travel, the car, coach and to a lesser extent the train compete with each other. For business people, the car, plane and first-class rail travel are the favoured competitors.

How to Carry Out a SWOT Analysis

The following steps need to be done separately for each major market segment.

Strengths and Weaknesses

To be a strength or a weakness, the element under consideration has to matter to the customers concerned. In fact, it has to be such an important factor in the customers minds that they would not buy without it. However well designed a personal digital assistant (PDA) may be, if it can't dock with your PC, you probably won't buy it. These are known as critical success factors (CSFs), and it is your performance against these that confirms your strengths and weaknesses.

Critical success factors	(%)	Amazon.com		Barnes & Noble	
		Score, 1–10	Weighted score	Score 1–10	Weighted score
Location	30	10	3.0	5	1.5
Opening hours	20	10	2.0	4	0.8
Range of books	20	9	1.8	2	0.4
Merchandizing	20	9	1.8	2	0.4
Staff	10	5	0.5	8	0.8
Total	100		9.1		3.9

Table 8.1   Critical success factors (CSFs)

Table 8.1 shows a hypothetical strengths and weaknesses analysis for Amazon.com and Barnes & Noble back in 1997, when Amazon was just picking up steam. The market segment we will assume to be busy professionals, married and living away from the city centre. It almost doesn't matter which city – Paris, London, New York, Tokyo, Sydney, the problems are the same. The bookshops are shut when you reach the office, and very often when you leave. No major bookshop is likely to be sited in the leafy suburb your family is living in. Location is the most important single factor, accounting for 30% of customers' reason to buy. Next comes opening hours, followed by the range of books, the way they are merchandized in the shops and the product knowledge of the staff. We could debate the precise ranking and weighting of each factor, but it would make little difference to the result. Barnes & Noble had a comparative strength in their people – they had 29 000 compared to Amazon's 2100 – and everyone will attest to how much Barnes & Noble's shop staff are smart about books. However, they were weak in almost every other respect. Amazon was strong where it mattered. They had 4.7 million books on their 'shelf', compared to Barnes & Noble's 175 000, and they were open 24 hours a day, every day. Sure, Barnes & Noble, and other booksellers, had made strides (or 'concessions', if you take the vocabulary of the more conservative booksellers) and were open in the evenings and part of each weekend. But adding up the weighted scores gave Amazon a nearly 2½ times competitive advantage over Barnes & Noble, more than enough to seize the market and become the most valuable bookseller in the world, as Figure 8.1 demonstrates.

This, of course, does not necessarily spell doom for bricks-and-mortar booksellers. In the past, new innovations didn't kill off old ways of doing business. They just forced them to re-focus and compete in different ways. Despite dire predictions, the plane has not supplanted

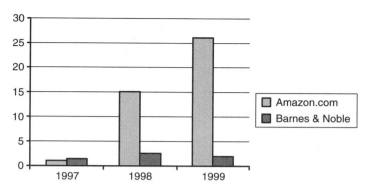

Figure 8.1 Amazon.com vs. Barnes & Noble:
Market capitalization, end year, $bn.
Source: Primark DataStream

the train – in Europe, with its own technological advances, the train has more than kept up. Neither has television replaced radio. Radio has just found new products and markets and with the advent of digital radio, is undergoing something of a rebirth in 2000.

Interestingly enough, Internet strategists claim that you need a three-to-one advantage to not merely capture market share but to make money too. Perhaps that is a problem Amazon needs to address in turning high sales into high profits.

Amazon's 20% share slide in July 2000 suggests that shareholders are beginning to wonder if this particular emperor has any clothes on at all. Crossing a risky business model, B2C, with a risky financial strategy, 99% debt funding, supported only by a thin gross margin (22%), Amazon (and a few dozen more such firms) looks increasingly more like a proposition for Las Vegas, than a serious Wall Street stock.

The ratings and the critical success factors are arrived at by market research, which you need to do regularly to decide the future strategic direction.

Opportunities

It is important to recognize that an idea, invention or innovation is not necessarily an opportunity to grow your business with. As we saw with Bookham Technologies, business growth has to be a market-driven process. That is despite, in their case, it taking a decade to develop the technology to exploit the market opportunity. An opportunity has to be attractive, durable and timely. It is centred around a product or service that creates or adds value for its buyer or end user. Working out what is attractive to you is fairly straightforward. Estimating the likely life of an opportunity, or whether the time is right for its launch, is not so easy. In a way, that is the essence of an entrepreneur's skill. It also explains in part why most firms start and stay small, or fail!

With opportunities, you are looking for those that will bring the maximum benefit to the business while at the same time having a high probability of success. The benefits you are looking for may vary over time. In the early years, cash flow and early settlement periods may feature high on the list. Later, fast growth and high margins may be more important.

Intuit (Figure 8.2) saw that the opportunity created by on-line account preparation was so great, whilst clearly matching their skill set, that despite uncertain signals from their customer base, they had to enter the market.

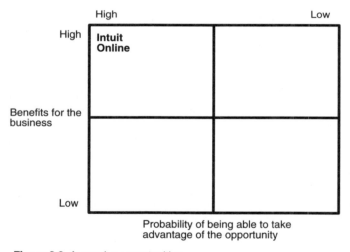

Figure 8.2 Assessing opportunities

Threats

Threats can come from all directions. Changes in the political or economic climate, new legislation or the impact of hackers and computer viruses can all have an impact on your business. One business founder found, to his dismay, that his new site linked into dozens of pornography sites, the work of professional hackers this time. This set his operation back 2 months. New technological developments happen faster in the Internet world, at such a rate that it would be financial ruin to be deflected from your strategy by all of them. So you need to decide which you can safely leave aside, for now. Changes in the demographic profile of populations (more older people and fewer of working age), or changing fashions, hit all business, old- and new-economy alike.

There are always too many potential threats for you to consider, so you need to focus on those with the greatest possible impact that seem most likely to occur. Merrill Lynch (Figure 8.3) clearly saw the demographics of the customer base, largely made up of an older group of share traders, as being a certain threat, with a high impact on the business – one that had to be addressed.

The question 'so what?' is a good one to apply to all aspects of your SWOT analysis. Once completed, the SWOT will provide the ingredients and framework for developing your growth strategy.

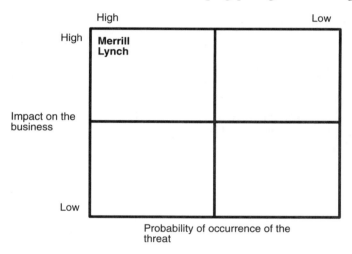

Figure 8.3 Reviewing threats

Action Checklist: SWOT Analysis

Carry out a SWOT analysis on each of your most important product/market areas, using the tools discussed above.

Part 1. Strengths and Weaknesses

❏ Initially, use your own view of what matters most to customers.
❏ Repeat the process after discussing what other entrepreneurs believe the critical success factors to be.

❑   Repeat the process with your newest front-line staff.
❑   Use a customer focus group to establish the critical success factors and carry out your analysis again.
❑   How far apart were the views of each of the above groups on what constitutes the critical success factors? If you are close to your customers, there should be little difference. If there is a large difference, what can you do to make sure the gap is narrowed and stays that way?

Part 2.   Opportunities and Threats

❑   Initially, use your own view of what constitutes the most attractive opportunity and the most serious threat.
❑   Repeat the process with your management team.
❑   Repeat the process with your newest front-line staff.
❑   Use a customer focus group to establish main threats and opportunities and carry out your analysis again.
❑   How far apart were the views of each of the above groups on what constitutes the main threats and opportunities? If you are close to your market, there should be little difference. If there is a large difference, what can you do to make sure the gap is narrowed and stays that way?

How Could We Do Better? 9

Market segmentation, SWOT and critical success factor analysis using market research are the essential first steps in determining your marketing strategy. This chapter puts forward a framework to help you review your products/services, markets and the way you do business, to see ways in which you might do even better.

How to Develop Marketing Strategy

Figure 9.1 illustrates the two major strategic options to pursue when aiming for growth. They are not mutually exclusive, but each has a different strategic focus.

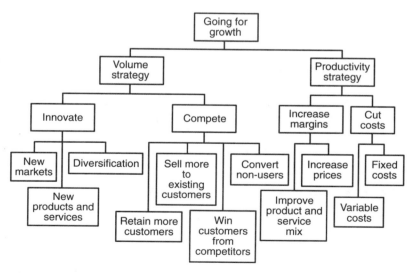

Figure 9.1 Developing marketing strategy

Building Volume

Increasing volume can have the effect of growing profits at a much faster rate. Once past break-even, fixed costs have been covered and each extra pound of contribution is largely retained profit. This can be particularly true for Internet companies, where the marginal cost of each extra sale can be quite small. Lastminute.com and Leisurehunt.com, a new Internet business offering a worldwide hotel search and booking service, incurred virtually no extra cost for every extra order received, once their sites were up and running. There are two principle strategies that can help you grow sales volume.

Innovation

This area of marketing strategy (Figure 9.2) concerns developing and launching new products and services and entering new markets. It is inevitably a higher-risk strategy than competing to retain and grow the existing customer base using existing products and services. Ansoff's growth matrix, as it is generally known, is a useful way of reviewing your growth strategies. Too heavy a dependence on one type of growth strategy might be viewed as risky if, say, all your hopes for growth were pinned on a successful entry into the Albanian market.

	MARKETS	
	Existing	New
Existing PRODUCTS/ SERVICES	**Business development** PeaPod's local sales blitz	**Market development** Motley Fool's entry to Germany, France, UK
New	**Product development** Amazon's Music NeXT workstation Amazon's tools and hardware	**Diversification** AOL's acquisition of Time Warner

Figure 9.2 Innovative growth for Internet businesses

New Markets

This may mean simply taking existing proven products and services into new geographic areas or new market segments. For example, Motley Fool's entry into the German market involves a modest change in a well-proven product, as for its entry to the UK, French and Italian Markets between 1998 and 2001. CommTouch Software, with a successful NASDAQ IPO worth $678 million behind it, has expanded from its base in Israel to have 10.4 million active e-mail users in 150 countries working in 20 languages. E-Loan is a USA-based, SoftBank-backed on-line consumer lending company that went public on NASDAQ in July 1999. By November they had established operations in Japan and in 2000 started up in the UK, Australia, France and Germany, learning something from each new market as they went along.

New Products and Services

At one end of this spectrum are truly new and innovative products, at the other are relatively modest product or service line extensions. Amazon's Music and Video/DVD business could be seen as product line extensions. Their Tools and Hardware operation looks more like a new product – new to them, of course, not to the thousands of other businesses in that sector. Intuit's adding paper cheques, forms and envelopes, and so creating a new financial supplies business, was truly selling new products into its existing market place. Launching new products can be a risky path to growth. Most new products are unsuccessful. Steve Job's NeXT workstation is a good example of the risks you run with new products. The workstation was generally recognized as being technologically superb, but it was launched into a market already dominated by Sun Microsystems and Hewlett-Packard. It failed. A new product has to be two or three times better in some respect – price, performance, convenience, availability – to dislodge a well entrenched rival.

They don't have to be your new products and services, of course. Alliances, affiliations, joint ventures and the like abound on the Internet, as they do elsewhere. The case studies below are just examples of thousands of such mutually beneficial strategies that can boost growth quickly.

Kozmo.com

Starbucks (NASDAQ: SBUX), the company that rewrote the book on tapping consumers' expendable income, has entered into a 5 year, $150 million marketing agreement with on-line delivery E-tailor, Kozmo.com, blending Starbucks's bricks-and-mortar assets and retail strength with Kozmo.com's 'E-mmediate' Web-based delivery of everything from Twinkies to DVD players.

The deal, which includes Kozmo.com giving the coffee merchant $150 million, will reportedly benefit both parties extensively. Kozmo.com intends to use the association to carve out a deeper toehold in Starbucks's home town, Seattle, to expand its presence in other Starbucks-saturated service areas, such as Boston, New York, San Francisco and Washington, DC.

Starbucks customers will now be able to purchase their beans on yet another on-line retail outlet, as Kozmo.com will deliver coffee-by-the-pound and other products. The bean behemoth estimates that of the 10 million customers who visit its stores weekly, approximately 90% are Web users.

'This alliance defines the benefits of a truly integrated clicks-and-mortar strategy for our customers', said Howard Schultz, Starbucks's chairman and CEO, in a prepared statement. 'In fact, the similarities between Starbucks and Kozmo.com customers make this a value-enhancing proposition for everybody'. Ultimately, Kozmo.com, founded in 1997, plans to make use of this new connection by utilizing Starbucks's 2100-plus stores in 34 US cities. Other Kozmo.com partnerships include TicketMaster and Amazon.com. Starbucks expects the deal to add $0.01 to earnings per share during the remainder of 2000 and roughly $0.05 per share in 2001.

iVillage

On-line women's network *iVillage* (NASDAQ: IVIL) and personal care products merchant Unilever (NYSE: UN) have created an independently managed dot-com to market beauty products on-line. Unilever and iVillage plan to invest up $200 million in cash, intellectual property, marketing and other resources, to fund the entity. The company will focus on beauty needs and beauty-related services, content and commerce solutions. The market has been quite crowded of late. Alley-based *Ingredients.com* launched last fall, hot on the heels of *ibeauty.com*. NYC-based *Beauty.com* was picked up by Drugstore.com for $42 million in stock, just 2 months after its launch. Forrester Research predicts that the on-line health and beauty products industry will grow from $509 million in 1999 to $10.4 billion in 2004.

This venture increases iVillage's reach and further underscores their ability to effectively leverage the iVillage brand and assets both online and offline'.

Unilever, which currently has 276 000 employees in 88 countries, supplied the capital. iVillage's contribution was its beauty channel, along with several other properties and advertising support. The new company, based in New York, will look to generate revenues through advertising, sponsorships, and E-commerce sales of beauty and personal care products.

iVillage.com's rich, independent editorial content, coupled with Unilever's marketing prowess, will create an unparalleled force in the beauty and personal care marketplace, both parties hope.

Diversification

This is the riskiest strategy of all – selling things you know little about to people you know even less about. Sure, you can do market research and buy in industry expertise, but that's still more risky than selling music to people who already buy books from you. Merrill Lynch's on-line business is pretty close to diversification. They are offering a Web-based service only recently developed, to a market of younger Internet-literate clients, when their existing customer base are generally older people. This is the riskiest strategy of all, so how do they succeed? By hastening slowly, and sometimes by acquisition, and above all by listening to customers and front-line staff. AOL's acquisition of Time Warner was a diversification, and the risk involved was not lost on the stockmarket, where their shares were quickly marked down. Beware of the lure of *synergy* – the mythical two plus two equals five. Unless you can quantify the value-added in an acquisition or diversification, for example in better buying with quantity discounts or by being able to spread your costs over a bigger sales volume, don't bother.

But if you can get acquisitions right, the growth through diversification, or even in your own sector for that matter, can be phenomenal. Cisco Systems has bought 52 companies over the past 15 years and set aside a further $10 billion for future deals. William Nuti, senior vice-president, in an interview for *Sunday Business* in April 2000, is quoted as saying, 'Management consultants who do this for a living come to Cisco to learn how to acquire and integrate companies successfully'. It has to be said that most important research studies of the past 30 years into mergers and acquisitions, as a strategy to create shareholder value, have detected little evidence to be quite as sanguine as Mr Nuti. Many other firms who felt that they had got acquisition and diversification strategy in the bag have gone the way of the dinosaur. Remember conglomerates?

Competition

Competition is not as exciting as launching new products but is the area where most young businesses consistently achieve the largest and most profitable part of their growth.

Retain More Customers

Every business loses customers. What is not generally appreciated is that even if you can win more new customers than you lose, you are still missing out on a major growth opportunity. Bain & Co., the American consulting group, has demonstrated that by hanging on to an extra 5% of your customers each year you can double profits. As on average companies lose and find half their customers every 5 years, there is plenty of scope for improvement. The reasons that 'loyalty' improves profitability are: retaining customers costs less than finding and capturing new ones; loyal customers tend to place larger orders; and loyal customers don't always place price first, whilst new ones do. E*Trade, the on-line stock brokerage (about which more later), discovered that even after a number of significant 'setbacks', more than 95% of customers stuck with them. People who put their assets into online brokerage tend to stay put for a long time.

A model such as the customer dynamics one (Table 9.1) helps keep track of customers as a means of improving retention and understanding how customers' needs change. Expectations at the courtship stage are not the same as at the wedlock or deadlock stages. Checking on customers who have not re-ordered within a set period is one way to use this framework, and Web-based systems are ideal to handle the flow.

Stage	Courtship	Engagement	Honeymoon	Wedlock	Deadlock
Customer attitude	Suspicious	Wary	Trusting	Bored	Disenchanted
Supplier's goal	Get trial or first order	Get them signed up	Increase usage/traffic	Maintain volume	Sell in new products and services

Table 9.1 Customer dynamics

A half-hearted approach has appeared in the 'others who bought this book have also bought one of these' screens that are now popping up on many E-booksellers' sites, as a way to stimulate interest. A much better model is being developed by Tesco.com (and others), which actually monitors an individual's behaviour over time, to tailor specific offers that should appeal.

A more aggressive approach is taken by AOL, who make it 'difficult' for a customer to quit the service. The only way out is via a live salesperson who, armed with an offer of several months' free usage and no telephone charges, whips the recalcitrant back into line.

Successful growth marketing strategies for entrepreneurial firms are explored in more detail by Barrow and Brown (1997).

Sell More to Existing Customers

Winning customers' early business during what is known as the 'courtship' phase does not mean that you are either their only or their main supplier. Winning more of their business, by becoming their chosen business 'partner' or preferred supplier, is clearly a priority. This can involve sharing information and carrying out joint promotions.

Winning Competitors' Customers

This is never easy, and in doing so your attention should be focused on added value rather than price cutting: there is no point in growing unprofitably. You need constant market intelligence to reveal when a competitor's quality is down, deliveries are late or a trusted sales-person has left. These moments of weakness are the best times to probe a competitor's defences and 'assault' their customer base. E*Trade had begun by offering trades at $35, but after seven price cuts in the war to win customers, they decided enough was enough. They did not want to engage in Pyrrhic price wars, where there would be no winners. Unlike most Web start-ups, they were profitable. So they held the line at $14.95 and then went on to pursue a value-added strategy, using retained profits for finance. They surrounded their transactions with mountains of well-organized information and lots of easy-to-use services that made customers want to return to this middle ground again and again.

Convert Non-users

There are inevitably many non-users of whatever you and your competitors sell. Lots of people eat at home and never go to restaurants, for example. AOL's strategy here is encapsulated in their 'Do a friend a favour' campaigns. Sending disks to existing customers with the message, 'Get your friend on line with AOL and once both you and your friend have been on line for 60 hours or more, you will receive £30 FREE', AOL hope that once they have broken their duck, a proportion will remain as customers. Sixty hours on-line sounds like quite a big duck, and in itself says something about the way the market is shaping up. It used to be that 'A FREE 10 hour Internet trial' was enough to hook a customer, but clearly times are changing.

Improving Productivity

Improving productivity is a constant requirement for a growing business. It is not something to be done only during recessions, cash flow crises or in other troubled times. Productivity needs to be improved by reviewing both your costs and your margins.

Cutting Costs

Costs need to be constantly controlled and balanced against the need for the business to be able to deliver products and services in a satisfactory manner. This means looking at both the fixed and variable aspects of cost. We will be looking at this aspect of generating growth in Chapter 18, 'Slowing Down the Burn Rate'.

Increasing Margins

This can be the result of cutting costs. It can also result from external market appraisal leading to changes in your product or service mix, or even from increased prices. Margins are something Internet firms and analysts in the sector focus on, and rightly so, as many have pretty dismal ones. PeaPod, by focusing on margin strategies, got its percentages up from 20% in 1999 to 23% in 2000. While this may not sound great in itself, it represents a 15% improvement and is perhaps the most significant action any firm can take in the short run, to improve its position.

Product Mix

Analysis of product mix requires that your accounts give you accurate costs and gross margins for each of your product or service lines. Once you know what product/service/markets make you the most money, your pitch can be slanted accordingly. So, if E-Toys or PeaPod or any E-tailor has this margin data, they can shift the emphasis of their marketing to sell more high-margin than slow-margin products. As the rest of their costs will remain fairly static (it costs as much to deliver a high-margin bottle of wine as a low-margin own-brand water), profits for the same amount of effort will rise. On-line category killers, such as Monster.com and CareerMosaic, have not only destroyed the classified jobs ads business for many local newspapers by their global reach, but have opened up big non-user markets too. They reach people who are not even really looking for a job. By letting them post their resumés in a database, the sites attract coveted professionals who aren't really looking but want to hear about opportunities all the same. But where this strategy really scores is by getting a client base with a higher spend capacity onto their system, thus increasing margins.

Increasing Prices

This is always difficult. Reducing prices is usually done with a fanfare of publicity. Some people believe that an increase in price is best accomplished by stealth. This is rarely the way to generate long-term customer loyalty. The most successful companies seek to combine price increases with improvements in the product or service. That was the strategy pursued by E*Trade (see above), with some success. Pricing is not generally regarded as an area in which new Internet businesses have been successful. We will look in more detail at pricing in the next chapter.

Action Checklist: How to Do Better

Go through each element of the marketing strategy chart and see what possible actions could be taken under each heading and with what possible result. This can be best tackled by making up a table, as in Table 9.2 below. Use the customer dynamics matrix (Figure 9.3) to categorize your customers and consider strategies to manage them from courtship to wedlock, and prevent deadlock occurring.

Strategy	Action	Information required	Expected result
1. New markets			
2. New products			
3. New services			
4. Diversification			
5. Acquisitions			
6. Customer retention			
7. Sell more to existing customers			
8. Win competitors' customers			
9. Convert non-users			
10. Improve product and service mix			
11. Increase prices			

Table 9.2 Marketing strategy chart

Stage	Courtship	Engagement	Honeymoon	Wedlock	Deadlock
Percentage of our customers					
What we could do to improve on this					
Target percentage to aim for					

Figure 9.3   Customer dynamics matrix

The E-marketeer's Toolkit 10

The marketing mix, as this toolkit is usually known in old-economy circles, is the way in which strategy can be developed and implemented. Using the mix in different proportions can result in very different 'products'.

In business, these 'ingredients' are price, product, promotion and place. A change in the way these elements are put together can produce an offering tailored to meet the needs of a specific market *segment*. For example, a hardback book is barely more expensive to produce than a paperback. However, with a bit of clever publicity, by bringing hardbacks out a few weeks before the paperback edition, and with a hefty price hike, an air of exclusivity can be created which satisfies a particular group of customers.

How to Use the Marketing Toolkit

The *product* or *service* is what people use, but what they buy are the underlying benefits they confer on them. The founder of a successful cosmetics firm, when asked what his business did, replied, 'In our factories we make perfume, in the shops we sell dreams.' The work we have done in earlier chapters should have brought this into sharp focus. Figure 10.1 shows how Schwab has managed the introduction of new products and services to sustain its growth. Not all product and service introductions have revenue streams of their own, but their impact can be felt elsewhere, as the case below demonstrates.

Estée Lauder

Estée Lauder's Clinique website, which sells make-up and skin-care products, was launched in late 1998. Lauder spend over $980 million a year on advertising, out of a gross margin of over 70%. By way of contrast, they only spend $35 million a year on research. So investment in a website was fairly small beer.

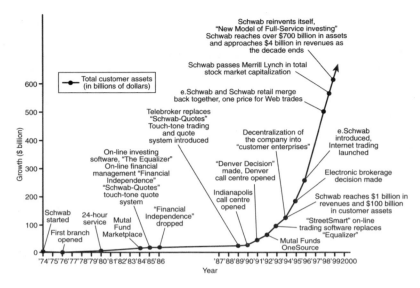

Figure 10.1 New products and services fuel Schwab's growth

From the start, the site was a great success and by mid-1999, Clinique had registered more than 200 000 new customers. After careful analysis, Angela Kapp, Vice-President and General Manager for Esteé Lauder Online, concluded that 90% of the people weren't transacting any business there. They just gathered information before visiting a store to buy. In one study, Clinique established that 68% of women registered on the website said they would rather purchase at a store. Far from cannibalizing sales from the stores, the website has proved to be largely a new service for existing customers. Sales overall are well ahead of preceding years, and on-line sales have risen to significant proportions too.

Pricing

Most aspects of your business are all about creating value for your customer. Pricing, as Tom Neagle of Boston University has observed, is the time 'when you grab a chunk of that value and put it in your own pocket'.

Deciding what is a fair price is a problem that has taxed economic man ever since money was invented in the fifth century BC. Things are made more complicated by the fact that most useful things, such as water (before designer water), seem to have a low value, while the least useful, such as silk, have a high value. Value, like beauty, is in the eye of the beholder. This degree of subjectivity means that companies have a great deal of discretion in the area of pricing.

A good quality product, priced too low, often does not have its quality recognized by the public. There is a strong belief that you get what you pay for. Economists offer conflicting advice, ranging from charging what the market will bear, through marginal cost (just enough to cover direct costs and a small contribution to overheads), to where your supply and demand curves intersect. Few growing companies find these concepts helpful. So, according to *Management Today*, over 80% of companies price by reference to their costs. They either use cost plus a percentage, or a cost multiplier (e.g. three times materials).

While it is important to know your costs, this is only one element in the pricing decision. In addition you have to take account of the market place, your competition and the way you position the product (e.g. luxury item). Frequently, resistance to increasing prices can come from your own team, eager to blame price for poor sales. It is important to make detailed price comparisons with your competitors, using a scoring system such as that in Table 10.1. You should also experiment with different prices in different market segments, to get a feel for what the market will bear.

Product/service attributes	Worse			Same	Better		
	−3	−2	−1	0	+1	+2	+3
Design							
Performance							
Packaging							
Presentation and appearance							
After-sales service							
Availability							
Delivery							
Colour/flavour/odour/touch							
Image							
Specification							
Payment terms							
Others							

Table 10.1 Pricing comparison with the competition

If your product or service scores a high positive figure and you price below the competition, then you may be giving the wrong signal to your customers and losing potential extra profit. Price points are another strategy for managing a 'pricing for profit' strategy. Look at the On-line Brokers chart (Table 10.2). This is a

	Set up fee (£)	Dealing commissions (£)				Administration charges	
		1000	9000	10 000	25 000	Annual	Exit per company
Barclays Stockbrokers www.barclays-stockbroker.co.uk	Nil	11.99	39.99	39.99	39.99	Nil	Nil
Cave & Sons www.caves.co.uk	Nil	15	40	40	40	Nil	10
Charles Schwab MM www.schwab-worldwide.com	Nil	12	36	36	50	1 each	10
DLJ Direct www.dljdirect.co.uk	Nil	14.95	37.50	37.50	37.50	Nil	15
e-cortal www.e-cortal.com	60	12	16.32	16.32	16.32	60	Nil
E*Trade www.etrade.co.uk	Nil	14.95	24.95	24.95	24.95	50	10
Fastrade www.torrie.co.uk	Nil	15	25	30	30	Nil	10
Goy-Harris Copyright www.ghcl.co.uk	35.25	20	20	20	20	35.25	Nil
Halifax ShareXpress www.sharexpress.co.uk	Nil	12.50	22.50	22.50	22.50	Nil	15
Hargreaves Lansdown www.hargreaveslansdown.co.uk	Nil	9.95	9.95	9.95	9.95	50	12.50
iDealing www.idealing.com	Nil	10	10	10	10	20	15
James Brearley Icon www.jbrearley.co.uk	Nil	20	20	20	20	25	5
Killik & Co. www.killik.co.uk	Nil	30	30	62.50	125	5 each	25
NatWest Stockbrokers www.natweststockbrokers.co.uk	Nil	15	41	46	61	Nil	10
Nothing-Ventured www.tdwaterhouse.co.uk	50	19.50	35.25	42.75	62.25	50	10
TD Waterhouse www.tdwaterhouse.co.uk	Nil	12.95	25.99	35.99	65.99	Nil	10
Redmayne Bently www.redm.co.uk	15	12.95	25	39.95	39.95	100	5
The Share Centre www.sharepeople.com	Nil	10	50	100	250	5 each	15
Sharepeople www.sharepeople.com	Nil	17.50	17.50	17.50	17.50	42.58	10
Stocktrade www.stocktrade.co.uk	10	14.50	20	49	100	10	15
Xest www.xest.com	20	20	20	20	20	45	Nil

Table 10.2   On-line brokers

schedule of charges showing the range of prices for different activities in May 2000. Xest charges the same price for all deals up to £25 000 and makes a small set-up charge. Schwab and E*trade, along with several others, make no charge to join, and have a sliding scale thereafter – that strategy presents no barrier to entry, but may not make anyone feel like staying after their first trade. However, once you have paid £50 to Nothing-Ventured, you may feel compelled to stick with them and do some day trading to get your money's worth.

But even with something as difficult to differentiate as selling a share, it is possible to send signals that support a higher price. Established firms can trade on fear of the unknown with a new player. Those who have had fewer glitches and no crashes when volumes get too high, a rather important factor these days with dot-com investments, can trade on that. And then there are all the services – charts, industry information and the user-friendliness of the website itself – that all surround the price.

As you can see from Table 10.2, pricing on the net can be anything but transparent.

Real Time Pricing

The stockmarket works by gathering information on supply and demand. If more people want to buy a share than to sell it, the price goes up until supply and demand are matched. If the information is perfect, that is every buyer and seller knows what is going on, the price is optimized. For most businesses this is not a practical proposition. Their customers expect the same price every time for the same product or service. And in any case they have no accurate idea what the demand is at any given moment in time. But for an Internet company, computer networks have made it possible to see how much consumer demand exists for a given product at any time. Anyone with a point-of-sale till could do the same, but the reports may come in weeks later. So on-line companies could change their price hundreds of times each day, in certain circumstances, in some markets, and so improve profits dramatically. Easyjet.com, a budget airline operating out of Luton (just north of London) does just this. They price to fill their planes, and you could pay anything from £30 to £200 for the same trip, depending on the demand for that flight.

Promotion

Doing business without advertising, it has been said, 'is like winking in the dark'. You know what you are doing but no-one else does. Whilst promotion and advertising can be an intangible activity, the bills for it are not. The Internet Advertising Bureau, an industry association, said that revenues were on course to reach $4.4 billion, up more than 130% on the $1.9 billion achieved in 1998. But the yield per dollar spent is actually dropping. The cost of attracting new customers to on-line retail sites increased by 15% to $38 per customer by the end of 1999. Multi-channel retailers' costs dropped to $11 per customer, whilst pure play sites spent $82 on each new account. As we saw from the E*Trade case above, advertising may win customers but that may not make you money. So perhaps the real answer is to do better advertising. That may have less to do with the advertisements themselves and everything to do with the way the campaign is planned.

The answers to the following five questions will help you become more successful in this area.

1. *What do you want to happen?*   There is no point in informing, educating or pre-selling, unless it leads generally to the opportunity for a sale. The first question to ask is, what does the potential customer have to do to enable you to make a sale? Do they have to visit your showroom, 'phone you, return a card or send an order in the post? Do you expect them to order now, or to remember you when at some future date they have a need for your services? The more you can identify a specific response, the easier it is to set objectives, e.g. 'we want to generate 400 phone calls for information'.

Alibris.com

One corner of the book market not being fought over by Amazon and Barnes & Noble came alive on the Internet in 2000. For decades, the antiquarian trade has remained the corner of the book market, attracting fiercely independent booksellers who savour the 'Eureka' moment of spotting a rare first edition in the back of an old bookshop, or in a bundle bought at auction. But that all changed with the arrival of Alibris, an on-line used-book seller that has Wall Street ambitions, Silicon Valley money and a strategy that is rolling away one of the last bastions of the book market where small dealers still hold sway.

There are now more than 11 000 rare and used book dealers and shops in the USA, up from 9000 in 1996. With financial resources totalling more than

$60 million in venture capital, Alibris is a mix of Internet start-up and industry upstart, a 2 year-old company with a daring national advertising campaign aimed at building a mighty brand on the spines of old books.

There are other existing online services for used books with a larger pool of dealers – at least for the moment. Advanced Book Exchange, which is based in Victoria, British Columbia, Canada, offers books from more than 6000 dealers, compared with about 1500 that Alibris says have joined its fold. But it is Alibris's eye-catching ads that have propelled the company to the forefront. The ads promote not leather-bound first editions of Charles Dickens but what might best be described as baby-boomer classics – books that were hugely popular somewhere between 35 and 50 years ago and whose covers, hard or soft, are invoked to trigger Proustian memories.

One Alibris ad features a battered copy of Lewis Padgett's 1950s-vintage science fiction book, *Mutant*. The ad reads: 'April 11, 1977. Freaked you out so bad you had to bury it. Jan. 25, 2000. Unearth on Alibris for son who shares your sci-fi gene'. Other ads feature titles ranging from Jack Kerouac's *On the Road* to *Phyllis Diller's Housekeeping Hints*.

In the next 5 years, said Martin Manley, chief executive of the company, Alibris hopes to spend at least $100 million to market its titles.

Alibris's splashy presence is causing a minor industry revolt. Some defiant dealers are refusing to supply books for the Alibris website, which draws titles from booksellers lower in the literary chain and then inspects and marks them up for sale. Others are testing a cooperative website of dealers. Then there are booksellers who are happily working with the high-profile newcomer, arguing that Alibris is trying to do what the vast majority could never afford: expand the rarefied demand for rare and used books into a mass market. The hostilities that Alibris has provoked among some traditional booksellers mirror the same tensions that other industries are facing over issues of consolidation and the loss of personal connections.

It is not as though Alibris is simply introducing new technology to the business. The Internet has already helped increase the number and reach of independent dealers. The Internet has enabled many sellers of used books to expand their customer base to the entire world. But the vast majority of these dealers are tiny operations. By contrast, Alibris has a growing staff of 100 at its administrative offices in Emeryville, California, a warehouse of books in Sparks, Nevada, and another distribution warehouse planned for England. And Alibris is moving aggressively to expand its database. Last October, it announced the purchase of Bibliocity, an electronic source of rare and antiquarian books. Meanwhile, Alibris has been eyeing ABE, with its list of almost 4 million titles and 18 million copies.

2. *How much is that worth?* Once you have a clear promotional objective, it becomes easier to put a figure on how much achieving it is worth. So if every 100 phone calls results in 10 quotes for business, every 10 quotes produces one order. Average orders are worth £5000 at an operating margin of 20%. Then any advertising cost less than £1000 will result in extra profit.

3. *What message will help achieve your objective?* Here you need to see exactly what benefits your potential customers are looking

for. Then you can produce the message that will convince them they are going to be at least satisfied and hopefully delighted.

4. *What media should you use?* Not all methods of communication have an equal impact. You need to chose the right one for the objectives you have chosen. Web-bases advertising may not be best for all aspects of your promotional strategy. For detailed negotiations, the direct or telephone sales force may be best. To reassure customers that you are good people to do business with may call for public relations. Meeting large numbers of new potential customers face-to-face for the first time may be most efficiently tackled at a trade show.

5. *How will we measure results?* Once again, with a clear objective it is very easy to measure results. But not many people do.

Selling

The sales process is an area that has been changed out of all recognition by the Internet. For over 60 years an immense and, until recently, growing mass of uniformly dressed salesmen travelled the globe. IBM alone has 30 000 salesmen; Oracle another 10 000; the next four biggest software companies have another 50 000 between them. The argument for retaining a sales force resides in the complexity of pricing, incentive discounts and so on that have always been the salesman's stock in trade. Having a deep relationship with a small number of people, say 30–50 client companies per salesman, was the reason the numbers became so vast.

The Web was not thought of as being much use as a primary selling tool because it could not manage the depth of information required to sustain a valuable relationship with clients. In the beginning (1995–1998), Internet penetration was low, and relationship maintenance tools were few and far between. But that is changing fast (Figure 10.2). The Internet has now penetrated almost every office and most homes. Oracle is leading the way, taking away the salesman's stock in trade, pricing. In their place are menus of greatly simplified pricing options and a shift of 80% of its sales efforts to the Web. The savings won't just be in salesmen. The paper-based or computer-incompatible systems the sales forces use make for an administrative nightmare. They also make buying habits, trends and preferences impossible to track. With new Web-based systems, companies such as Oracle could have the equivalent of an intelligent checkout till and be able to have a deeper relationship yet, with even more customers.

You need to review carefully the 'moments of truth', those points

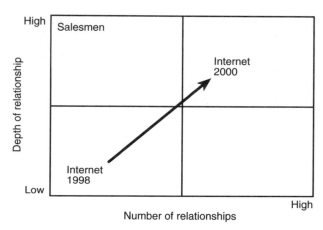

Figure 10.2 Web sales, the new new salesman

of contact between you and your customers, that add up to a sale being won or lost, to make sure you have the most cost-effective route to market.

The *Encyclopaedia Britannica* case below is not merely a vivid example of how changes are happening to the sales process. It also shows how a salesforce bent on protecting its own position (and who can blame them?) could bring a long-established company to its knees.

Britannica.com

In 1768, three Scottish printers began publishing an integrated compendium of knowledge – the earliest and most famous encyclopaedia in the English-speaking world. They called it *Encyclopaedia Britannica*. Since then, *Britannica* has evolved through 15 editions, and to this day it is generally regarded as the world's most comprehensive and authoritative encyclopedia.

In 1920, Sears, Roebuck and Co., an American mail-order retailer, acquired Britannica and moved its headquarters from Edinburgh to Chicago. Ownership passed to William Benton in 1941, who then willed the company in the early 1970s to the Benton Foundation, a charitable organization Britannica grew under its American owners into a serious commercial enterprise, while sustaining its reputation as the world's most prestigious and comprehensive encyclopaedia. The content was revised every 4–5 years. Brand extensions, such as atlases and yearbooks, were added. The company built one of the most aggressive and successful direct sales forces in the world. By targeting middle-income families and focusing on their aspirations for their children, the company developed a marketing proposition as compelling as the intellectual content of the product itself.

By 1990, sales of *Britannica's* multivolume sets had reached an all-time peak of about $650 million. Dominant market share, steady if unspectacular growth, generous margins, and a 200 year history. Since 1990, however, sales of *Britannica*, and of all printed encyclopaedias in the USA, have collapsed by over 80%.

The CD-ROM came from nowhere and destroyed the printed encyclopaedia business. Whereas *Britannica* sells for $1500–2200 per set. CD-ROM encyclopaedias, such as *Encarta*, *Grolier* and *Compton*, list for $50–70. But few people pay even that: most copies are given away to promote the sale of computers and peripherals. With a marginal manufacturing cost of $1.50 per copy, the CD-ROM as freebie makes good economic sense. The marginal cost of *Britannica*, in contrast, is about $250 for production plus about $500–600 for the salesperson's commission.

Britannica's executives at first viewed the CD-ROM encyclopaedia as an irrelevance. This perception was entirely reasonable. Microsoft had licensed the text for its encyclopaedia from Funk & Wagnall's, whose third-rate, nearly defunct product survived only as a periodic promotional item in the aisles of supermarkets. Microsoft dropped its name in favour of *Encarta* shortly after buying it. The addition of public domain illustrations and scratchy sound recordings too old to bear a copyright hardly made for a serious rival to the *Britannica* – or so it seemed.

As revenues plunged, it became obvious that whether they ought to be or not, CD-ROM encyclopaedias were serious competition. Britannica executives reluctantly considered creating their own CD-ROM product, only to encounter a technology constraint: the content of *Britannica* was too big for the medium. *Encarta*, with its 7 million words, could fit easily onto a CD-ROM, with plenty of room for illustrations and interactivity. *Britannica*, however, had more than 40 million words. It was impossible to create an interactive version within the capacity limits of a CD-ROM. The technology was not ready for the content, so the company's executives decided to wait.

Sales continued to plummet. In response, the company put together a text-only CD-ROM version of *Britannica*, only to encounter another crisis: a revolt by the sales force. Even if priced at a significant premium over *Encarta*, a CD-ROM product would have to be sold through a completely different channel. To avert a revolt by the sales force, Britannica executives decided to bundle the CD-ROM as a free bonus for buyers of the multivolume set. Anyone who wanted to buy the CD-ROM alone would have to pay $1000, which compared to a list price of *Encarta* at $70!

This decision kept the sales force happy, but did nothing to stem the continuing collapse of sales. Losses mounted. In May of 1995, the Benton Foundation finally put the company up for sale. It took 8 months and rejections from nearly everyone in the industry, including Microsoft, before a buyer was found. Finally, in 1996, financier Jacob Safra agreed to buy the company, for less than half book value, itself a figure much diminished in recent years.

Amongst the many lessons to be learnt from Britannica was that their salesforce, built up over decades and the envy of the industry was obsolete. Parents until 1990 bought encyclopaedia to address their concerns about their children's knowledge. Britain's own market research showed that the typical encyclopaedia was opened less than once a year. But the salesman, playing on parents' concerns and their natural desire to do something to help their children advance, still closed the sale and pocketed $600. For the price of the old *Encyclopaedia Britannica*, parents in the 1990s could get a PC *and* an encyclopaedia.

Britannica is now trying hard to come to terms with the new climate. Their first launch on the Web was on 19 October 1999, when they offered free access to the contents of the 32-volume encyclopaedia, plus news from the *Washington Post* – and paid advertisements. After a splash launch the site was overwhelmed. It was re-launched in May 2000, in a much quieter manner. The official traffic count was around 15 million clicks. Britannica also runs a subscriber service without advertisements, aimed at schools and colleges.

Action Checklist: Price, Promotion and Selling

❑   How many new products and services have you launched in the past 12 months?
❑   How successful would you say these were?
❑   What good (and) bad lessons have you learnt about your capacity to launch new products/services?
❑   How do you price your product or service?
❑   How does your value proposition compare with that of your competitors?
❑   Does real-time pricing have a role to play in your pricing strategy?
❑   How much do you spend on advertising and promotion, and how effective is each major element of that?
❑   Where do your competitors advertise?
❑   How effective is your human salesforce?
❑   Do you use the Web for sales activity, and with what results?

Remember the Van

11

All businesses have some similar elements. Someone sells and someone buys. The deal is not consummated until the goods change hands and the cash clears. E-businesses have had rather more problems with these areas of business than have old-economy firms. Despite re-branding delivery and calling it by new-economy-sounding names, such as 'logistics' and 'fulfilment', companies such as E-Toys greeted the new millennium with the same old problem. They failed to deliver thousands of toys in time for a critical, and not-to-be-repeated that year, date.

Some examples of how dot-coms got this aspect of their marketing strategy wrong, and what if anything was done to put things right, are given below.

Shopping.com

This company opened its doors as a discounter in 1998, and got a rush of orders at Christmas. It couldn't handle the volume. The local Better Business Bureau received nearly 300 complaints which, when you consider that most complaints never happen, is a pretty stunning figure.

Compaq Computer Corp. bought the fledgeling company after Christmas and immediately offered $250 gift certificates to anyone who filed a complaint. They also put in place a programme that made it clear to customers that service was the primary goal. Compaq later sold the company after restoring some credibility to it.

Jungle.com

Launched in 1999 to a fanfare of PR, Steve Bennett's new business, having hived off his first company, Software Warehouse, got off to a less than auspicious start. Jungle.com kicked off in August with a multi-million pound giveaway. But operations failed to perform. Orders failed to arrive, e-mails and telephone calls fell on deaf ears. Bennett said that he was most concerned about not ending up like Boo.com, whose website launch was beset by delays. He pressurized his programmers to deliver on time, but although launched as planned, that was about all that actually went as planned. The programming team really needed another month, and it showed. Customer service was 'lousy' for weeks. Originally they had three people in customer service: within 3 months they had 30.

Bennett has these words of advice based on this experience: 'Never stint on customer service'. His business was nearly jeopardized because of operations failures in the early weeks. He also recommends outsourcing servers, as you just can't afford for them to go down.

eBay

This company grew very rapidly following its IPO in October 1998. It was at the time the largest on-line auction site, where sellers are drawn because of the large number of users, which increases the size of the potential market for things being auctioned. This in turn creates a wider selection of goods to sell, and so creates a virtual and expanding circle. The increase in demand put real pressure on eBay's ability to keep up. According to the *San Jose Mercury News*, in June 1999 eBay failed to keep up with this demand. For some eBay customers, the 22 hour breakdown in June 1999 was the final straw. While eBay assured its customers it had everything under control, many did not believe them. Customers defected. Demand was down 18% the morning after the crash.

During the weekend after the crash, eBay changed its policy, extending auctions when systems failures occurred. Previously, eBay had extended the time only for those auctions that were scheduled to end during the down period. After the crash they changed the policy to allow a 22 hour extension, following any 2 hour breakdown in service. In May 2000, one of eBays competitors, QXL, announced Europe's biggest Internet acquisition, a £627 million all-paper deal to buy rival German auction house, Ricardo. This created a pan-European player of sufficient stature to challenge eBay. eBay itself is a profitable business, unlike many others on the Internet. Its 138 employees are responsible for $229 million in revenues and $10.8 million in net profits. Their gross margin is 71%, which compare with E-tailors' margins of 25%.

IBM

On 18 January 2000 an irresistible offer appeared on IBM's website. They offered ThinkPad I Series 1400 laptops for $1, rather less than the $1199–1899 price tag that usually accompanies the model. Customers jumped at the opportunity to stock up on grade-A equipment priced to move. Even those buyers who ordered more than 10 laptops were given order numbers and sent confirmation e-mails. But IBM.com staff spotted their error before the goods were shipped. As a consolation prize, IBM offered free shipping to anyone who elected to reorder at the list price.

IBM is not alone in making this type of error. Ashford.com, Land's End and Buy.com have all had pricing glitches. But this is not a new problem. Prices are incorrectly marked up in shops too. By some estimates, over 25% of shop products are incorrectly priced, most often in the retailer's favour. The bottom line is that E-tailors and retailers are not legally obliged to honour pricing glitches. However, if you have taken the product away from the shop, it's hard to see what can be done to get it back. But perhaps

E-tailors should think about going the extra mile, and think about all the favourable PR they could be wallowing in.

Complaints

Monitoring complaints is one way of keeping track of how your operations and fulfilments services are running. Complaints are a fact of life in any sizeable business, but the trends can reveal significant information, and now Internet firms in the consumer field can get a rare insight into how many complaints other E-businesses are getting. Consumer complaint group eComplaints.com officially launched its on-line complaint forum in May 2000 as a medium for disgruntled users to seek compensation from companies whose customer service has been unsatisfactory. The site publishes laments in a public database and then notifies the company in question, asking them to respond. Site users answer a brief series of personal questions, enter their complaint, and then decide what personal information they'll allow to be available on eComplaints.com. Complained-about companies are notified via e-mail or fax. eComplaints.com already has its share of competition from sites like epinions.com and Bizrate.com, which rate products and overall commercial performance.

In May 2000, the site listed complaints against several hundred companies. Some of those mentioned in this book were there. A partial list is given in Table 11.1, which shows the number of complaints received for each company.

Company	Number of complaints
Amazon	0
Barnes & Noble	0
Schwab	0
Easyjet	1
Buy.com	9
eBay	9
Microsoft	9
Dell	11
E*Trade	11

Source: eComplaints.com

Table 11.1 Most complained-about companies in May 2000

Action Checklist: Remember the Van

❏   How many complaints have you received about your product or service? Break that down into different types of complaint, e.g. service, product quality, delivery, etc.

❏   What is the trend?

❏   How do you think your competitors are doing?

❏   How good is your website, relative to others in your business? Rate it on a scale of 1–5 for all the important factors, e.g. speed, ease of use, etc.

❏   What major failures in systems have you had, and what have you learnt from them?

❏   What major failures have others in your industry had, and what have you learnt from them?

❏   What checks do you have in place to ensure that information, including price, is right?

❏   What is your policy for dealing with complaints?

❏   How does that compare with others in your industry?

❏   Have your facilities been overwhelmed by demand or suffered a breakdown? Why?

Part III

Management, the Forgotten Art

Management's theoretical basis comes from an era eons before the Internet. Taylor's *Principles of Scientific Management* was written in 1911; Henri Fayol's *General and Industrial Management*, first published in 1916, was printed in English in 1949; Chester Barnard's *The Functions of the Executive* was penned in 1938. The subject of management was extended in 1940s by the likes of Mary Parker Follett's *Dynamic Administration* (1941) and in the following decades Frederick Hertzberg (*The Motivation to Work*, 1959) Abraham Maslow (*Motivation and Personality*, 1954), Peter Drucker (*The Practice of Management*, 1954), Douglas McGregor (*The Human Side of Enterprise*, 1960) and Philip Kotler (*Marketing Management: Analysis, Planning, Implementation and Control*, 1994) have all played their part in raising a generation of managers' understanding of their art.

In the E-economy, the focus of attention is on new technology and new business models. The key players are often young and almost invariably inexperienced. No-one at Boo.com had experience of managing a sizeable business and the founders of Lastminute.com are both people with some expertise in staff functions but no history of managing teams or of running businesses employing hundreds of people of differing cultures in different countries.

For many E-entrepreneurs, management is an abstract concept, most likely to be either ignored or reduced to a sentence or two in the business plan. Unfortunately for them, it's management and people that make businesses successful, and business models have but a modest part to play in the process.

Getting people to do what you want them to do, because they want to do it, is what management is all about. It's a 'heads up and walk about' activity, unlike the Internet, which seems to attract people who apparently often prefer to keep their eyes on a computer screen whilst sitting, or occasionally lying, down. Life is spent in cubicles rather than in contact, or so it would seem.

Stop Being the Hero 12

From the start, the founder of most dot-com businesses makes the entire running. He or she is up in front of the VCs, raising money, dousing fires at the bank, smoothing crises with suppliers and smiling at the cameras. Martha Lane Fox, eat your heart out!

But heroes make lousy managers and unmanaged businesses go downhill. A new management style is needed for the new economy . . . welcome back *the strategist*. But strategists are in short supply in the dot-com world. As one former finance department employee of failed E-tailor, Boo.com, said:

> When I joined it was the coolest place to work. But though the management had great vision, they had no idea how to get there. It was extremely chaotic and spending went out of control.

Alongside the drawn face of Kajsa Leander, co-founder of the collapsed Boo.com, which appeared in London's *Financial Times* on Saturday 2 May 2000, was a telling quote:

> We came in early and worked late. I haven't had a social life for the past 2 years.

One of her employees was reported in the same paper on the same day as seeing the past 2 years in a rather different light:

> It's not often you get to spend $130 million. It was the best of fun. We thought we were the next Microsoft, so profits didn't matter.

Both parties seem to have missed the point. The employee clearly had no understanding of Microsoft's business. Their business model and Boo's were miles apart. One, Microsoft, sells shovels. Boo.com, on the other hand, was one of thousands of hopeful but weary miners panning for gold. Also profits do rather matter to Microsoft, and they have always been pretty good at making them – so much so that the US government is hell-bent on breaking them up. No government yet has used anti-trust legislation to fragment a loss-making business.

Ms Leander may also have been misguided in believing that hard work alone is the way to get a new business into great shape. In fact, it has rather less to do with the amount of work you do than the nature of the work itself.

For some businesses, what prevents them from growing is that they still operate as a one-man band, despite often having dozens of employees. The founders of such firms seem either not to recognize the need to build a management team or to be incapable of doing so successfully. At Boo.com, for example, there was no chief operating officer, they took 6 months to recruit a chief financial officer, and 4 months to find a technology officer; and, as you can see from the Boo case in Part I, no sooner did some key staff arrive than they left. Hardly surprising, then, that Ms Lander felt over-worked. Most bosses of their own firms work long hours. Nearly a third, in a recent study, admit to working 60 hours a week or more. This is in sharp contrast to employees in small firms, where only 3% work the same long hours. Yet there is little evidence of a direct correlation between excessive work and excessive profit.

RBR Networks

Rory Sweet and Ben White, for example, both in their early 30s, built up their company, RBR Networks, starting out in a London basement with just £600. Within 4 years they had sold the company to a South African software and Internet provider for £25 million. Sweet admits that neither he nor his partner had a background in computing and he confessed that, 'Half the time we didn't get up until 11 am and only worked until 1 pm'. Their 45 employees ran the business, while the founders planned the strategy. As well as taking their staff out for a curry to celebrate, Sweet and White set aside £1.5 million as a loyalty bonus for their team.

What Sort of a Boss Are You?

In my study into entrepreneurial behaviour (Barrow, 1998b), I looked at the relationship between entrepreneurs and the teams they built up, and its likely impact on successful growth.

The first element studied was how much time the owner-manager spent on routine management tasks, such as marketing, selling, analysing figures, reviewing budgets or arbitrating between

Figure 12.1 Relationship between the entrepreneur and his or her key staff in a growing firm

managers. On average, with the exception of the group of entre-preneurs who were still preoccupied with basic non-management functions, such as delivering their service or making their product, e.g. architects, small builders, retailers, etc., over 85% of an en-trepreneur's working day was spent on these routine management tasks. The owners' behaviour can be more easily understood by showing this graphically, as set out in Figure 12.1. A low score on the vertical axis indicates either that most time is spent on basic non-management functions, or that most time is spent on strategic issues, such as new product or market development, improving market share, acquisitions and divestments or diversification. A high score indicates that the owner/manager is still largely preoccupied with routine management tasks.

The second element examines what level of business skills has been attained by the key staff, and this is plotted on the horizontal axis of Figure 12.1. Here, a low score would be where most of the management team were relatively new to their tasks or largely untrained for their current jobs. An example (true, believe it or not) of this would be an unqualified book-keeper trying to produce the management accounts for a £5 million business. A high score would be where people were mostly either specifically qualified or trained for their current job. If we had replaced the unqualified book-keeper in our earlier example with a fully qualified accountant who had been in post for a year, then this would merit a high score.

The different types of key staff identified in The Cranfield Model are described below. They are characterized as male purely for ease of description, although clearly they could just as easily be female.

The 'artisan' in The Cranfield Model is typified by low occupation with routine management tasks – because most of his time is spent producing a product or delivering a service. The level of business skills in the company is also low, as most of the artisan's staff are employed helping in 'production', or carrying out primary tasks such as book-keeping or selling. The owner/manager is very much 'one of the boys' still. Artisans can encompass professional firms, such as architects and surveyors, software houses, games companies, website designers, consultancies, owners of small retail chains such as chemists, video stores and proprietors of hotels and restaurants.

Little time is available either for routine management tasks, such as analysing performance or reviewing methods. Every hour that can be sold is sold, and little time is left over to either improve the quality or profitability of today's business or to consider strategy for tomorrow. The artisan entrepreneur devotes all his time to the area of the business he either knows or likes the best, whether or not that is what is actually best for the business at that particular stage in its life.

The artisan has low growth prospects, relative to his market. His training and development needs are to raise his awareness of the importance of management as a business task of greater importance than whatever operational aspect of the business he is particularly interested in.

From the available evidence, Boo looked very much like an artisan-led venture. Boo asked the big consulting firms, such as Andersen Consulting, to build their whole system, but according to Ms Leander, 'They didn't have the experience'. Ms Leander, a former model, set about building the site in-house. The site was 6 months late, hard to access and generally viewed as a disaster in the industry. Boo spent £500 000 a month taking 3D photographs of its products to put on the site.

It seems highly unlikely that much strategic management in any serious sense of the word took place at Boo after the initial concept was sold to investors. The investors didn't help themselves much by not setting any performance targets for the company. Board meetings were reputed to have been held by mobile phone.

The 'hero', by contrast, probably heads up one management function, such as sales or production. But, for example, if he heads up sales he will do little selling, except for handling some key accounts. His time is now spent on managing the business. As the level of business skill among his employees is still relatively

low, he will take the lead in initiating routine management procedures. He will introduce them to the firm, and be the only person
who really understands them. To his managerially illiterate team he
will consequently be seen as a hero.

Unfortunately the hero has a Herculean task on his hands.
Shedding the 'doing' tasks is relatively simple, as the working skills
in most dot-coms are technical and available, albeit at a price. But
passing out routine management tasks will almost invariably require that the owner/manager trains up his own management
teams. There are relatively few well experienced and trained managers available to the new or small dot-com company, as the overall
pool of such people is small and the demand is great. There was a
queue of recruitment consultants outside Boo's various offices as
soon as their failure was announced (one of Boo's staff told an
interviewer he planned to take a long weekend and start work again
on Tuesday. He didn't know where yet, but he did know he'd have a
job). The Hero has a high capacity for improving the performance of
his firm but still has low growth prospects relative to his market. He
has no time for strategic thinking and no depth of management
experience to handle growth effectively.

His training and development needs are to help him raise the
general level of management skills in the business, whilst at the same
time increasing his own grasp of motivation, leadership, organization
design and development and of strategic management issues in
general. If a hero fails to do this, as most do, he becomes a meddler.

The '*meddler*' raises the level of management skill, either by training or recruitment, but then fails to let go of routine management
tasks. Despite having a highly qualified CFO in place for the last 18
months of Boo's existence, it seems highly likely that Boo's founders
took the lead in the search for cash to fund the high burn rate. At this
stage, the owner-manager probably has no functional responsibilities
and has assumed the role of managing director. Typically, he spends
much time second-guessing subordinates, introducing more refined
(but largely unnecessary) management systems. He also goes on
courses or reads books that make him even more knowledgeable and
sometimes better at routine management tasks than his own subordinates, who anyway are by now doing a perfectly satisfactory job
of managing today's business. He gets in early, and leaves late and
practises 'management by walking about'.

One owner-manager in the study still gets in to let in the cleaning
staff and leaves at 8.00 pm 'when the neighbouring car park closes'.

The meddler's problem is that he can't let go of routine management tasks, because his day will feel empty. He's been used to a

70–90 hour week, with only 10 days' holiday each year. Once his management team is in place and trained, he is out of a job. Until he reduces his involvement with routine management tasks, he will limit the growth capacity of his firm, for two reasons. First, his management team won't take on more responsibility if the reward for taking on the last lot of responsibility was being nagged and criticized. Second, he is too busy checking on people to develop sound strategies for growth. At Boo there were even staff to second-guess the staff. There were three creative directors for a business with just $0.5 million a month in sales revenue coming in.

Most owner-managers become meddlers once they have managers. They actually work more hours, spending the extra time checking and overseeing the work they are already paying others handsomely to do. The result of this meddling is much unhappiness all round. Overheads soar and motivation plummets. Either the boss has picked the wrong team (which happens all too frequently), in which case there is a recruitment problem, or else the team is not being managed and motivated properly.

Boo may well have suffered from both these failings. They hired some 'very expensive staff' who had worked in big companies (not start-ups). Apple's Steve Jobs made this same mistake when he thought Apple was about to become a big company and take on IBM. More likely still, the boss simply does not know how to stop working and start thinking. To grow a business successfully, three tasks have to be implemented. The day-to-day business *operation* has to be carried out effectively. *Business improvements* have to be carried out to make today's business better. But most importantly, a business *strategy* has to be developed to point the business in the best direction for the future. In dot-coms, the future is almost always being made *now*, so by far the most important task for the owner-manager is to plan the future strategy of the business.

E*Trade's founder, Bill Porter, stepped back from day-to-day management as quickly as he could build a team to take over. He spent his time 'defining corporate DNA', which is a new new word for strategy.

Some 90% of the potential to add value to a growing business lies in shaping its future competitive strategy *now* and in making the business better. But owner-managers spend barely 10% of their time on these tasks, if they spend any time at all, preferring to spend 90% of their time on day-to-day operations (Figure 12.2). Without any clear strategic direction, it is hardly surprising that many SMEs (and a few not so small firms) are either standing still or going round in circles.

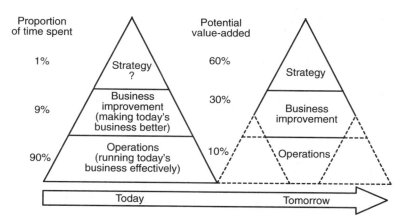

Figure 12.2 How entrepreneurs spend their time

As nearly 90% of entrepreneurs are either heroes or meddlers, according to the Cranfield study, it follows that most entrepreneurs are a significant barrier to growth in their own firms.

The *'strategist'*, is the most desirable type of entrepreneur to develop a growing business. He develops the management skills of his team to the highest appropriate level and in depth. He may introduce a staff function to help his line managers in such areas as personnel and market research. This will free up his key managers to think strategically too.

He will devote roughly 10% of his time to management tasks, such as monitoring performance, coordinating activities, resolving conflict and helping manage today's business. A third of his time will be spent motivating, counselling, developing his management team and helping them to manage change. This activity is aimed at improving the existing business. The final 60% of his time will be spent on developing strategic thinking to form the shape of the future business.

The natural path of development for the relationship between the owner manager and his team, is to pass from artisan to hero to meddler and for the lucky few on to become strategists. For a more detailed study of entrepreneurs' management styles, See Barrow, Brown and Clarke (1997).

You can use the questionnaire below to see whether you are a hero, a meddler or a strategist.

Action Checklist: What Kind of a Boss Are You?

Complete the following questionnaire to find out if you are a strategist, a hero or simply a meddler when it comes to managing your business.

Instructions for Completion:

1. Complete the questionnaire below, scoring each question 1 for agree and 0 for disagree.
2. Transfer your completed scores to the profile grid (Figure 12.3A).
3. Total each column of the profile grid.
4. Plot your personal histogram (Figure 12.3B) using the profile scores from the grid. Figure 12.3C shows characteristic histogram shapes.

❑   **Q1**   I don't believe in asking anyone to do a job I can't do myself.

❑   **Q2**   Sod's law says that if things can go wrong, they will go wrong. I'm here to keep my finger on the pulse.

❑   **Q3**   I've managed to free up my time so that I can spend almost 2 days a week on engineering tomorrow rather than managing today.

❑   **Q4**   Few people would be in any doubt that I'm the boss.

❑   **Q5**   I live, eat and breathe the job 24 hours a day. My spouse and family would probably say they suffer.

❑   **Q6**   I believe in a high and continuous investment in appraising, training and developing the management team.

❑   **Q7**   I'm quite happy to roll up my sleeves and get stuck in.

❑   **Q8**   Sometimes the only way to get something to happen is to do it yourself.

❑   **Q9**   I place a high reliance on regular downward briefings.

❑   **Q10** I try to spend as little time as possible on the day-to-day management processes.

❑   **Q11** I would bet that 10–20 potential crises hit my desk each day. My job is to solve them before they explode.

❑   **Q12** I'm usually the first person in the office and the last to leave in the evening. I rarely take holidays longer than 1 week.

❑   **Q13** I communicate primarily by setting the vision of where we're going and the values or 'way we do things round here'. I'm not interested in the detail.

❑   **Q14** My job is to make the decisions around here, and I do.

❑   **Q15** I don't believe in creating distance. I'm very much one of the gang.

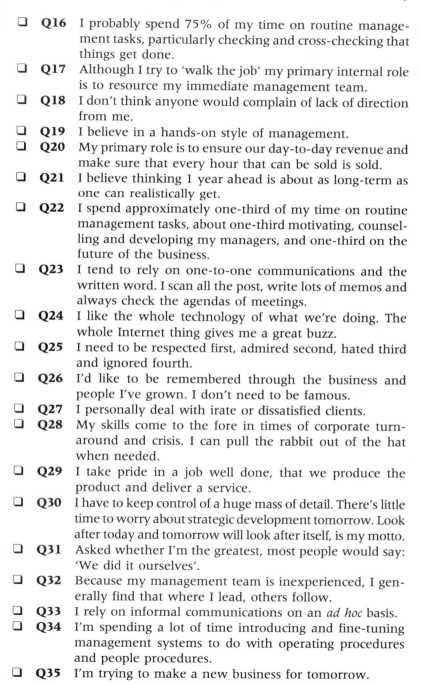

❑ **Q16** I probably spend 75% of my time on routine management tasks, particularly checking and cross-checking that things get done.

❑ **Q17** Although I try to 'walk the job' my primary internal role is to resource my immediate management team.

❑ **Q18** I don't think anyone would complain of lack of direction from me.

❑ **Q19** I believe in a hands-on style of management.

❑ **Q20** My primary role is to ensure our day-to-day revenue and make sure that every hour that can be sold is sold.

❑ **Q21** I believe thinking 1 year ahead is about as long-term as one can realistically get.

❑ **Q22** I spend approximately one-third of my time on routine management tasks, about one-third motivating, counselling and developing my managers, and one-third on the future of the business.

❑ **Q23** I tend to rely on one-to-one communications and the written word. I scan all the post, write lots of memos and always check the agendas of meetings.

❑ **Q24** I like the whole technology of what we're doing. The whole Internet thing gives me a great buzz.

❑ **Q25** I need to be respected first, admired second, hated third and ignored fourth.

❑ **Q26** I'd like to be remembered through the business and people I've grown. I don't need to be famous.

❑ **Q27** I personally deal with irate or dissatisfied clients.

❑ **Q28** My skills come to the fore in times of corporate turnaround and crisis. I can pull the rabbit out of the hat when needed.

❑ **Q29** I take pride in a job well done, that we produce the product and deliver a service.

❑ **Q30** I have to keep control of a huge mass of detail. There's little time to worry about strategic development tomorrow. Look after today and tomorrow will look after itself, is my motto.

❑ **Q31** Asked whether I'm the greatest, most people would say: 'We did it ourselves'.

❑ **Q32** Because my management team is inexperienced, I generally find that where I lead, others follow.

❑ **Q33** I rely on informal communications on an *ad hoc* basis.

❑ **Q34** I'm spending a lot of time introducing and fine-tuning management systems to do with operating procedures and people procedures.

❑ **Q35** I'm trying to make a new business for tomorrow.

❑ **Q36**   Most of our people are concerned with getting product out, or tasks such as book-keeping and selling.

❑ **Q37**   I spend a lot of my time on personal business training programmes, making external presentations, etc. I'm known in the industry, and they do tend to ask for me rather than any of my staff.

❑ **Q38**   I've made a big investment in trying to train my team and drag them kicking and screaming into new ways.

❑ **Q39**   Turning managerial 'mice' into 'men' is one of the challenges I most enjoy.

❑ **Q40**   Survival today is the name of the game.

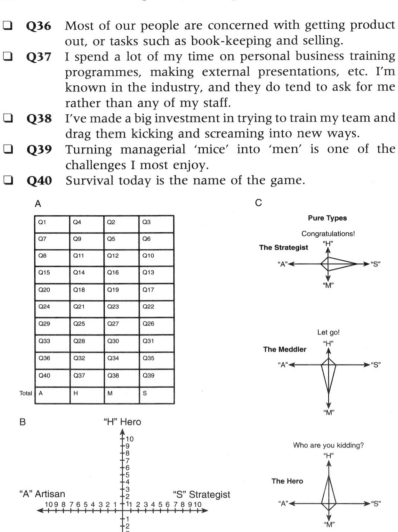

Figure 12.3 Profile grid (A), histogram (B) and shapes of histograms for pure types (C)

Greed Is Not Enough   13

If we were to believe all we read, the only thing Larry Ellison, the founder of Oracle, has on his mind is money. Not whether he is worth $51 billion or $61 billion. Those figures mean little to him, we are told. His company, set up in 1977, with three rogue computer programmers, now employs 43 000 people. Although it nearly collapsed at one time when it promised more than it could deliver, its fortunes have soared since. He is not concerned whether he has enough to support three ex-wives, or his own private airforce, or even his custom-built Mercedes cars and the drop-head Bentley. The figure that Ellison is reputed to have in his mind is how far ahead or behind Bill Gate's net worth he is on any one day.

Jim Clarke, founder of Netscape, Healtheon and Silicon Graphics, had something similar on his mind as he was building and selling three separate billion-dollar firms. Sure, he was interested in having the biggest computer-controlled yacht in the world. But he also wanted to be richer than Larry Ellison. That was when Ellison was worth a mere $11 billion.

Money is seen as the driving force in the E-world. Money from VCs – money for burn rate and money to motivate key staff. And yet money as a motivator has the shortest shelf-life of all and perhaps the least predictable set of outcomes. But what really motivates great people to deliver stunning results, time and time again? And how do you go about recruiting, appraising, motivating and rewarding staff in E-businesses?

Management and Motivation

Management is the art and science of getting people to do what you want them to do, because *they* want to do it. This is easier said than done.

Most entrepreneurs believe that their employees work for money and their key staff work for more money. Pay them enough and they'll jump through any hoop. This view is not borne out by most of the research, which ranks pay as third or even fourth in the reasons why people come to work. David Pottruck, the Co-CEO at Charles Schwab, believes that 'the business leader has to show empathy and respect for the people who are performing a critical function for the company'. Understanding why people work is the key to successful motivation. The 'theory' of motivation and management is contained in the following classic concepts.

Theory X and Theory Y

These theories were developed by Douglass McGregor, an American social psychologist, to try to explain the assumptions about human behaviour which underlies management action.

Theory X makes the following assumptions:

- The average person has an inherent dislike of work and will avoid it if possible. So management needs to put emphasis on productivity, incentive schemes and the idea of a 'fair day's work'.
- Because of this dislike of work, most people must be coerced, controlled, directed and threatened with punishment to get them to achieve the company's goals.
- People prefer to be directed, want to avoid responsibility, have little ambition and really want a secure life above all.

Despite being the antithesis of everything that 'enterprise' and 'growth' stands for, this view still persists amongst many owner managers. But whilst theory 'X' does explain some human behaviour, it does not provide a framework for understanding behaviour in the best businesses. McGregor and others have proposed an alternative.

Theory Y has as its basis the beliefs that:

- Physical or mental effort at work is as natural as either rest or play. Under the right conditions, hard work can be a source of great satisfaction. Under the wrong conditions, it can be a drudge, which will inspire little effort and less thought, from those forced to participate.
- Once committed to a goal, most people at work are capable of a high degree of self-management.
- Job satisfaction and personal recognition are the highest 'rewards' that can be given, and will result in the greatest level of commitment to the task in hand.

- Under the right conditions, most people will accept responsibility and even welcome more of it.
- Few people in business are being 'used' to anything like their capacity. Neither are they contributing creatively towards solving problems.

BATM

Dr Zvi Marom was born in Tel Aviv 46 years ago with a typical background of many second-generation Israelis: his mother a pre-war immigrant from Poland and his father a refugee from Hitler's Germany. Marom has little good to say of the stockmarket, although in 2000, for a brief period, he was a paper billionaire. In his view the market for Internet stocks is based only on the business model, 'I offer to burn your money, and don't complain afterwards because we told you so'.

Marom started BATM, known as Batman to city traders for the shares' ability to defy gravity, in 1992. He made sales and profits from Day One and never sought outside finance until he raised $10 million by floating his company on the Alternative Investment Market (AIM) in 1996. He has a clear vision of what business the company is in: 'What the Internet requires is three things: the road, the traffic lights, and the storage for all the information'.

BATM are concerned only with the traffic lights and his target is to be best. Their main competitor is the giant Cisco Systems, but despite that, IBM became an early buyer and recently Marom has forged alliances with 3M, Nokia, Sun Microsystems and Samsung. In fact, both 3M and Samsung have taken small stakes in the company.

The secret of BATM's success, according to Marom, has been in assembling a team of like-minded boffins (he worked at CERN in Switzerland, where the early work on the Internet was carried out) from larger corporations. In Marom's view, 'This is still an industry where very talented young people want to see how far they can stretch their brains and who are less concerned with how much they can get in options'.

A growing business depends critically for its success on everyone giving of their best all the time, and on few resources being diverted into 'overhead'-type activities which push up costs. They also need to 'out-think' larger competitors, as they cannot out-spend them. For these reasons, those entrepreneurs with growth in mind may need to critically re-think the way they manage.

Hertzberg's Hygiene Factors

Frederick Hertzberg, an American professor of psychology, discovered that distinctly separate factors were the cause of job satisfaction and job dissatisfaction. His research revealed that five factors stood out as strong determinants of job satisfaction:

- Achievement.
- Recognition.
- Responsibility.
- Advancement.
- The attractiveness of the work itself.

When the reasons for dissatisfaction were analysed, they were found to be concerned with a different range of factors:

- Company policy.
- Supervision.
- Administration.
- Salary.
- Working conditions.
- Interpersonal relationships.

Hertzberg called these causes of dissatisfaction 'hygiene factors'. He reasoned that the lack of hygiene will cause disease, but the presence of hygienic conditions will not, of itself, produce good health. So the lack of adequate 'job hygiene' will cause dissatisfaction, but hygienic conditions alone will not bring about job satisfaction.

Misunderstandings about Money

One of the biggest mistakes you can make is to assume that money alone is the way to motivate staff. Figure 13.1 gives a graphic example of how minor the motivating effect of a salary increase is by itself. In fact, it is not so much the amount of money awarded that is important – expectation is all. The S-shaped curve shows that the effect of a salary increase on job satisfaction and, therefore, performance, depends on what you expected. Thus, if you expected a salary increase of £2000 and this is what you got, then the effect is zero. If you expected an increase of £2000 and were given £3000, then your job satisfaction will increase. You will have a warm glow but the feeling soon tails off! Similarly, if you expected £2000 and were given £1000, you will actively be demotivated!

In fact, the problem is not so much that of motivating people, but of avoiding demotivating them! If managers can keep off the backs of employees, it is quite possible that they will motivate themselves. After all, most of us want the same things: a sense of achievement or challenge, recognition of our efforts, an interesting and varied job, opportunities for responsibility, advancement and job growth.

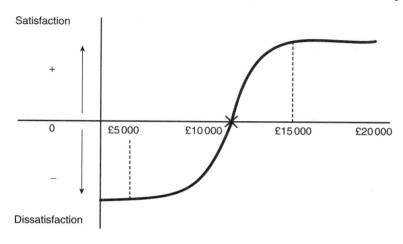

Figure 13.1 The effect of a salary increase on job satisfaction

What Else Can You Do?

Even money can be made to seem more interesting and motivational if you put a bit of thought into it. Microsoft was reported recently to be handing out extra-large stock options in order to retain key staff. They reportedly gave some high-level executives options to buy as many as 200 000 of its shares, worth $14.5 million at the time. But they didn't wave a cheque book on its own. They promoted more than 30 managers to vice-president, not an action to be recommended in a new dot-com – it might confuse the switchboard. But that action is a clear recognition that some people have egos, and titles stroke some egos. Microsoft also encouraged top executives to take as much holiday as they need to balance their work and family lives.

Research by Hewitt Associates, who specialize in people strategy, suggests that dot-com companies (and others) must become more creative if they want to keep staff. Companies need to start introducing standard crèche facilities, care for elderly or handicapped family members, flexible hours, home working, long sabbaticals and more creative job roles. Cynics point out that the company benefits by getting more output for very little extra cost. Well, to some extent that's the name of the game.

One final observation on money, especially in the form of employee stock options. More than 30% of these schemes are in the red, as of

March 2000. New accounting rules mean that re-pricing them down will count against profits, which will in turn hit profit bonuses. Employees could be tempted to do some of their own re-pricing and move on elsewhere. Potential new recruits will be more sceptical in future about taking a large slice of 'pay' in the form of possible options to come in after a possible IPO. For a start, the IPO may never happen, and if it does, they can't sell for 6 months, during which time the shares could slide, causing misery rather than motivation.

One interesting variation on the equity stake theme is being used by one of Silicon Valley's leading PR companies, Alexander Ogilvy. Despite having 230 staff in 14 offices around the world, they claim not to have enough staff to take on all the clients who would like to be part of their fold. Merrill Lynch Online, Web-MD/Healtheon, Nortel Network and *Red Herring* magazine are amongst the client list.

One factor that makes the company fairly selective about who it works with is their scheme to swap a portion of fees for equity in their clients. They have established an employee equity pool and taken stakes in key clients such as IdeaLab and E-Toys. The company claim that having the ability to participate in the upside of their clients' success is a useful tool in attracting and retaining key staff. It also keeps everyone focused on customer service.

A wide range of other perks (Table 13.1) are on offer to employees in E-economy firms, ranging from being allowed to wear casual dress (almost essential) to on-site childcare, of little appeal perhaps because few have them.

Perk	(%)
Casual dress	82
Flexible hours	60
Personal development training	49
Employee entertainment/company product discounts	40
Free food or beverages	36
Telecommuting	27
Fitness centre	16
Recreation facilities	9
Bringing children to work	7
Bringing pets to work	5
Mothers' and babies' room	5
Concierge service	2
Take-home meals	2
On-site childcare	1

Reproduced by permission from Shaffer (2000).

Table 13.1 Perks used to attract and retain staff in Internet companies

It is the 'motivators', such as recognition and advancement, that produce satisfaction. In a growing company it should be possible to create a virtuous cycle, with well-managed people producing excellent results, which in turn allows scope for recognition and advancement. This improves morale further and acts as spur to even greater achievements.

Healtheon Floats

In mid-February 1999, Healtheon went public. The company was the founder of Netscape, Jim Clarke's third Internet flotation. By 5.30 pm the employees had assembled in the main reception area, in front of a television set. The NASDAQ opened up 64 points, or better than 2%. Yahoo! was up almost 10 points. An imbalance of orders had caused Healtheon's stock to be suspended, so no price was yet shown. About 8% of the company, or five million shares, were on offer to the public, but the demand was greater. Morgan Stanley Dean Witter and Goldman Sachs, who were handling the IPO, had drummed up a lot of interest.

What Healtheon's employees wanted to know was, how much would people who had not got as many shares as they had wanted in the IPO pay to top up their portfolios. The initial price had been $7. Pavan Nigam, a graduate of a top Indian Institute of Technology (ITT), was chief of the engineering team at Healtheon. He owned, by way of options, 1 million of the 69 million shares outstanding. Between them, key staff at Healtheon owned 15 million shares, a bit more than Clarke himself.

It was nearly 2 hours before trading started, and by 9.15 am the excited engineers knew that there was demand for 40 million shares. When the price reached $21½, the 400 people in the room went wild. Between them they were worth $300 million. By the end of the day the price had reached $33. Pavan Nigam was worth $33 million, and his two most senior team members were worth $10 million and $3.5 million, respectively. Healtheon was one of the most successful IPOs ever.

But just 6 months previously Healtheon had pulled an IPO at short notice. The market, and sentiment about the company, made a float impossible. Pavan's concerns on that day was the fear of every new Silicon Valley company – mass exodus. No E-business can readily withstand pessimism, and there was a lot of that at Healtheon. It got so bad that Pavan made up a 'Loyalty Matrix'. He knew that the first 10 engineers he had hired were loyal to him. He called them and told them to draw up their own loyalty matrix and work on any doubtful candidates.

This would not have been the first failed IPO in which a trickle of deserters became a torrent. But now, with dozens of these loyal staff turned into millionaires overnight, the problems were different ones. One employee, a dollar millionaire, is on record as saying that he had doubts whether the sacrifice had been worth it. Months of 20 hour days and cliff-hanging suspense had eaten deep into his family relationships. Another resented the public knowledge of his new status. Everyone came up to him – people he barely knew – shaking him by the hand. He had been brought up never to talk about his finances in public – good or bad news alike. He deeply resented the intrusion.

Had Healtheon's float been pulled again, it seems unlikely that the key staff could have been held together a second time. A 'bonus' that can't be guaranteed carries very great, even fatal, risks.

Action Checklist: Monitor Your Team's Level of Motivation

❑ How would you assess your company's morale right now? Please explain why.

❑ What action would help to move company morale up and increase your job satisfaction?

❑ How well does the management team manage?

❑ How effective are your internal communications, up, down and across? What improvements would you suggest?

❑ How clear is everyone, yourself included, about what is expected of you (targets, etc.)?

❑ How adequately are you and your key team rewarded and recognized for good performance?

❑ How well does the appraisal process work? Any recommendations?

❑ How fully are you using everyone's talents? How could we do better?

❑ What do you believe people like most about working for this business? What is special about us?

❑ To what extent does everyone feel part of the total team? How could we involve everyone even more?

Great Team, Great Results 14

However talented the soloists are, in the end it's orchestras that make enough noise to wake up a slumbering share price or bring a reluctant VC into a new funding round.

But teams don't just happen. However neat the CVs and convincing the organization chart, you can't just turn out a 'team in a box'. The presumption that people are naturally going to work together is usually a mistake. Chaos is more likely than teamwork.

Cultures in Internet businesses have very different pedigrees. In Schwab's business, for example, people came from financial services, retail and, more recently, technology. The company's roots were in financial services. Their competitors were banks and brokerage firms and their employees had moved around the sector in search of the ultimate accolade, to become a vice-president. The focus was inward, towards 'hierarchy and title', according to Schwab's co-CEO. Their second cohort of employees came from retailing, the staff of their one-time expanding branch network. For retailers, the focus is outwards towards the customer. Their success is measured in the market and the best salesmen have the greatest respect and power. The third group in Schwab, and the most recent, were the technologists. For these people, success is measured by technical expertise. Titles are irrelevant and their main concern is for the completion of the project. Their loyalty is not to the hierarchy but to the principles of the project itself.

Healtheon (Nearly Sinks)

Back in 1996, Healtheon did not look as it was going to make its 400 strong team of engineers into millionaires. Far from it. For most of 1996, the engineers did what they were told by their sales force. This sales force had been put together by David Schnell, a former Venture Capitalist, who was CEO. The sales force told the engineers that the key to the whole business was to write the software that would allow corporate employees to interact with their health plans over the Internet. The engineers wrote the software, but nobody actually wanted it. Blue Cross/Blue Shield did not want it. They were very pleased with the product, but their own focus had shifted away from technology.

The sales force had led the engineers, and the whole company, up a blind alley. Worse than that, they had lost track of the vision. The sales focus was talking to big companies about helping their employees handle their health plans. But this market was a drop in the ocean when compared with the $1.5 trillion health care industry that had been Healtheon's vision – the vision they had sold the VCs and the reason why Pavan Nigam, Healtheon's chief engineer, had joined the firm.

When Pavan realized what was going on, he and his engineering team were angry. In his words, 'We engineers took over the business'. Initially, they pushed the salesmen aside, and eventually kicked them out. They went on the road themselves. They intended to bring their project to a successful conclusion.

Building the Team

The young, entrepreneurial business needs to give little attention to its internal communication. Its people tend to be a highly motivated small team who spend a lot of time together at work and socially. As the business grows in numbers, sheer size will start to crack the foundations of its camaraderie, and the introduction of new people without the original motivation will change the flavour of relationships. The problem for many E-businesses is that whilst they may start with a handful of people, the ramping-up process can start very early. Boo.com started with 12 or so people and within a year had over 400 on the pay roll. It is at this point that you will find yourself consciously having to introduce ways and means of getting the team together and keeping them facing the right way. Involving your team in the preparation and presentation of the business plan can, in itself, be a good way of providing coordination to a growing business. In Healtheon, for example, the chief engineer did presentations to VCs and others on the company's strategy in the run-up to the IPO.

In addition, you will probably have to start putting in processes to address what happened quite naturally in the early weeks and months. Friday night beer busts, go-carting races, ballooning, are amongst the myriad of corporate get-togethers that are regularly used to foster team work. For example, Letsbuyit.com, the UK E-tailor, took more than 100 staff on a skiing weekend to Switzerland in January 2000 as part of a corporate bonding session. They may have got a dividend from this investment in their team sooner than expected, as the company, due to a backlash against dot-com stocks generally, had to pull its proposed IPO on the German Neuer Market technology index by June. Companies galore are in the business of inventing new and exciting bonding concepts for new and old teams in the industry. It is amazing how many businessmen expect a team to work as a team without any practice. After all it (presumably!) does not work this way for football teams. The way to build a team is to find many formal and informal ways of bringing them together: cascade briefings, state-of-the-nation addresses, lunches, social events, special project teams, happy hours. And remember, if you don't foster team spirit, some entrepreneur's networking event, such as a First Tuesday, might spirit them away altogether.

Fun is actually quite compatible with profit. The importance of informal contact between people, as a way of building productive networks, cannot be over-emphasized, but again it will not happen without the mechanisms to make it happen.

It is absolutely clear that the more you are trying to grow and change the business, the more you will have to communicate. Briefing groups are an excellent discipline for downward communication, but there is a lot more to it than that. You need processes to ensure upward communication and especially to coordinate across the barriers which your organization will establish as it grows. There are plenty of examples to help here and plenty of ways of building your team: for example, Outward Bound programmes and internal team-building events – giving everyone the same language.

Cisco Systems

Cisco was founded in 1984 by a small group of computer scientists from Stanford University seeking an easier way to connect different types of computer systems. Cisco hardware, software, and service offerings are used to create Internet solutions, so that individuals, companies and countries have seamless access to information – regardless of differences in time and place. Cisco solutions provide competitive advantage to their customers through more efficient and timely exchange of information, which in turn leads to cost savings, process efficiencies and closer relationships with their customers, prospects, business partners, suppliers and employees.

Cisco is one of America's great corporate success stories. Since shipping its first product in 1986, the company has grown into a global market leader that holds No. 1 or No. 2 market share in virtually every market segment in which it participates. Since becoming a public company in 1990, Cisco's annual revenues have increased from $69 million in that year to $16.7 billion in the year to April 2000. As measured by market capitalization, Cisco is among the largest in the world. They employ approximately 30 589 people worldwide.

Cisco Connection Online (CCO) is the website that generates much of the company's revenues and profits. The idea for the website came from Chris Stinton, a relatively junior staff member. The problem that CCO set out to solve was caused by the company's four-fold sales increase between 1995 and 1998. Its engineering support staff had already doubled to 800. Unless something new was done, at least another 1000 engineers would have to be hired, at a cost of $75 million.

A further bonus of $250 million accrued to Cisco from the savings made by distributing software over the Internet, rather than making and mailing disks to customers. What was arguably Cisco's greatest idea came from way down the organization. It is also what the company sees as its great strength – teamwork.

William Nuti, Senior Vice-President at Cisco and one of the company's top five executives summed up their culture in a recent interview published in *Sunday Business*. He said that the Cisco culture was one of teamwork. Cisco now has its third chief executive officer in its 15 year history. Nuti claims:

> 'In the Internet economy, it is going to be teams rather than individuals that win. I have never met an individual in my life who can accomplish a goal as succinctly and is as results-driven as a team of people focused on a common goal.'

Recruiting the right people and training and developing your current employees is the foundation of a successful team. But creating the winning team is about more than just picking the best people. The characteristics that research has consistently shown to be essential in building winning teams are described below.

Balanced Team Roles

Every team member must not only have their 'technical' skills such as being an accountant or sales person. They must also have a valuable team role. Belbin (1984), an expert in team behaviour, has identified eight team profiles that are essential if a team is to function well. Any one person may perform more than one of these roles. But if too many people are competing to perform one of the roles, or one or more of these roles is neglected, the team will be unbalanced. They will perform in much the same way as a car does when a cylinder misfires. These are the roles identified by Belbin (1984; see also Table 14.1.):

- *Chairman/team leader*.   Stable, dominant, extrovert. Concentrates on objectives. Does not originate ideas. Focuses people on what they do best.
- *Plant*.   Dominant, high IQ, introvert. A 'scatterer of seeds' who originates ideas. Misses out on detail. Thrustful but easily offended.
- *Resource investigator*.   Stable, dominant, extrovert and sociable. Lots of contacts with the outside word. Strong on networks. Salesperson/diplomat/liaison officer. Not an original thinker.

- *Shaper*.   Anxious, dominant, extrovert. Emotional and impulsive. Quick to challenge and to respond to a challenge. Unites ideas, objectives and possibilities. Competitive. Intolerant of woolliness and vagueness.
- *Company worker*.   Stable, controlled. A practical organizer. Can be inflexible but likely to adapt to established systems. Not an innovator.
- *Monitor evaluator*.   High IQ, stable, introvert. Goes in for measured analysis, not innovation. Unambiguous and often lacking enthusiasm, but solid and dependable.
- *Team worker*.   Stable, extrovert, but not really dominant. Much concerned with individuals' needs. Builds on others' ideas. Cools things down when tempers fray.
- *Finisher*.   Anxious introvert. Worries over what could go wrong. Permanent sense of urgency. Preoccupied with order. Concerned with 'following through'.

Shared Vision and Goal

It is essential that the team has ownership of its own measurable and clearly defined goals. This means involving the team in business planning. It also means keeping the communications channels open as the business grows. The founding team knew clearly what they were trying to achieve and, as they probably shared an office, they shared information as they worked. But as the group gets larger and new people join, it will become necessary to help the informal communication systems to work better. Briefing meetings, social events and bulletin boards are all ways to get teams together and keep them facing the right way.

A Shared Language

To be a member of a business team, people have to have a reasonable grasp of the language of business. It's not much use extolling people to improve return on capital employed or reduce debtor days if they have only the haziest notion of what those terms mean, why they matter or how they can influence the results. So you need to develop rounded business skills across all the core team members through continuous training, development and coaching.

Compatible Personalities

Whilst having different Belbin team profiles is important, it is equally vital to have a team who can get on with one another.

They have to be able to listen to and respect other people's ideas and views. They need to support and trust one another. They need to be able to accept conflict as a healthy reality and work through it to a successful outcome.

Good Leadership

First-class leadership is perhaps the most important characteristic that distinguishes winning teams from the also-rans. However good the constituent parts, without leadership a team rapidly disintegrates into a rabble bound by little but a pay cheque.

Chairman/team leader	Company worker
Stable, dominant, extrovert Concentrates on objectives Does not originate ideas Focuses people on what they do best	Stable, controlled Practical organizer Can be inflexible but likely to adapt to established systems
Plant Dominant, high IQ, introvert A 'scatterer of seeds', originates ideas Misses out on detail Thruster, but easily offended	*Monitor evaluator* High IQ, stable, introvert Measured analysis, not innovative Unambitious and lacking enthusiasm Solid, dependable
Resource investigator Stable, dominant, extrovert Sociable Contacts with outside world Salesperson/diplomat/liaison officer Not an original thinker	*Team worker* Stable, extrovert, low dominance Concerned with individuals' needs Builds on others' ideas Cools things down
Shaper Anxious, dominant, extrovert Emotional, impulsive Quick to challenge and respond Unites ideas, objectives and possibilities Competitive Intolerant of wooliness and vagueness	*Finisher* Anxious, introvert Worries over what will go wrong Permanent sense of urgency Preoccupied with order Concerned with following through Gets things done, whatever

Source: after Belbin (1984).

Table 14.1   Belbin's team profiles

Using Belbin might just have saved Steve Jobs some heartache at Apple in the early days. When he thought Apple was about to become a big company, he went out and hired big company people, only to find that they were useless. They couldn't actually do anything, so he fired them. In the process he probably set Apple's strategy with the Macintosh back months, as he set about recruiting from within and growing his own people. The factory was run by a 32 year-old English graduate with no experience of manufacturing but with a wealth of experience in managing during periods of change, in all probability with elements of 'Chairman' and 'finisher' profiles.

People cannot just be picked and put into teams because of their particular professional or job skills. If the team is to function effectively, the balance of behavioural styles has to mesh too.

Appraisals

Appraisal lies at the heart of assessing, improving and developing people's performance for the future of the business. However, to be an effective tool, appraisal needs to be approached seriously and professionally by all involved.

David Pottruck of Schwab believes that appraisal can easily be misused or even become irrelevant if it devolves into merely a form or process rather than the documentation of the relationship between two people. It should not end up as the 'boss', simply probing for areas of weakness and bringing them to people's attention. Pottruck claims that he grew the most when he received objective feedback for improvement. Schwab uses a 360° feedback appraisal process, where peers, direct reports and subordinates all contribute to the process – so long as any criticism is made in the best spirit, and is constructive in its approach.

In 6 years Barrie Haigh built his company, Innovex, from an £8 million a year turnover business, based in Henley-on-Thames, UK, to a global business with operating subsidiaries in 20 countries. The business was sold in 1996 to Quintiles for £580 million, turning Haigh, from moderate obscurity, into the 57th richest person in the UK overnight. The appraisal process had a major part to play in that achievement.

Innovex

Innovex is a major part of the new Healtheon/Web-MD and Quintiles Transnational collaborative venture. Healtheon/Web-MD is an end-to-end Internet healthcare company connecting physicians and consumers to the entire healthcare industry, whilst Quintiles Transnational Corp. improves health care by bringing new medicines to patients faster and providing knowledge-rich medical and drug data to advance the quality and cost-effectiveness effectiveness of health care.

Research carried out by the Gallup Organization in February 2000 revealed that over 6 million people in the UK alone are now using the Internet regularly to keep up to date with the latest treatment options and medical information. Nearly a third of the patients surveyed also said they question and challenge their GPs' diagnoses with medical information they have gathered elsewhere – with 13% of patients using the Internet as an information source. Men and younger patients are the most likely to surf the Web before visiting their doctors (17% of men and 22% of 16–24 year-olds), using a whole range of UK and US medical websites.

In order to help GPs face up to the challenge of Internet-savvy patients, a free health information service – InnovexHealix – was launched into GP surgeries across the UK, in January 2000. With GPs facing greater time pressures, it is increasingly hard for them to keep up-to-date with the latest medical developments from traditional health information sources. The average GP practice has over 7000 registered patients and will see around 100 patients a day – that's over 35 000 consultations a year. GP practices are inundated with health information, ranging from magazines, newspapers, videos and sponsored newsletters to flyers and competitions, in addition to regular visits from pharmaceutical representatives. Every week, GP practices receive up to 20 kilograms of health information in the post – that's the same weight as a 10 year-old child. InnovexHealix provides this information – filtered to remove duplication and summarized and reviewed by GPs, as a one-stop medical information system, which is simply downloaded via the Internet onto GPs' computers.

Growth and change has characterized Innovex's development since it was set up by Barrie Haigh, initially to help Pharmaceutical companies to recruit sales teams. Haigh recognized that he would need to create more sophisticated processes in anticipation of significant growth through merger and acquisition. At the time, Innovex had a fairly half-hearted appraisal system. Not all managers carried out appraisals, some interviews took only half an hour or so, assessment of areas for improvement was distinctly lacking, there were no clear objectives, people were assessed against personality characteristics (such as common sense), rather than results. Yet the great issue for Innovex was the lack of depth of management resource.

This could easily become a limitation on its phenomenal growth plans. There were no obvious successors to the top players, and managers were already 100% stretched in their current jobs. The requirement was to grow people capable of running businesses in the UK and Europe. There were significant gaps between the management 'animal' of today's business and the one Innovex would need for the future. As Barrie Haigh said, 'The key is to look hard at our people, look hard and develop'. He recognized that the mechanism for doing this was appraisal. Innovex then put all its managers and support staff through appraisal interview training, took a good look at its appraisal system and revamped it along the following lines:

- Appraisal is seen as a discussion between people who work together, rather than simply a boss/subordinate relationship.
- Open two-way discussion. Both appraiser and appraisee prepare for the interview in advance.
- Results-orientated rather than personality-orientated. The appraisal interview starts with a review against objectives and finishes by setting objectives for the year to come.

- The appraisal discussion is kept separate from salary review.
- The appraisal starts with performance and only later moves on to reviewing potential.
- The appraisal format is a narrative, rather than a 'tick boxes and rating'. process. It covers a discussion of achievements, areas for improvement, overall performance, training and development and career expectations.
- Plenty of time is allowed for each appraisal interview (one and a half hours, on average).
- Appraisals are carried out at least once a year, with more regular quarterly reviews.
- Training needs are identified and acted upon by those concerned.
- New staff are appraised during their first 3 months.

Adding to the Gene Pool

Most Internet companies ultimately have their growth limited to their ability to recruit and retain people. During periods of high growth it is difficult in any industry to find the right people, and right at the start of a new industry it's hardest of all.

The frenzy has led to some pretty bizarre recruitment practices. In the first place, 'head-hunters' are more prevalent in the E-business world than anywhere else. Not only professional head-hunting firms but also a myriad of part-time freelances operate in the field. And everyone is invited to join in. One US head-hunting firm offers $2000 for every referral who gets appointed. Refer 10 and you win a Ferrari. Entranet, an E-business solutions supplier based in Reading, UK, offered £50 000 to anyone who could recommend a team of 10 Java programmers to join the business. They had to up the anti from the £3000 a head they had been offering. It's hardly surprising that people in Internet firms spend a fair chunk of their working day fending off telephone calls from head-hunters. Internal telephone directories regularly go missing, and new staff are grilled in debriefing sessions to grass on their dissatisfied former co-workers. Pre-film advertisements at cinemas in Silicon Valley are not for the local McDonalds or a curry house; instead job advertisements offer immediate interviews at any hour of the day or night at Internet firms within 15 minutes' walk. The public address system announces new vacancies at Cisco, while you park your car. Then there are the bonuses for teams to switch mid-game. Many of the engineering team at Healtheon were recruited from Netscape, where they had all worked with the founder of both firms, Jim Clarke.

Yet despite this volume of 'out of the box' recruitment activity, the vast majority of new externally generated appointments come via fairly conventional routes (see Figure 14.1).

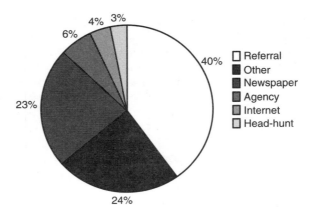

Figure 14.1 How Internet staff are recruited.
Reproduced by permission from Wilson (2000)

However you go about finding staff, good disciplines are required. The six-step plan below should put you on the right track. First, you may need to change your attitude to the whole process. Most entrepreneurs dislike the task, do it as little as possible and fit it around their other 'more important' tasks. Finding good staff is *the* number one job for the boss. He or she needs good people to delegate to. The current team need a stream of new people who do not need to be carried and who can bring new, fresh and innovative ideas with them to stimulate everyone on to greater things. So recruitment has to become a routine task, like selling or monitoring cash flow, the elements of which are addressed everyday. Furthermore, you need a budget to carry out the recruitment and selection task, just as you need a budget for equipment and rent. Most Internet start-ups don't have a recruitment budget. It is hardly surprising that a task upon which no money is spent so often goes wrong.

- *Step 1: review your business goals.* The starting point for any recruitment activity is a review of exactly what your short- and medium-term business goals are. If you have recently updated your business plan, then your goals will be fresh in your mind. If not, then you need to do so. For example, if, like Cisco, you plan to sell, service and despatch software via your website, then the people needed will be quite different from those required if you plan despatching physical products.
- *Step 2: define the job(s).* You need to set out the scope and responsibilities of the job before you start recruiting. Too many Internet firms don't get round to preparing the job description until the person is in place, or worse still they don't have job

descriptions at all. The argument advanced is that, as jobs in the E-Business world have a short shelf-life and people move jobs every 6 months or so, why bother? In fact, the shorter the life of the job, the more important it is to have a description.

The job description should include the measurable outcomes that you expect, as well as a description of the tasks. So, for a salesperson you need to spell out what the sales target is, how many calls should be made, what the customer retention target is, and so on.

- *Step 3: profile the person.*   With the job description done, you can begin to put some flesh onto the sort of person who could do it well. If you are looking for a salesperson, then communications skills and appearance will be important factors to consider, as might their personal circumstances, which may have to allow them to stay away from home frequently.

  As well as qualifications and experience, keep in mind their team skills (Belbin) and that all-too-rare business savvy. Unless a good proportion, ideally everyone, actually knows what business is about, rather than just how to design a good website, new staff could rapidly become just more passengers.

- *Step 4: advertise the job.*   (a) *Internally.* Don't overlook your existing staff if they could be promoted into the job, even if they need some additional training. About a fifth of growing firms have filled new jobs by promoting from within. Also, your staff, suppliers or other business contacts may know of someone in their network who might be suitable. (b) *Externally.* Press advertising is still a popular external source of new staff. Nearly a quarter of Internet appointments come via this route. About 10% have used recruitment agencies or executive search agencies (head-hunters). The Internet is now exploding onto the recruitment market. But despite the 'noise', only a small percentage of jobs are actually filled from advertisements on the Internet. The type of vacancy will determine the medium. The Internet might be right for design engineers, but a leaflet drop on a housing estate would be better when looking for shift workers.

  You also need to give as much thought to your job advertisement as you would to your latest new product. Using a recruitment consultant does not excuse you from doing the job description and person profile yourself. Much of the frustration expressed by those using consultants is that they have to spell out exactly what they are looking for. It may be hard work and more costly, but on average recruitment agencies are twice as successful at filling vacancies with the right people than are entrepreneurs working on their own.

- *Step 5: make your selection.*   Advertising is intended to give you a reasonable choice of applicants. If you get it right, you should end up with enough applicants to have a choice to make. First, screen out the people who don't meet your specification. 'Phone them if you need to clarify something, for example to establish whether they have experience of a particular software package. Then interview your short list, using, where possible, either a skills test or a psychometric test. There are many self-administered tests, custom-designed for different types of work. They probe intelligence, mental aptitude and whether the applicant's personality is suited to the job. Let the applicants meet others in the business. This will give them a better feel for the company and you can get a second opinion on them. When Apple was developing the Macintosh, the entire Mac team was involved in every new appointment. Applicants spent a day with the team, and only when the team decided a person was suitable did they let them in on the project. Then, if their eyes didn't light up, they showed them the door.

  You need to end up with at least three people you would be happy to appoint. Offer the job to the best candidate, keeping the others in reserve. You must have a reserve in case your first choice lets you down, accepts but then changes his or her mind, or quits, or is fired after a week or two. One Internet business took 6 months to fill a key post after four appointments went wrong. One was offered more money to stay with his current employer. One had an unbeatable offer in Australia. One lasted a month but was useless. The final one left at the end of the first week as she found the rest of the office 'unfriendly'. It took 8 months to fill the job satisfactorily and held the company's growth back a year. Boo.com had similar problems in filling its CFO appointment.

  Always take up references, preferably on the phone. Don't take 'testimonials' at face value.

  Having made an offer that is accepted stay close to the applicant until he or she arrives. Keep him or her posted of developments, put him or her on the memo/e-mail list and invite him or her to social events.

- *Step 6: make them welcome.*   Having got the right people to join you, make sure they become productive quickly and stay for a long time. The best way to do this is to have a comprehensive induction process showing them where everything is and the way things are done in your business. Set them short-term objectives and monitor performance weekly, perhaps even daily at first, giving praise or help as required.

For further thoughts on developing people in entrepreneurial ventures, see Barrow and Creagh (1997).

Tellme Networks

Mike McCue has worked out the secret of attracting star employees to his Silicon Valley start-up – free pizza. Free pizza at midnight, to be precise, pizza that McCue – respected Netscape veteran and now CEO of Tellme Networks – will personally deliver to the Stanford computer lab, hoping to persuade a handful of top students into quitting school and joining his start-up.

Even months before its launch in May 2000, Tellme had generated some serious buzz. For one thing, the company brings together one-time arch-rivals in the browser wars – McCue and 22 year-old Web whiz Angus Davis, a fellow Netscapee, are teamed with Hadi Partovi, an erstwhile leader of Microsoft's Internet Explorer team. Former Netscape CEO, Jim Barksdale, and ex-Microsoft executive, Brad Silverberg, who haven't exactly seen eye-to-eye on anti-trust issues lately, both invested in Tellme and sit on its board. And the company has raised $47 million funding from the Valley's competing venture capital firms – Benchmark Capital (which funded eBay, Webvan and Red Hat) and Kleiner, Perkins, Caufield & Byers (Amazon, AOL and Netscape).

The service promises to combine the power of the Web with the convenience of the telephone by creating what's being called a 'voice portal'. Tellme will offer content and commerce via a toll-free number, with users navigating the service through simple voice commands. It's not the entire Web on the 'phone, but rather an interactive service powered by voice-enabled XML files – sort of a scaled-down Yahoo!-by-phone. Tellme is only one player in this hot new sector: more than half a dozen voice portals are involved in a mad-scramble replay of the original Net portal rush.

'It's not hard to get money these days', McCue says, in what has become a Valley truism. 'It's getting the right people that's difficult. I spend 60–80% of my time on recruiting. It's by far the most important thing that we're doing. We're assembling the DNA of a company that's going to be around for the next 100 years.'

'Building for the long term is the difference between a great company and a mediocre one that gets bought by somebody', McCue says.

McCue's company could have staged their guerrilla recruitment drive during the day, but Stanford officials aren't crazy about start-ups raiding their computer science department for talent. Besides, Tellme isn't interested in any student engineers who think they have something better to do than sit in front of their computers at midnight. 'We're basically looking for people without lives,' says McCue. But the mission is dead serious. With the launch date approaching, McCue desperately needs to hire more good people, especially coders. To that end, he's staged late-night pizza frenzies at Harvard, MIT and UC Berkeley, hoping to cherry-pick the top two or three students in the computer science and business programmes. So far, the plan's paid off: for about $1000-worth of pizza, Tellme has landed two students from Harvard Business School and made serious offers to 20 other college students.

'I'm very, very aggressive about people quitting college to join Tellme,' says 32 year-old McCue, who passed up academia for IBM, later launching his first start-up, Paper Software, which he eventually sold to Netscape. 'I just tell them "Hey man, the time to go to school is during a recession. Not now. Not when you have opportunities like this" '.

Once on campus, hungry hands grab the pizzas, and McCue begins his pitch. A brief explanation of what they plan to do is followed by the invariable questions:

- How much money do you have ($53 million first round financing).
- How many people (55 and growing).
- When do you IPO (soon).

As the questions skew toward stock options, McCue winds up with a recruitment pitch. 'We're looking to hire the best,' he says. 'We're building something that'll be used by literally anyone with a telephone, billions of people. So check us out at tellme.com or send us e-mail.'

A handful of students circle McCue, peppering him with questions. This time, the queries are incisive. How accurate is your voice-recognition system? What about the international market? Do you have any partnerships with wireless companies? This is the reason that Tellme came to the lab – to find the half-dozen top students who have a passion for what the company is doing. Half an hour later, McCue climbs back into his car, clutching a fistful of résumés, and five possible hires, out of which maybe two will be the right fit.

Action Task: Building the Team

❏ Using the Belbin profiles, try to identify the characteristics of your current team(s) – Chairmen, Plants, Finishers and so forth.

❏ Do you see any obvious gaps in your team(s)?

❏ What recent appointments have been made from within and were they successful?

❏ What is your staff turnover rate? Is it going up and how does it compare with others in your sector?

❏ How do you recruit key staff? Which methods work best for you and why?

❏ How many and what type of new staff will you need to meet your growth plans over the next 12 months?

❏ How are appraisals done and are they seen as helpful?

❏ What happens after an appraisal by way of action and follow-up?

❏ Who appraises you?

❏ Who appraises your boss/chairman?

Managing Change 15

Peter Drucker, the management guru, says that the first task of a leader is to define his or her company's mission. In a world where product and service life cycles are shrinking, new technologies have an ever shorter shelf-life and customers demand ever higher levels of both quality and service, entrepreneurial leadership means inspiring change. Whilst managers may accept the status quo, leaders must always challenge it. In adapting the business to an increasingly volatile and competitive environment, the boss must become the change master in his or her firm.

But recognizing the need for change falls a long way short of being able to implement it successfully. Few people like change and even fewer can adapt to new circumstances quickly and without missing a heartbeat.

By definition, a business seeking fast growth must be able to manage a fast rate of change. Entrepreneurs must see change as the norm and not as a temporary and unexpected disruption, which will 'go away' when things improve.

How to Manage Change

Change management is a business process, like many other processes in business. Following a tried and proven procedure can improve your chances of getting it right more often. The five rules below show how you can break down change management into its elements. The rules work just as effectively outside of your organization as in it.

Rule 1: Tell Them Why (or Better still, Help Them to Find Out for Themselves)

The first rule in managing change is to explain to your staff the business case for change. For example, if a new competitor with a

lower cost base has entered the market, making you appear un-
competetive, you may want to change working practices to help
restore the balance. Explaining the background to the changes you
want to make will help people see the changes as an opportunity to
be competitive, rather than a threat to existing work practices.
Encyclopaedia Britannica's sales force were unable to recognize the
threat posed by Microsoft's *Encarta*. They saw it only as an inferior
product, failing to see that it was in fact a completely new value
proposition. Instead of paying $1000 for a book, parents paid the
same for a PC, getting the book for free.

Better than just explaining is to encourage staff to look outside the
business for themselves, identify potential problems and suggest
their own solutions. Not only might they have great ideas for
change, perhaps better than yours, but they will be more willing
to accept them and take responsibility for making the changes
succeed.

The benefits of change are not always obvious. So spell them out
in much the same way as you would explain the benefits of your
product or service to a prospective customer.

Rule 2: Make It Manageable

Even when people are dissatisfied with the present position and
know exactly what needs to be done to improve things, the change
may still not happen. The change may just be too big for anyone to
handle. But if you break it down into manageable bits, it can be
made to happen.

Individual resistance to change is a normal reaction. By understanding why people are resisting, it will be possible to help them see
the problem as manageable. The first step is to anticipate the impact
of the change on the people involved:

- Get an overview of the forces at work, both in favour of and
  against the change (see Table 15.1).
- Make a list of those most affected by the change. Put each person
  into one of four categories: (a) no commitment; (b) will let it
  happen if others want it; (c) will help it happen; (d) will make it
  happen.
- Examine how each person will be affected by the change. Look
  at career prospects, working hours and conditions, team membership and so forth.
- Will retraining be necessary? Often, a fear of failing is the
  principle reason why people won't try something new.

- Now see how the proposed change can be broken down into smaller parts, so that people can 'eat their elephant a bite at a time'.

---

1. What is the problem? (Write it down and define it in specific terms: who is involved, what is the magnitude?)
2. Where are we now?
3. Where do we want to get to? (Define the desired end result and try to make it measurable)
4. What are the things going *for* us? – driving forces. (List all the forces, organizational, individual, motivational, which are helping the change along)
5. What are the things going *against* us? – restraining forces. (List all the sources of resistance to the change)
6. What *action* can we take to maximize the driving forces and minimize the restraining forces?

Table 15.1   The process of force field analysis

Rule 3: Take a Shared Approach.

Involve people early on. If you ask them to join you in managing change only at the implementation stage, it will be too late to get their full cooperation. Give your key participants some say in shaping the change right from the start. This will mean that nobody feels the change is being imposed and more brains will be brought to bear on the problem.

Open, face-to-face communication is the backbone of successful change. It gets across the 'why' of change and allows people to face up to problems openly. It also builds confidence and clears up misunderstandings.

While open communication is vital, it is risky to announce intended changes until you have some committed participants alongside you.

Rule 4: Reinforce Individual and Team Identity

People are more willing to accept change and to move from the known to the unknown if they have confidence in themselves and their boss. Confidence is most likely to exist where people have a high degree of self-esteem. Building up self-esteem involves laying stress on the positive rather than the negative aspects of each person's contribution. Exhortations such as, 'you guys have had it too easy for too long', are unlikely to do much for people when you are faced with major competitive pressure. The importance to the change project of each person, both as an individual and where appropriate as a team member, needs to be emphasized.

To survive, a positive, confident climate for change need lots of reinforcement, such as:

- Rewards for achieving new goals, and as quickly as possible.
- Highlight success stories and create as many winners as possible.
- Have social events.
- Pay personal attention to those most affected by the change.

Rule 5: Change Takes Longer than You Think.

Most major changes make things worse before they make them better. More often than not, the immediate impact of change is a decrease in productivity, as people struggle to cope with new ways of working while they move up their own learning curve. The doubters will gloat and even the change champions may waver. But the greatest danger now is pulling the plug on the plan and either adopting a new plan or reverting to the status quo.

To prevent this 'disappointment' it is vital to both set realistic goals for the change period, and to anticipate the time lag between change and results (Figure 15.1).

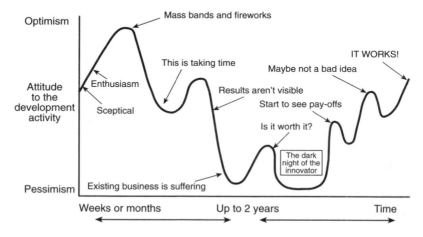

Figure 15.1 The long dark night of the innovator

Schwab – A Cautionary Tale

The President and CEO of Schwab, David S. Pottruck, says:

'To really gain engagement and commitment in a business, we need a different standard of communication than one of "tell and instruct". Moving a new model into a business environment was a real challenge and took some modification. Ultimately, I want the engagement of everyone in the company, but unlike a marriage, the business requires that I also have the ability to move fast, to make decisions quickly when I need to. Business leadership is not only about facilitation or consensus; it is about ultimate responsibility. Even as I encourage dialogue and listen carefully to everyone who contributes, my responsibility is to make decisions that are the best for the whole of the business, and to continue to have the participation of those who disagree with me. It requires that I understand other people's point of view – and that I can acknowledge our differences.'

A few years ago, Schwab decided to open their branches for a few hours on Saturday. They announced the decision without much input from field managers. The plans did not differentiate between branches where potential customers would actually appear on Saturdays and those locations that would not get foot traffic at the weekend. To compound the communication problem, at the same time that they were looking at Saturday hours, they were 'announcing' the opening of a call centre in Denver, which would require many people to move from their base in Chicago to Colorado.

It didn't go down that well. Many people in the field operation were vehemently opposed to this idea; especially, and understandably, people who worked in branches that had no Saturday traffic. The company struggled with the decision between listening to people threaten to quit. David Pottruck, company CEO at Schwab, took the opportunity to address the issue at a manager's meeting in Chicago. Here is what he said:

'When I decided to speak to all of you about these changes, I was quite excited. As you know, we have been considering both locating a call centre in the Mountain states and opening the branches for a few hours on Saturday for some time. But as I reflected on the impact of these changes, it occurred to me that opening a new call centre did not require me to move from my home, and in fact, I was not going to work any more hours on Saturday than I already do . . . (but) for many of you, an occasional Saturday away from the family will be something new, and certainly, these changes will cause some disruptions in the family patterns of your staffs.

It also occurred to me that it was you, not me, who were going to tell your staff about moving or working Saturdays.

Given these thoughts, I quickly realized that you might not be as excited about these moves as I am, even though these changes are for the good of the company and ultimately will create more opportunity for all of us.'

He went on to outline the reasons for the change and the shifts made in the implementation before taking questions from the group.

The next day, he got a number of voice-mail messages from people at that meeting. Remarkably, their comments were much more about the 'caring' part of the remarks than the 'content' regarding the changes. It was a real lesson in leadership. People wanted to be heard and acknowledged. Eventually, they made changes to the plan that made it work much more efficiently. The move and the open-Saturday implementation went much better after that.

The Change Star

Unfortunately, managing people through organizational change is not a straightforward step-by-step process. It is messy and it involves doing lots of things at the same time. The change star model (Figure 15.2) has proved a useful framework to help get people through the change process as quickly and painlessly as possible.

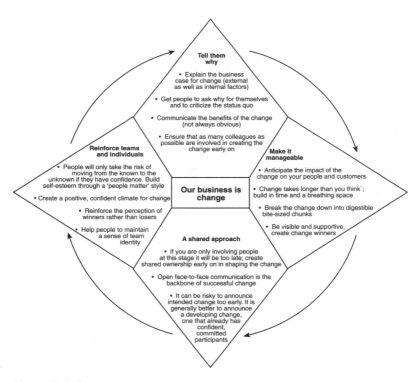

Figure 15.2 Change star model

It starts from the belief that, if an entrepreneur has to make an assumption about how people react to change, it is wisest to assume that change hurts. The change star model provides four pointers to help you convert the perception 'Change hurts' into the perception that 'Our business is change'.

There is no right place to start on the star – it is an iterative model. Tell them what may seem the obvious start point but, unless you have 'made it manageable', it may be that the resistance you will meet will make the change too hot to handle. Similarly, you cannot afford to wait until the later stages of the change to adopt a 'shared approach'; this must come right at the beginning. The fourth pointer of the star talks about the need to 'reinforce teams and individuals' in order that people feel safe enough to take the risks of change. This climate of positive thinking and that people matter cannot be built overnight. If you have a punitive culture where people 'keep their heads below the parapet' and come out of every meeting with their boss feeling uncomfortable, then it will be a long time before your employees will feel they can risk making mistakes without being cut off at the knees. A detailed illustration of how to use the change star is given in Barrow et al. (1995).

Action Checklist: Managing Change

❑ How well did the last major change you experienced (imposed!) go?
❑ Are there things you will do differently the next time?
❑ For the next change you have in mind go through the force field analysis process outlined in Table 15.2.
❑ Prepare a plan to implement your next change, using the change star framework (Figure 15.2).

Key players	No commitment	Will let it happen	Will help it happen	Will make it happen

Table 15.2 The force field analysis process

New Blood, New Broom 16

The great paradox about entrepreneurship, especially in technology companies, is that the skills and attitudes required to get a business up and running are usually not the best to manage its growth.

A powerful example of the difference between entrepreneurs and managers was given in a study conducted by Ohio State University a few years ago. They took 124 entrepreneurs and 95 professional managers from big, successful and well-established companies. They asked both groups a series of identical questions. First, they were asked factual questions with two possible answers, for example, 'Which cause of death is more frequent in the USA, cancer or heart disease?' Then they were given business decisions, for example, 'You must replace a foreign-made machine that has just broken down with one of two alternatives: either an American machine recommended by a friend, who had bought one which had not broken down, or another foreign-built one which was statistically less likely to break down than the American one'. The entrepreneurs we evenly split on these types of question. However, 90% of managers went for the foreign machine.

Among the conclusions drawn from this study were:

1. Entrepreneurs were much more confident that they were right, especially when they were wrong.
2. Entrepreneurs prefer hunches to data. They are happy to extrapolate from very small samples, whereas managers would look to 'statistical significance'.

If you think about that it makes perfect sense. Entrepreneurs can't wait for hard evidence before they launch into a market. Once that evidence is available, the opportunity will be crystal-clear to others. They will have lost their advantage. In the Internet and technology worlds, where so much store is set on first-mover advantage, this would pose a serious drawback. It also suggests that one side-effect of being decisive on the basis of not much evidence is that entrepreneurs are going to get things wrong more often than not. The high failure rate amongst new and small firms is ample evidence of this.

Managers, on the other hand, are more inclined to be rational, consistent and more concerned with the efficient deployment of resources, once they have been allocated.

Get Out of the Way

Start-ups need entrepreneurship, growing businesses with hundreds of staff need managing. So the big big question is, can the founder make the transition from caterpillar to butterfly, or perhaps it is really the other way around.

Jim Clarke, entrepreneur extraordinary, with 3 billion dollar start-ups under his belt, knew his place in the business food chain. It was in having great ideas and a vision and in getting someone else, a manager, to take over the venture almost from the moment of birth. With Healtheon, he sought the help of venture capitalist John Doerr, of Kleiner, Perkins, Caufield and Byers, to find 'a guy with gray hair and soothing manners who could speak to the CEOs of large health-care companies in their own language'. Clarke used a VC because VCs straddle both worlds, the world of visionaries with dangerous ideas and the world of serious executives, who get things done and usually done right. VCs usually had been to business school and owned suits, even if they didn't always wear them. VCs kept their ties on hooks on the backs of their office doors, so they could go either way. Doerr identified Mike Long, who had spent 20 years building a computer services business in Austin, Texas, called Continuum. In 1996 Continuum sold itself to Computer Sciences for $1.7 billion. Up to that time it was the seventh-largest deal ever done in the computer industry.

Doerr called Long more than 100 times over a 6 month period to talk him out of his safe computer company and into the Internet revolution. It took a further 6 months for Long to extract himself from his old company. He arrived at Healtheon to find a chaotic and demoralized group of 100 people, and managed it towards a successful IPO 2 years later.

Caught in the Web, the Internet design and consulting company, started in 1995 by Bobby John and Aziz Hurzook while they were in York University together, is another example of founders seeing their role as being other than being the CEO. The company started with two people, a cell phone and a Visa card, and has grown into a million-a-month operation heading for an IPO. At that point the founders decided they needed a different animal to run the business. They recruited Peter Jones, a former president of Apple Canada to join them in March 2000. He was introduced to John and Hurzook through a mutual friend. They met every day for about a week and a half. Jones saw something of the early days at Apple about the firm, and decided to join. It could have taken 6 months to find Jones using a search agency and a further 6 months to get him free of his current job, as it did at Healtheon. But Jones was taking a 'breather' after leading Shared Network Services through its merger with BCE Emergis, so he was available immediately.

Not everyone feels ready to let go of their 'baby' as soon as the two examples above. Jonas Svensson, founder of Spray, one of Europe's largest Internet portals, has strong views about preserving his company's 'tribal collective values'. His company is based in Stockholm, which in 2000 had 900 Internet companies, one for every 850 residents, and more than any other European city. He and his co-founders don't want to answer to anybody. Their business, which began as a few friends tinkering with computers in 1995, now employs 3000 people in Sweden, France, Italy, Norway and Germany. One of Spray's board members, a leather-clad academic, claims that entrepreneurial firms in Sweden need to be managed differently. Quoted in an article in a recent edition of the *Economist*, this Spray director asserts:

'At outposts of American tech firms, they're still ticking manuals and reporting to Santa Clara. This business is growing too fast to be closely managed from the centre. You have to pick the people carefully, then leave it to trust'.

Or Be Pushed Aside

Financiers' love affair with Internet companies and with E-businesses in general has been too hot for it not to have the inevitable cooling down. But what may happen, as it has happened in other sectors (Bio-technology for example) is a small ice age. In May 2000, the the NASDAQ composite, the FTSE techMARK 100 and the Neuer Markt All-Share index were all down to half their high point, reached in January 2000. In fact, they were headed right back down to the plateau of a year previous (Figure 16.1). More than 60 US IPOs were postponed or cancelled in April 2000, as were a dozen European IPOs. Those that did get away were trading below their

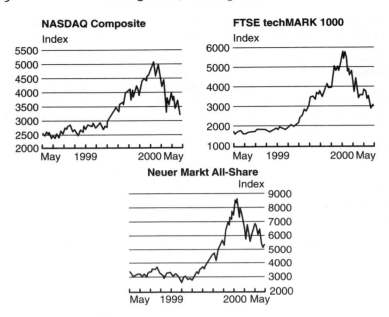

Figure 16.1 Collapsing share prices

offer price within days. egg, the Internet arm of Prudential, the UK insurance group, scaled its pricing back to about £1.4 billion, compared with earlier estimates of £4 billion. Various industry watchers about this time were suggesting that, at the current burn rate, two-thirds of Internet firms would run out of cash anywhere between 6 months and 2 years hence.

It's at this point that the financiers usually reassert control. Power drains away from the E-entrepreneurs along with their cash and radical changes in structure are imposed from outside. So if you can't build up a better team and become a more effective manager, or find one yourself, you may have them pushed upon you.

The case below is a good example of a shooting star founded by people with no management experience. Just a good idea, a few years (between them) in staff jobs and a business plan.

Lastminute.com

Just a couple of months after its UK listing, with its shares trading at 60% below its March 2000 offer price, Lastminute.com, the start of the UK Internet world, was under new management. Only a few weeks before that, the story of the birth of the new business had been breathlessly peddled around London in a burst of PR activity, aided by a photogenic founder. It needed some story to turn less than £200 000 a year's turnover into a business that was eventually, however temporarily, valued at £400 million.

The idea behind Lastminute.com belongs to Brent Hoberman, the less visible of the founders. After a lifetime (aged 31) of trying to book hotels, restaurants and air tickets at the last minute – and being frequently disappointed – he decided that he and others like him deserved a better deal. After all, he reasoned, there were millions of empty hotel beds, unfilled restaurants and spare seats on aeroplanes. All that was needed was for the link to be made. Hoberman, who lives in Notting Hill, London, met his co-founder, Martha Lane Fox, while they were both working at Spectrum, a management consultancy.

Fox was not convinced by the idea, or of starting a business, and moved on to Carlton to work on its pay-TV channels. Hoberman had helped launch the British Internet Auction House, QXL.com and, while he never empathized with that business, he felt convinced about the Internet and about Lastminute's concept. After twisting Fox's arm quite hard, they set out to put a business proposal together.

Both the entrepreneurs have privileged backgrounds – Oxford for both of them, and Eton and Westminster, respectively. Both had entrepreneurial families – Hoberman's grandfather started with one shop in South Africa and built up a chain of 250. He claims always to have wanted to be an entrepreneur. Fox's late grandfather started the up-market estate agents Lane Fox, and her cousin and aunt are well-established interior decorators in London. Her ambitions leant more towards being an actress, as her performance in the run-up to Lastminute's UK listing revealed. Despite this privileged background, both had to work hard in getting their plans accepted. Her network helped, but in the end it was learning to write a business plan at Spectrum, and Brent being brilliant at Excel, that really counted.

Both founders have worked hard – long hours and lots of travel. But nothing prepared either of them for the transition from a Notting Hill kitchen table to being a stockmarket player in 2 years. By the time the company had 700 000 customers and 200 employees, it was becoming clear that the founders needed help. Fox was quoted as returning from Paris having received something of a shock. Lastminute's Paris office had a staff of 30; when she had been there earlier in the month, there were only 10 people in the office.

On 16 April 2000, the financial pages of the London press carried this comment:

New Blood in at Lastminute

Troubled Internet Company Lastminute.com will announce the appointment of a new tier of senior management to run the business this week. Shares in Lastminute.com – founded by Brent Hoberman and Martha Lane Fox – fell to an all-time low on Friday and are now trading at 60% below last month's offer price.

The company is bringing in three senior executives to strengthen the management of the business, both in the UK and internationally. Charles McKee has been appointed Executive Vice-President, David Kelly joins to head the UK team and Helen Baker joins as Head of Supply for the UK. McKee, who will be responsible for international expansion, was a general manager at Virgin Atlantic Airways, with responsibility for global distribution. He joined Virgin in 1992 as Vice-President for Asia and the Pacific, before being appointed Senior Vice-President for North America. Kelly, who will be responsible for the day-to-day running of the Lastminute.com business in the UK, was the director of customer service at Amazon.co.uk. Baker will work with existing suppliers in the UK.

'These appointments add a great deal of depth to our management team, bolstering the existing senior expertise and freeing up the time of other senior executives to focus on their core roles,' said Brent Hoberman, chief executive of Lastminute.com.

The dramatic fall in the share price has been embarrassing for both Lastminute.com and investment bank Morgan Stanley, which raised the top of the price range on the eve of the flotation.

Lastminute was a hugely important deal for Morgan Stanley. Over the past year, it has missed out on almost all of the major European Internet flotations.

Non-executive Directors

A further way to inject new talent into the business with experience of growing companies and overcoming major obstacles is to bring in non-executive directors. Typically, a non-executive director will be an executive director somewhere else, or has been so fairly recently. For Internet firms that are stuffed full of bright, talented, young and inexperienced people, having some older people around with a depth of business experience and an extended range of contacts can prove invaluable.

Non-execs can open doors to potential clients, banks, venture capital firms, possible alliance partners and even competitors. They can help resolve internal disputes, give guidance – perhaps even respectability – to proposals on directors' remuneration, your own in particular. And they can give an aura of gravitas that will make the business community take your company more seriously than it might otherwise.

Very often, the pool from which non-executive directors are drawn includes successful entrepreneurs who have sold their successful business and are looking for a new challenge. They have a track record of creating value, which is a rare and valuable commodity in the Internet world, where that is seen as the main goal by investors, employees and often suppliers too.

Beenz.com

Philip Crawford, one of Europe's most prominent information technology executives, currently sits on three dot-com boards. The 48-year-old was, until recently, head of worldwide operations for EDS, the IT services group. As head of the UK arm of Oracle, the US database giant, he built a $250 000 business into $1 billion within 3 years. He was also the only non-US executive to sit on the main Oracle board.

While Oracle was easily the first choice for big company projects, small groups, and particularly Internet start-ups, were less enthusiastic. This was a problem, not only because they were losing out to their competitors, but also because the new Internet companies would be the big players of tomorrow.

The first move Crawford instigated was to order his sales force to dress down when visiting dot-com companies. Out went suits and ties, in came open-necked shirts and chinos as a means of forging better customer relationships. His second initiative was to use his most senior management, himself included, to win new Internet start-up business. He felt that if these new companies felt valued through their relationship with senior Oracle management, that would reflect with better sales.

This was also how he joined the board of his first dot-com. Charles Cohen and Philip Letts were meeting Crawford to decide on the database system for their company, Beenz.com, which mints an on-line currency similar in concept to Green Shield Stamps. They left with not only an Oracle system but also a new non-executive director.

It was a move actively encouraged by Larry Ellison, Oracle's chief executive, as part of the company's new outreach strategy to Internet start-ups. Mr Crawford took a small stake in Beenz and was then involved in helping the company build its US strategy when it eventually relocated from London to New York. He was then instrumental in bringing in a large personal investment from Ellison in a high-profile move that brought great publicity for the start-up.

The Beenz board meets monthly, usually in New York. The meetings begin with formal board tasks, before moving on to areas where Crawford and the other non-executives bring their experience to bear. Philip Letts, the chairman, is very good at utilizing the four non-executives, getting them to use their contacts, open doors, make introductions.

In addition to the Ellison investment, Mr Crawford has been able to make several other introductions for the company. Jonathan Rowland, founder of Jellyworks, was brought into Beenz as an investor. He was also instrumental in initiating Beenz's joint venture with Oracle in Japan.

Action Checklist: Are You the Right Person to Run Your Business, Now?

The answer should be 'Yes' to at least seven of these questions for you to be the right person – less than five 'Yes' answers and you should start looking for your replacement now, before someone does it for you.

❑ Do you have sufficient cash, or cash flow, to run the business for the next 2 years without raising more money? If the answer is 'Yes', you can put off answering the rest of these questions until your answer becomes 'No'.

❏ Do you enjoy managing large teams and feel comfortable doing so?
❏ Are you really good at recruiting and selecting leaders?
❏ Have you fired anyone in the last 2 months?
❏ Do you find having your performance appraised and evaluated a valuable experience?
❏ Can you translate a big vision into the key steps needed to get results?
❏ Do you spend at least a third of your time planning strategy and less than a third either travelling or in discussions on technology or operational issues?
❏ Do you understand the financial accounting information fully?
❏ Do you work less than 10 hours a day?
❏ Do you have non-executive directors on board, and do you make the best possible use of them?

Part IV

Real Money for Virtual Firms

One factor that surely separates old-economy goats from the new-economy sheep is their capacity to consume cash. Burn rate, the new new word for overtrading, features high in every E-entrepreneur's vocabulary. Cash truly is king. Not in the old-economy sense, where cash piles were stashed aside as war chests to fund hostile takeovers. In the new economy, cash is consumed in gargantuan proportions to win customers that one day may be worth having. Amazon, by its fifth year of trading, and something of an old man in the world of E-tailers, was still burning cash at a rate of millions a day, with profits still on some distant horizon. The key survival measure in the E-economy is not how much profit you are making, or perhaps even will make, as your backers will probably be long gone before that happens. Rather, it is the number of months your last round of finance will last at the present rate of cash consumption.

Valuing and measuring performance in E-businesses has been notoriously difficult. Even where companies are making profits, as for example with Yahoo!, it is hard, not to say impossible, to support the valuations, even at the scaled-down figures now prevailing. Even factoring in a 60% compound growth for the next decade or so makes the figures still seem high. Even Microsoft, in a fast growing 5 year period, only hit a compound growth rate of 57%. Despite the new paradigm arguments, normal service looks as if it's about to be resumed. By ignoring normal investment criteria, such as price: earnings ratios, investors have allowed Internet firms to 'proliferate like some species of jungle animal without any natural predators', as Evan Swartz, a former editor at *Business Week*, aptly put it. But it looks like the predators are back. And the changes may not be gradual, with numerous minor alterations to the ecosystem. It could be more of a cataclysmic shock, such as that which swept the dinosaurs off the Earth. Investors have started to recognize that certain much-touted business models really don't work; that profits – not revenues, site hits, page views, PR coverage or IPO road shows

– are what finally matters. Those profits have to be real profits. Not profits before 'special one-time expenses', or excluding write-offs for acquisitions or any other accounting slight of hand. Real bottom-line profits are what is finally needed, even from virtual businesses. All the omens are that a shock is being delivered to the business system, with five of the seven preconditions for a major change of economic 'ecosystem' already on the radar (Table IV.1).

By the spring of 2000, the surviving Internet firms were beginning to look hard at ways, usually old old ways, of surviving in turbulent times. To survive and turn a business round, you need a control panel to tell you what is happening, just as with an aeroplane or a car. You also need a few levers and pedals linked to the business that will allow you to assert, reassert perhaps, a measure of control over the firm's destiny.

In Part IV we will look at ways of slowing down the burn rate or taking on more fuel, whilst managing the external financial PR which can provide a much needed canister of oxygen when the air supply is running out.

	1929	1972	1989	2000
High valuations based on dubious justifications	✓	✓	✓	✓
'This time is different'	✓	✓	✓	✓
High participation in market	✓	✓	✓	✓
Debt-financed speculation	✓	✓	✓	✓
$US declining	✓	✓	✓	
Rising interest rates	✓	✓	✓	✓
Capital flight	✓	✓	✓	

Table IV.1   Difficult times ahead

Reading the Dashboard 17

During the early months and years of any business, cash is more important than profit. Cash is what determines whether or not a business will survive. Profit is the signal that it has all been worthwhile. If profits don't come through in a reasonable amount of time, the business will be unable to sustain itself. Going back to raise more money will be impossible. While many people will take a risky investment, few want to back a proven loser. That rule always applies in the longer term. However, in the short term things can be different. Sectors come into favour, markets indulge in over-exuberance. But eventually sanity returns. Business is not about sentiment, but about the profitable allocation of resources. If profits don't come through, a business will die. As Darwin put it in his book, *The Origin of Species*, 'We forget that though food may be superabundant, it is not so at all seasons of each recurring year'.

E-economy firms have been given longer to deliver profits than most conventional firms might have been (most, but not all – the Channel Tunnel is nearly through its first decade without any sign of a real profit). That indulgence has in part been because of the size of the opportunity that the financiers see in Internet firms, partly through ignorance of the technology and its implications, and partly because the public has been carried away with enthusiasm (or greed). That has meant that no financier is really taking much risk, as they expect to package their investment up and sell it on quickly to the public via an IPO. In the old economy, a VC might hold an investment in a private company for a decade or so, and even then the exit would be more than likely via a trade sale at a fairly modest value. In the new economy, VCs have seen an easy exit available, sometimes within months of making their investment. This has made them both more adventurous and more tolerant. Times are changing.

E-entrepreneurs need to keep track of key numbers if they are to survive and grow. As well as being the entrepreneurs' control panel, showing what is happening to the business, a firm grasp of the numbers give the financiers more confidence in the face of mounting losses. It has to be said that the ratios for most Internet firms make sorry reading. One can only assume that there is no-one in the driving seat to read the instruments, or perhaps the dashboard has been covered up to prevent an attack of vertigo.

Ratios Rule

Numbers on their own are not a good gauge of the performance of a moving target. Knowing that a car has used 10 gallons of fuel is fairly meaningless unless you know how far it has gone in using that fuel. If has gone 100 miles, that represents 10 miles per gallon, which does not sound great. If it has gone 400 miles, then that sounds a much better 40 miles per gallon. That measurement of performance is a ratio, and ratios are the best tool for getting a feel for how a business is performing. Several ratios are required to get a good understanding.

Look at Table 17.1. The figures are abstracted from Cisco Systems' filed accounts. The figures for the quarter ending January 2000 are unaudited. All are in millions of dollars. The performance looks healthy enough. In the first place, the company, unlike most other Internet firms, is making a profit. Better still, the profits, whether gross, operating or net, are growing. Again, an unusual feature for the sector. But it is only when we show the percentages that the true measure of Cisco's results shine through (Table 17.2).

Now we can see that not only has Cisco grown its sales and profits, by every measure of profit, substantially, but they have become more profitable. Their operating income (profit) has risen from 16% to 24%, which means that nearly 25 cents in every dollar of sales is operating profit. Net profitability has nearly doubled from 10% to 19%.

	Quarter ending January 2000	Quarter ending January 1999
Sales turnover	4350	2845
Gross margin	2814	1857
Sales and marketing costs	924	576
Research and development	598	372
Operating income	1059	466
Net income	825	282

Table 17.1 Figures from Cisco Systems' filed accounts (millions of $US)

	Quarter ending January 2000	(%)	Quarter ending January 1999	(%)
Sales turnover	4350	100	2845	100
Gross margin	2814	65	1857	65
Sales and marketing costs	924	21	576	20
Research and development	598	14	372	13
Operating income	1059	24	466	16
Net income	825	19	282	10

Table 17.2 Figures shown in Table 17.1, with percentages added

All that has been achieved while increasing their marketing and R&D spends, both in absolute terms and as a percentage of sales. Until we use ratios, we just can't get a real measure of performance.

There are many financial ratios, but we will concentrate on the key ones needed to help kick-start profitable growth. The accounts used throughout the rest of this chapter are of Amazon.com and Barnesandnoble.com, an abstract of which are given in the case study at the end of the chapter. The figures given are for the first quarters of 1999 and 2000 for each company. This allows comparisons for each company against its past, to show the trend, and also against a competitor, to show the relative performance. The analysis that follows is not intended to be a critique of Amazon.com or of Barnesandnoble.com, it is just a way to make the ratios more relevant. There is no realistic way a couple of quarters' results can be seen as anything more than a straw in the wind, by outsiders at any rate.

Measures of Growth

Internet companies set great store by growth. Three useful measures of growth are:

- Sales growth, which tells you if the firm is getting bigger.
- Profit growth, which tells you if it is just getting bigger without getting any better. We would usually use net profit, the bottom line, in this calculation. But we can gain some insight from seeing how the gross and operating profits are moving.
- Headcount growth is also a number worth watching. With people come costs – office space, equipment, mistakes and so forth. The faster you are piling on people, the greater that future expense will be.

It can be seen from the case study below (see Table 17.3) that Amazon.com has grown its sales by 96%, quarter on quarter – an impressive figure, however one that was exceeded by Barnesand noble.com, who grew sales by 143%. Neither company made either an operating or net profit. However, Amazon.com grew its gross profit by 98% and Barnesandnoble.com by 108%.

We could usefully drill down deeper into information governing growth performance. For example, we can see that Amazon's expenses, or perhaps in their term's 'investments' in technology and sales, are growing in both absolute terms and as a percentage of sales, while Barnesandnoble.com is spending more money each quarter, but the rate of expenditure is slowing down relative to sales growth.

Headcount data is not given for both quarters, but we will look again at this area when we look at profitability.

Profitability and Efficiency

The usual ratios to measure profitability, or the efficient use of resources, are given below. Where data is available on Amazon.com and Barnesandnoble.com, it is used.

Gross Margin

Deduct the cost of sales from the sales, and express the result as a percentage of sales. The higher the percentage, the greater the value we are adding to the goods and services we are producing:

$$\text{gross margin} = \frac{\text{gross profit} \times 100}{\text{sales}} \%$$

Amazon.com is making a 22% gross margin, a figure which has been static when compared with the same period last year. Barnesandnoble.com, in contrast, has seen its gross margin decline from 23% to 19% over the same period.

Operating Margin

In this case, we not only deduct the cost of sales, but we also take off expenses (other than financing charges such as interest, and taxation). This is a measure of how well the management is running the business (it is assumed that financing decisions are taken by the owners, and interest and taxation set by the government of the day – so they are out of management control and accountability.

$$\text{operating margin} = \frac{\text{operating profit} \times 100}{\text{sales}} \%$$

Both companies we are using are making operating losses. For Amazon.com, the loss has accelerated from -18% in 1999 to -34% in 2000. The operating loss at Barnesandnoble.com is much higher at -66%, but relatively static.

Drilling down further into the operating expenses, we can see that Amazon is still accelerating its spending on technology and marketing, up from 8% of sales to 11%, and 21% to 24%, respectively. Barnesandnoble.com, in contrast, is slimming down from 11% to 8% in terms of spending on technology, and 59% to 41% on marketing.

Net Margin

This is the *bottom line*. It represents the sum available either to be distributed as dividends or retained by the business to invest in its future.

$$\text{Net margin} = \frac{\text{net profit} \times 100}{\text{sales}} \%$$

The bottom line is something that not many Internet firms have seen appear. Whilst Cisco has managed a respectable 19%, Amazon was losing 54% in 2000, a figure that has accelerated up from 21% in 1999. Barnesandnoble.com has actually cut its losses slightly from 13% to 12% over the same period.

Return on Capital Employed (ROCE)

This is the primary measure of performance for most business. If, for example, you had £10 000 invested in a bank and at the end of the year they gave you £500 interest, then the return on your *capital employed* (ROCE) would be 5%:

$$\text{ROCE} = \frac{500 \times 100}{10\,000} \%$$

In a business, this ratio is calculated by expressing the operating profit (i.e. profit before interest and tax) as a percentage of the total capital employed – both in fixed assets and in working capital.

$$\text{ROCE} = \frac{\text{operating profit} \times 100}{(\text{fixed assets} + \text{working capital})}\ \%$$

which, if you think about it, is the same as saying the return on the shareholders' funds plus the long-term loans, i.e. the 'financed by' bit of the balance sheet.

Internet firms on average have made no return on the capital invested in them. There are dozens of other measures of efficiency and profitability that may be more appropriate in one industry and less so in another, but ultimately ROCE is a good guide as to how well a business is being run.

A useful generic model to help understand the factors affecting ROCE is shown in Figure 17.1. The left-hand side of Figure 17.1 is a cut-down income statement (profit and loss account) and the right-hand side is a slice of the balance sheet, showing what our money is tied up in. An increase in sales or a decrease in costs could result in an increase in profit. If the working capital, inventories and debtors, for example, and the fixed assets (buildings, equipment, etc.) don't rise, then the return on capital employed will improve. The same result can be achieved by reducing the investment in fixed assets and working capital required to produce a given level of profit.

You can expand this model to include all the elements that matter to any particular type of business. However, in the long run, all business have to produce a satisfactory return on the money invested in them, or the money will go elsewhere.

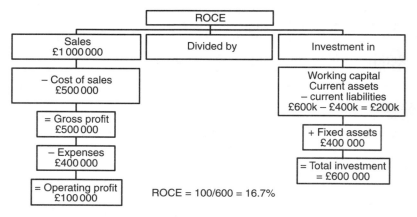

Figure 17.1 Factors that effect ROCE

Return on Shareholders' Investment (ROSI)

The shareholders are usually most interested in the net return on their investment. So here we are concerned with the profit left after interest has been paid on any loans and after the tax man has had his slice. The shareholders have invested not only their initial stake, but any profits left in the business.

$$\text{ROSI} = \frac{\text{net profit after tax and interest} \times 100}{\text{total shareholders' funds}}$$

Shareholders in most Internet firms are still holding their breath and waiting for a return.

Profit per Employee

If, as in most cases, your principle 'assets' are people, and not just capital assets such as machines, then you will need to monitor what value employees are contributing:

$$\text{profit per employee} = \frac{\text{net profit (after interest, but before tax)}}{\text{number of employees}}$$

We use profit before tax, as salaries and wages are a tax-deductible expense for the business.

Whilst neither of the companies are making net or operating profits, we can get a measure of how efficiently they are being used by looking at the sales and gross profit being generated per employee.

In 2000, Amazon.com's 7600 employees produced \$75 000 of sales and nearly \$17 000 of gross profit each in the 3 month period. Barnesandnoble.com's 1237 employees produced \$63 000 of sales and nearly \$13 000 gross profit per employee.

Stock Turn

This ratio provides a view as to how efficiently goods for sale are being used and processed through the business. For Internet firms this is a crucial measure, as to some extent this is the real value being created – the destruction of chains of supply along the route from producer to consumer. This is as true for Cisco on-line in the B2B (business-to-business) market as it is for Amazon in the B2C (business-to-consumer) market. The ratio is calculated as follows:

$$\text{stock turn} = \frac{\text{cost of sales}}{\text{inventory (stock)}}$$

We use cost of sales, rather than sales as we are not 'holding' our profit margins and indirect costs in the warehouse.

Both Amazon.com and Barnesandnoble.com are turning their stock over about 1¼ times a quarter.

Financial Strength

The big question for Internet firms is, will they be able to survive long enough to reach profitability? Surviving is about financial strength. Cash reserves are part of this equation, but cash in a business is a moveable feast. The figure in either the balance sheet or the bank may be meaningless in a fast-moving environment. Once again we have to fall back on ratios and trends to get a feel for how events are unfolding.

Current Ratio

A business has to be able to pay its way from day to day. In other words, its current liabilities, such as creditors or overdraft, must be covered by money expected shortly from customers (receivables/debtors) or fairly soon (from the sale of inventories/stocks and work in progress).

This ability to meet current obligations as they fall due is called 'liquidity'. It is measured by dividing the current liabilities into the current assets and expressing the answers as a decimal fraction.

$$\text{current ratio} = \frac{\text{current assets}}{\text{current liability}}$$

Anything less than one to one (1:1) (i.e. current liabilities being covered by current assets) means the company cannot realistically expect to be able to pay its bills as they fall due. The result will be inefficient work practices, e.g. moving from job to job, waiting for raw materials to come in from suppliers, who are upset at being kept waiting for payment, etc.

Anything over 2:1 means you may have too much money tied up in working capital, i.e. your stock levels are too high or you are taking too long to collect in your money, or you are not taking enough credit!

In the case of Amazon, the current ratio has moved up from an adequate 1.37:1 to a very comfortable 2.02:1. The figures for Barnesandnoble.com are of a very different order (8.66:1 and 6.66:1). Barnesandnoble.com is a subsidiary of the 'bricks and mortar' company of the same name, so the way in which inter-company factors such as inventories and receivables are treated may have contributed to this. Cisco, for example, had a current ratio of 1.54:1 in May 2000.

Gearing

The more borrowed money a business uses, as opposed to that put in by the shareholders (either through initial capital or by leaving profits in the business), the more highly geared the business is.

Highly geared businesses can be vulnerable when either sales dip sharply, as in a recession, or when interest rates rocket.

$$\text{Gearing} = \frac{\text{debt (long-term borrowings)} \times 100}{\text{debt} + \text{shareholders' funds}} \%$$

So Amazon.com long-term borrowing made up 99% of the capital employed in the business, up from 85% in the same quarter of 1999. This is high by any standards, and was brought about by the long history of losses which has all but wiped out the shareholders investment. Barnesandnoble.com has no long-term borrowings. Once again, its subsidiary status will have a bearing on these figures.

Interest Cover

Whilst gearing is important, it is equally important to look at a company's ability to service the interest on that borrowing. If you were fortunate enough to inherit £¼ million, you could buy a house or apartment for £½ million and only be 50% geared. What you might find a little difficult would be to find the £2000 per month to pay the interest on the loan. The calculation is as follows:

$$\text{interest cover} = \frac{\text{operating profit}}{\text{interest on long-term debt}}$$

Neither of the companies in our example has made an operating profit, so this ratio is somewhat academic. However, in the real old world, the financial community would be concerned if a business couldn't cover the interest on its borrowings at least two or three times. The only source of money for a highly geared company with a low level of interest cover is an investor. For a more detailed illustration of the ratio performance of entrepreneurial firms, see Barrows (1999).

Value

In the old economy, companies are valued on the basis of their profits (earnings) in relation to their share price via a price:earnings ratio. So if a company makes $10 million profit for its 1 million shareholders, its earnings per share is $10. If the share price is $100, then by dividing that by the profit per share we get a price:earnings ratio of 10. By new-economy standards that would be pretty low. Even by old-economy standards, where the main stockmarkets have reached general multiples of 15–30, that would be a low figure.

Cisco's price:earnings ratio doubled from 77.11 in 1998 to 147.97 on 31 January 2000. To make a business worth this valuation implies an incredible growth rate. Shareholders in Internet companies are not looking to current performance on which to base their valuations, but to some distant future date when massive returns will come in.

There is a certain perversity in the way Internet investors look at the relationship between company performance and company value, as Figure 17.2 shows. Even in the old economy, the link between short term performance and company values are tenuous to say the least. But as value is what investors ultimately want, you need to have this figure on your control panel, perhaps using more mature firms as a guide to what you should be aiming for. For a more detailed study of how entrepreneurial firms are valued by underwriters and venture capitalists, see Barrow et al. (1999).

Amazon.com

Jeff Bezos, Amazon.com's founder, came up with the idea for selling books on-line while he was working as a senior vice-president of D.E. Shaw, a New York-based investment management firm. According to *Wired*, Bezos was assigned to come up with profitable ideas for selling over the Internet. Bezos concluded that on-line book selling would be a good business because two of the USA's largest book distributors already had electronic lists.

Bezos realized that no single bookstore could carry a comprehensive inventory of the books in print. The distributors who carried thousands of titles acted as the warehouse for most stores, particularly smaller booksellers. When customers asked a store for a book it did not have in

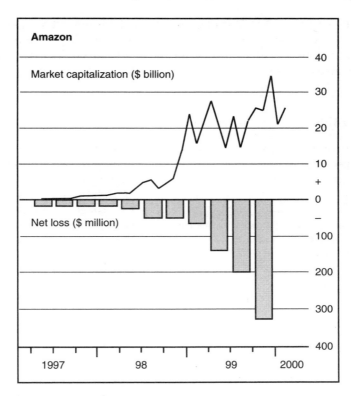

Figure 17.2 Amazon: the more they lose, the more they're worth!
Source: company reports, Primark Datastream

stock, they filled the customer's order through one of the two largest distributors – Ingram or Baker & Taylor. These companies' inventory lists were digitized in the late 1980s. The on-line inventory lists would enable Bezos to offer books on-line through the company he envisioned creating.

Bezos's firm was not willing to invest in the idea. Bezos and his wife then drove across country to Seattle to start Amazon.com. Bezos typed the business plan on his computer while his wife drove. He recruited one of the programmers he had met through his investigations for D.E. Shaw, Shel Kaphan, to become his first employee.

Kaphan and a contractor named Paul Barton-Davis built a prototype of the Amazon.com website in a converted garage of a rented home in Bellevue, Washington. Bezos raised the first $1 million of seed capital from 15 wealthy individual investors. The naming of Amazon.com was based on the importance of its relative size. Bezos reasoned that the Amazon River was 10 times as large as the next largest river, the Mississippi, in terms of volume of water and Amazon.com had six times as many titles as the world's largest physical bookstore. To deliver on this vision of huge relative size, Bezos and Kaphan started work on their website. They programmed the site to sound a bell every time the servers recorded a sale.

Amazon.com was launched in July 1995, and the bell started ringing – so often that within a few weeks, the noise had become unbearable and they disabled it. (At least two other entrepreneurs had used this technique years before: Virgin's Richard Branson and Julian Richer, founder of Richer Sounds.) Every week, the revenues went up. By the second or third week, Amazon.com was generating revenues of $6000 or $10 000 per week. By the end of early September 1995, revenues were $20 000 a week.

Bezos realized that not all activities should be conducted on-line. For example, he decided that Amazon.com should own its own warehouses, so that it could maintain quality control over the packaging and shipping of orders, which he saw as an opportunity to enhance the Amazon.com customer experience.

The reason for locating in Seattle was not just to be near a technology hub. It was to be near one of the distribution facilities of Ingram, Amazon.com's largest book supplier. Bezos recognized that this proximity to distribution facilities would allow for quicker turnaround on deliveries.

Bezos also focused on ways to enhance Amazon.com customers' experiences. He altered the website to make it easier to understand, streamlining the ordering process and responding immediately to each customer question. As Bezos noted, Amazon.com wants people to feel as though they are visiting a place rather than a software application.

Mean and Lean

Bezos was extremely selective about hiring. According to *Wired*, Bezos would interview candidates himself. Then, in hiring meetings, he would probe every other interviewer, occasionally constructing elaborate charts on a whiteboard detailing the job seeker's qualifications. If Bezos identified any doubt, rejection usually followed. One Bezos motto was that every time Amazon.com hired a new employee, he or she should raise the bar for the next hire, so that the overall talent pool was always improving.

Amazon.com is loath to spend on things that do not add value. According to *Upside*, Amazon.com's 1998 offices in downtown Seattle were located in a drab four-storey cube called the Columbia Building. Amazon occupied all four floors, above and behind the dry cleaner, print shop, and Indian restaurant on the street level. Amazon.com also leased space in two other equally inexpensive commercial buildings nearby.

Bezos has desks made from doors. The wood and the brackets cost about $70, and the labour is about $60. Bezos built the first four himself, but now hires carpenters to come in and build them 70 at a time. Bezos also refuses to spend money on office equipment such as monitor stands and extra chairs. Monitors are propped up on telephone books. Chairs for meetings are 'borrowed' from those who leave them unguarded.

This style contrasts with failed E-tailers Boo.com, whose senior staff had luxurious offices in London and travelled first class to most destinations.

Strategic Thinking

Bezos spends hours thinking about the future. He looks for ideas, explores his own site, and sometimes just surfs the Web (particularly on Mondays and

Thursdays, which he tries to keep unscheduled). He also catches up on
e-mail, wanders around and talks to employees, and sets up meetings that
are not part of the regular calendar. He also gathers new ideas from other
Amazon.com employees who are similarly searching for growth
opportunities.

Amazon.com continues to use its stock as valuable currency to make
acquisitions and to expand into new product lines. For example, in April
1999, Amazon.com purchased three companies that would enhance its
ability to offer personalized products and services to its customers.
Amazon.com has also been expanding the products it offers from books to
gifts, CDs, videos, and on-line auction services to compete with eBay.

Time Management

Bezos and his top executives manage their time as a strategic resource that
must be aligned with the company's objectives and strategies. According to
Wired, every 3 months, Bezos sits down with his assistant, Kim Christenson,
to examine and analyse his calendar for the quarter just passed. He wants
to know how much time he has devoted to each of the dozen or so
categories to which Christenson has assigned every meeting, phone call or
trip.

But Amazon remains a financial paradox – accelerating losses, growth
and market capitalization. The company's financial structure looks fragile,
when compared to Barnesandnoble.com, its arch-rival (Table 17.3). Of
particular note is Amazon's high dependence on debt financing. Equity
capital is all but eroded and may require constant priming.

Action Checklist: Reading the Dashboard

❑   Calculate your growth ratios and compare them with both your
    past figures and with other comparable companies ('compar-
    able' could be as seen through the eyes of an investor, rather
    than a directly comparable company).
❑   Do the same for your profitability and efficiency ratios.
❑   Use the ROCE chart above to extend the efficiency ratios for
    your business.
❑   Calculate and compare your financial strength ratios, both for
    past figures and competitors.
❑   So how does the control panel look?
❑   If you have not already done so, get your CFO to put these
    figures on your desk every month.

$'000, Q1 Compared	Amazon.com		Barnesandnoble.com	
	2000	1999	2000	1999
Sales	573 889	293 643	78 244	32 317
Cost of sales	445 775	228 852	63 051	25 016
Gross profit	128 134	64 791	15 193	7 301
Technology	61 244	23 402	6 364	3 519
Marketing and sales	140 111	60 717	32 204	18 909
Operating expenses	326 026	116 772	67 304	28 535
Profit (loss) from operations	(197 892)	(51 981)	(52 111)	(21 234)
Interest expenses	27 621	16 634	–	–
Net-profit (loss)	(308 425)	(61 667)	(9 000)	(4 044)
Current assets	1 270 949	1 012 178	398 763	505 614
Current liabilities	629 165	738 935	46 073	75 940
Inventories	172 257	220 646	8 918	3 886
Fixed assets	334 396	317 613	110 937	97 854
Accounts payable	255 797	463 026	12 089	19 204
Long-term debt	2 136 961	1 466 338	–	–
Equity	25 617	266 278	115 844	120 682
Employees	7 600	N/A	1 237	N/A
Gross profit (%)	22	22	19	23
Operating expenses (%)	57	40	86	88
Operating loss (%)	34	18	67	66
Net loss (%)	54	21	12	13
Debt to total LTC	99	85	0	0
Interest cover	Not covered	Not covered	N/A	N/A
Current ratio	2.02:1	1.37:1	8.66:1	6.66:1
Stock turn (x)	1.29	1.29	1.24	1.28
Sales growth (%)	96		143	
Gross profit growth (%)	98		108	
Sales per employee	75.51		63.25	
Gross profit per employee	16.86		12.77	
Technology spend as a percentage of sales	11	8	8	11
Marketing spend as a percentage of sales	24	21	41	59

Source: company filings (2000, unaudited).

Table 17.3   Amazon.com vs. Barnesandnoble.com

Slowing Down the Burn Rate   18

All businesses consume cash in much the same way as a rocket uses up fuel. The goal is similar too. A rocket needs to break free of the earth's gravitational pull and get into orbit, or beyond. In business terms, this is the point when a company reaches cash flow break-even, or equilibrium. Cash in and cash out are reasonably matched and the company is profitable. If the company wants to exploit new major opportunities, an acquisition for example, it may need to take on more cash to deal with a temporary imbalance, in much the same way as a rocket will need a burst of fuel to change direction.

In 2000 few Internet firms were in this happy position. Most were still burning fuel at an ever-faster rate, with an orbiting altitude seemingly as far away as ever. However, the distance to reach orbit can be travelled at different speeds, which will in turn govern the fuel consumption. It is also becoming clear that much of the fuel (cash) is being used up on activities that may have little to do with getting into orbit. Here are some areas to examine to see if you can slow down cash consumption, whilst still heading for growth.

Working Smarter

The learning curve (Figure 18.1) is a useful way of seeing how costs fall with increased experience of carrying out tasks.

There are two ways to deal with gaining experience and so reducing costs. You can buy in expensive and experienced people and hope they are already a long way down the learning curve. But doing that is risky. They may not graft easily onto your business and in any event there are few 'Internet-ready' staff available.

Or you can develop your staff quickly, so they can learn from their own and other people's experience. This requires training. Poor IT training is endemic in most firms. Millions are spent on new

Figure 18.1 The learning curve

software and little or nothing on training staff to use it. A recent survey conducted in the UK by Metrica Research found that one in three companies loses half a day a week per manager due to staff struggling to understand software.

But knowledge about software and technology in general is only a small part of the problem. A major American firm found that its productivity improved by 5–20% by the simple expedient of explaining to people why their jobs mattered. This action alone saved $9 million a year, net of training costs. In the service sector mistakes abound. At one stage the National Westminster Bank, a British bank now owned by the Royal Bank of Scotland, reckoned that basic mistakes by employees accounted for between 25% and 40% of the total cost of any service business.

Looking back to the ratios in the Amazon.com case, you can see that they sold $75,000 per employee per quarter, compared with Barnesandnoble.com, who sold $63,000 per employee. You could take the view, based on these figures alone, that Barnesandnoble.com has the opportunity to work 19% smarter, the percentage difference between those two results. If that opportunity could be realized, then Barnesandnoble.com would see quarterly sales rise by just short of $15 million, which on their then gross margin of 19% would result in $2.85 million extra profit dropping down to the bottom line. This in turn would reduce their current quarterly burn rate of $9 million by nearly a third.

Stop Doing What You Don't Do Best

Almost every part of the E-business value chain can be bought in. Websites can be designed and hosted, and technology can be rented. There are E-wholesalers and packers, such as Global Fulfillment.com, and Internet-only delivery groups, including iforce.com. Customer services can be handled by third-party call centres, such as 7-C.

World-pay and Netbanx compete with traditional banks to offer online payment processing. Almost every other aspect of business, from accounting and recruitment to payroll and human resource services, can be outsourced, often via the Internet itself. So you need to be very sure that you need to do everything yourself, all the time.

Boo.com took the view that they could develop their website themselves better than outsourcing from a consulting firm specializing in that aspect of business. They bet wrong and went bust as a consequence. By developing its own site, Boo took lots of risks, not confined to a technology bet. For example, it ramped up its employment to do this task in house, ending up with far more employees than anyone at the top had ever managed before. Also, the founders ended up being involved in developing the website, an operational task, when they could have more usefully been concerned with the company's strategy, which apparently no-one was thinking much about (see the Boo.com case, Chapter 1).

Two examples follow, one American and the other Japanese, showing how Internet firms have approached outsourcing to reduce cash requirements.

Kosher Grocer Inc

Not all the CEOs who move aggressively on to the Web are heads of large, publicly traded companies. Some successful Web sellers have revenues of less than $50 million. According to *Information Week*, Kosher Grocer Inc., an online retailer whose only full-time employees are its two co-founders, is one such company. Kosher Grocer has hired an Intel/SAP joint venture, Pandesic, to host Kosher Grocer's entire computer system. This system does all Kosher Grocer's accounting. Working with Pandesic, customers pay an up-front fee of $25 000–100 000, then pay 1–4% of their E-commerce revenues to Pandesic. For that, Pandesic provides and hosts an E-commerce catalogue and transaction-processing application based on Microsoft Site Server, as well as back-end fulfilment functions such as warehouse management, shipping and real-time inventory updates, based on a dedicated R/3 application.

Kosher Grocer's management realized that E-commerce could generate tremendous value for customers. According to Deborah Alexander, CEO and co-owner, Kosher Grocer had limited capital, so structuring a deal in this way was an affordable way for the company to grow. Alexander replaced IBM's Net.Commerce with Pandesic in late 1997, primarily because Kosher Grocer did not want to invest in back-end systems. Alexander noted that in light of the rapid pace of technological change, it did not make sense for Kosher Grocer to put all its capital into the technology.

Kosher Grocer is an example of a company that was clever enough to realize the benefits of E-commerce without sinking too much capital into the infrastructure needed to deploy it. Kosher Grocer was thus able to move aggressively despite its limited capital resources.

Monex

In 1999, Oki Matsumoto quit his partnership in Goldman Sachs, an American investment bank, before it floated on the stock-market, making its partners extremely rich. He compounded this act of folly by devoting himself to what many of his colleagues thought a crazy venture: setting up an on-line brokerage, Monex, which he now runs and owns in a joint venture with Sony.

On-line broking has been growing at a hectic pace in Japan. Monex already claims 57 000 accounts, producing 16 000 orders a day. Its staff of 40 are casually dressed, packed in a cramped office as if trying to replicate Silicon Valley in downtown Tokyo. Monex contracts out most administrative work, so in total about 140 people are employed full-time on its business.

The marketplace is already crowded. Besides Monex, there are other 'pure' online brokers such as E*Trade Japan, a joint venture between E*Trade and Softbank, a Japanese technology investor. And there are discount brokers moving online. The leader in this category is Matsui Securities, which has been offering on-line trading for 2 years.

Then there are the established securities houses. Of these, Nikko, in which Citigroup intends to increase its shareholding to 20%, has set up a specialist on-line brokerage.

Be Lean and Mean

Some E-businesses have lost the plot when it comes to controlling expenses. You only have to compare the behaviour of Cisco's top team, a highly profitable business, with loss-making Boo.com. Cisco's executives travel economy. If they want to upgrade, they pay themselves. That goes for long-haul flights as well.

When Cisco Senior Vice-President, William Nuti, was interviewed in London in April 2000, he boasted that he was the most-travelled executive in Europe, but still the cheapest when measured per mile. Tales abound of Boo's excessive spending. First-class flights, stays in expensive New York hotels and team dinners at the Ivy restaurant in London's Covent Garden are all part of the legacy at Boo. People quickly built their own empires. As well as travelling first class to Paris and New York, Boo executives would take all their executive assistants with them. The founders even had their property paid for.

A recent study of where 10 dot-com companies have chosen to locate their London offices, in fashionable areas of the capital (Figure 18.2), is in marked contrast to Amazon's Jeff Bezos's approach to expenditure (see Chapter 17). His offices in 1998 were behind a dry cleaning shop, with an Indian restaurant below in a drab inexpensive part of downtown Seattle (see case above). Office desks were made from old doors, computer monitors were propped on telephone directories and chairs for meetings were 'borrowed'.

Start-up Internet companies need to reassert an old-economy frugality if they are to slow their burn rate to manageable levels. This is one area in which leading from the front, as in Cisco and Amazon.com, can reap a rich cash dividend.

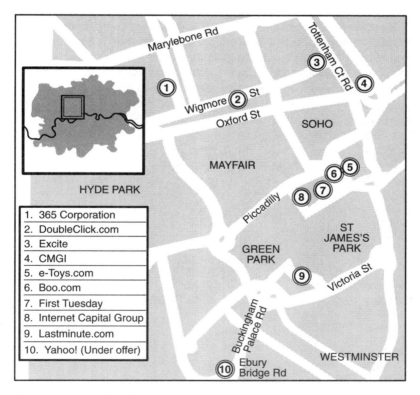

Figure 18.2 High-living Internet firms.
Reproduced by permission from Robinson (2000)

Postpone Expenditure

In April 2000, the 16 most well-funded firms were sitting on a cash pile of around a billion pounds (see Table 18.1).

But even those figures may not last long. Robert Bonnier, chief executive of Scoot.com, the on-line consumer directory service, has a cash 'pile' of £55 million, mainly as a result of their joint venture with Vivendi, the French conglomerate. But their present cash burn rate is £1 million a month, they are not profitable and they are still growing. If they, and others, were to follow the Amazon cash/ growth model, running through the amount of cash shown by the companies in Table 18.1 could happen in months rather than years.

The strategies being rushed to the fore include either postponing investments, or using 'paper', that is shares, rather than cash.

Karl Watkin, chief executive of Just2Clicks, faced with an uncertain future, promptly cancelled a cash and shares acquisition to renegotiate it as a purely paper deal. Few owners want to sell for shares alone, but as cash dries up they may have little option.

Acquisitions are not the only expenditure that can be postponed. Any capital purchase that is not central to the core mission has to be challenged. There are lots of 'nice' things to have, and there is certainly evidence that many E-businesses have had more money

Company	£ million cash in bank (estimate)
Lastminute.com	130
StepStone	127
QXL	80
gameplay.com	80
Freeserve	76
iii	75
The Exchange Group	60
Scoot.com	55
Just2Clicks	50
365 Corporation	50
freecom.net	40
NetStore	40
Paradigm	21
Letsbuyit.com	20
Affinity Internet	19
Oxygen	8

Source: company accounts and filings

Table 18.1 What UK's top dot-coms had in the bank in April 2000

'chucked' at them than their management had the experience to manage prudently. Letsbuyit.com raised £80 million from four rounds of financing, and when it had to pull its IPO had about £20 million left in the coffers. They immediately began to cut back overall expenditure, including postponing their proposed American launch, and a planned £67 million global advertising campaign was scaled back.

The problems are the same in the USA, where a Goldman Sachs study published in May 2000 suggested that at least 10 publicly traded E-tailors would need more cash to remain viable over the coming 12 months. Many of Internet were already cutting expenses to stay afloat.

Squeeze Working Capital

Working capital, the money tied up in stocks (inventories), debtors (receivables) and so forth make up a sizeable portion of any Internet firm's asset base. If you look back to the Amazon.com and Barnesandnoble.com figures in the case above, you will see that they had over $600 million and $300 million, respectively, tied up in this way (current assets minus current liabilities = money used to finance working capital).

Amazon.com's current ratio (for explanation of current ratio, see Chapter 1) grew from 1.37 in 1999 to 2.02 in 2000. This implies a 47% growth in working capital, which may or may not be needed. Were Amazon to be able to operate with the same level (not amount) of working capital as it had in the previous year, then it would need $300 million less to run the business. There is no special reason why working capital should rise as a proportion, just because a firm is growing fast. Cisco's current ratio in 2000 was 1.54, a period when sales doubled.

Examining each aspect of working capital can reveal rich seams of spare cash to be hewn out in times of need.

Use Equity as Cash

One other way to create more cash is to trade off your equity against some of the goods and services you need to allow you to grow. It can be a messy process, perhaps resulting in getting less for shares than had you waited for, say, an IPO. But surviving long enough to make a profit may call for fairly drastic measures.

People will probably only be interested in taking your equity for their goods and services once you have some venture capital on board. This saves them the difficult task of valuing your business, as they can 'buy' in at the last price at which shares changed hands. But there are many examples of companies taking a stake in small Internet firms, in return for services rendered, long before venture capital has been raised.

EmployeeService.com

In 1998, when Jay Whitehead founded EmployeeService.com, a human resources firm in San Francisco, he set aside 5% of the shares to pay bills. His banks wanted equity before they would lend him money. Both his landlords asked for equity in the firm before they would rent him office space. He gave equity to people who referred business to him, and equity to the firms that leased him office equipment. Cisco Systems wanted stock valuation information before they would even send a salesman to see him, and equity to put him on a priority list for new equipment.

Then it was Mr Whitehead's turn. When he offered his firm's services to Internet start-ups, he topped off his fee with equity in his clients: he took the cost of his firm's work in cash, and the profit in equity. Before long he was sitting on a portfolio of equity in more than a dozen firms, hoping more would go public than go bust, just like venture capitalists who once had this world of early-stage private equity to themselves.

A typical technology start-up will pay for legal services in part with equity (Table 18.2). Its public relations firm will take equity in lieu of some fees; so will its management consultants. There are venture branding firms, venture advertising firms, even venture

Law firm	Number of clients in which it has an equity stake	Total equity value at 12/99
Wilson, Sonsini, Goodrich and Rosati	34	230
Venture Law Group	16	62
Cooley Godward	17	45
Gunderson, Deffmer, Stough, Villeneuve, Franklin and Hachigian	11	31
Brobeck, Phleger and Harrison	12	22
Gray, Cary, Ware and Freidenrich	4	8
Fenwick and West	6	7

Source: *The Recorder*

Table 18.2 US law firms taking stakes in Internet clients

building engineers. Software companies will offer licence-fee discounts for equity. Venture head-hunters now try to take a third of a placed executive's first-year stock options along with a cut of salary. In tight office-space markets, such as San Francisco and New York, a venture landlord may take equity equal to 3% of a rent over the term of the lease, on top of the rent itself.

A start-up may trade equity for advertising space in magazines; it may even give equity to a television network for airtime. Equipment vendors are willing to cut a deal for equity; even the cleaning firm that comes in at night will discount its fees for stock.

For start-ups too, there are risks as well as benefits. On the upside, an equity stake aligns the interests of the service provider with those of the start-up, cementing a long-term relationship and reminding the service firm that the goal is to see the start-up succeed, not just to milk it for cash. On the downside, start-ups that give away equity indiscriminately in their early days may find that they do not have enough to keep their employees later. The smart ones pay cash for short-term relationships – a naming consultant, for instance – and save their equity for business marriages, such as their law or PR firm. Those that trade equity for a cheap database licence may feel locked into a single provider's technology. And any firm that gives away a per cent or two of the company to a head-hunter may find in a year or two that it has conducted the most expensive executive search in history.

Action Checklist: Slowing Down the Burn Rate

❑ Calculate your sales, gross profit and net profit (if you have one) per employee for the past four quarters. What does the trend look like?

❑ Compare these with any broadly comparable businesses. Do you work smarter than they do?

❑ What areas of the business that consume significant amounts of cash could you outsource?

❑ Can you identify any broadly comparable business that has outsourced any of these tasks successfully?

❑ Do you and your staff travel economy, everywhere? If not, why not?

❑ Are there any other areas of extravagant spending that does not yield any obvious benefit (e.g flash office, etc.)?

❑ Review your capital expenditure plans for the upcoming year. Are all of those really essential to achieving your primary goal?

❑ Get your CFO to produce the working capital ratios for your business for the past four quarters or so. What do the trends look like? What areas could you reduce without impairing your ability to grow?

❑ Now get the CFO to do the same for a couple of comparable businesses and see how you measure up to them.

❑ Have you used equity to buy goods and services? Do you know if your key suppliers have stakes in any of their customers? Can you now identify a relationship such as this, where you could swap equity for goods and services?

Jettisoning Passengers   19

Getting a business back on track for growth is not the time to be carry non-fare-paying passengers. The less baggage you are carrying, the further your limited cash resources will go. Some of that baggage may have a value that can be realized to swell your own funds, so giving you more time to get your core strategy to deliver results.

The following are areas to probe to see what you can safely dispense with, for the moment at any rate.

Selling Off Non-core Businesses

CorporateGear.com is a good example of a business undertaking a strategic review to decide which opportunities to concentrate on. They decided the B2B market was too attractive to miss, and that diluting their efforts with non-core activities, such as distribution, was a dangerous distraction. Selling off Cogear, their distribution business, as well as bringing in some welcome cash, allowed the management team to focus down on the main business.

CorporateGear.com

CorporateGear.com aims to be the leading business-to-business E-marketplace for the $60 billion US promotional products industry. Powered by proprietary software, CorporateGear links manufacturers, distributors and end-user corporations to an industry wide E-marketplace. CorporateGear works with manufacturers and distributors to help them lower costs, increase efficiency and compete more effectively, without having to invest and maintain their own technology platforms. CorporateGear's neutral business stance and transactional fee-based pricing model supports industry growth, rather than posing a competitive threat. The company's mission is to establish the preeminent business-to-business exchange for the promotional products industry.

David Verchere, the company founder, started the Verchere Group in 1995, a successful sales promotion agency that was folded profitably into

Cogear.com. Utilizing his strong industry knowledge and contacts, David, with a BA from the University of Montreal, has led the development of CorporateGear. The senior team includes Ashwan Khanna as CFO, with 15 years' experience in such companies as Price Waterhouse Coopers and Barclays/BZW, and Eric Jackson, formerly with Andersen Consulting as chief marketing officer. Jackson's experience at Andersen's included dealing with their 175 dot-com company clients.

Early in 2000 the company reviewed their growth options. They decided that the B2B market was more than enough for the company to go for, without the added distractions of their other activities (see Table 19.1).

Strong partnerships for distribution and logistics was one of the critical success factors the company identified when they set up, so they started their own distribution arm. But it rapidly became clear to Verchere that distribution was a completely different business in its own right, with a whole range of segments calling for detailed expertise. For example, whilst UPS is happy to transport books, CDs and stereos, they don't transport lumber, resin or hydrochloric acid. This takes specialized distribution and logistics players.

So, in May 2000 the company announced plans to sell its distribution arm, Cogear, in an effort to strengthen CorporateGear.com's grip on the promotional-products market by streamlining the company's expansion strategy, thus narrowing its focus to all things B2B.

	Conservative case	Middle case	Bullish case
Total B2B transaction revenue – 2003E($)	2481	2481	2481
Seller site sales (%)	90	85	80
Market maker sales (%)	10	15	20
Market maker transaction revenue ($)	248	372	496
Market makers advertising revenue ($)	5	7	10
Total Market Maker Revenue ($)	253	380	506
Compound growth rate (1998–2003E) (%)	237	259	275
USA (%)	63	63	63
International (%)	38	38	38
Net margin (%)	3	4	5
Net income ($)	8	15	25
PE multiple	50 ×	55 ×	60 ×
Revenue multiple	1.5 ×	2.2 ×	3.0 ×
Market capitalization (2003E) ($)	380	835	1518
PV (discount rate = 35%) ($)	154	339	617

Sources: Merrill Lynch Internet Research; Forrester Research; Veronis Suhler & Associates

Table 19.1 The B2B Market to 2003

Licence Off Technology

Whilst many Internet firms may be short of cash, they often have intellectual property rights (IPs) which are either not needed for their core business or could be usefully applied elsewhere. These IPs may have cost millions to develop and yet are a wasting asset on the balance sheet. The pharmaceutical industry has a long history of trading out unwanted IPs. Innovex, whose case we looked at in Chapter 14, made a healthy living out of what they called 'brand fostering'. This involved taking over drugs from such companies as Glaxo, where the product was too minor to get the sales force's attention, and put them into Innovex's product range, where they were a relatively big fish in a smaller pond. They shared the gross profit with the drugs' owner and returned it to them 5 years later, a much healthier and bigger selling product. Innovex agreed with the client an earnings multiple, so the more successful they were, the more money they got when the rights to the drug were returned to the original owner.

Yet2.com, based in Massachusetts, which started trading in January 2000, acts as a clearing house between buyers and sellers of IPs. The company's co-founder, Chris de Bleser, reckons the technology licensing market is worth about $100 million a year. He also believes there is a whole new class of IP deals between $5000 and $200 000 yet to be tapped into. So even if your surplus IP is small, it may be worth investigating selling it off. Whilst $200 000 may only be a couple of weeks' burn rate for a typical Internet start-up, that could just be the difference between living and dying.

Firing Staff

Many Internet firms take on too many people at the outset. Big visions and a rush to be first to market lead to overstaffing. Boo.com, Letsbuyit.com, BlaBla.com, a collection of 385 male-focused, pop-culture sites lumped together under a theme entitled 'hip, edgy and outrageous', and hundreds more Internet start-ups have been shedding staff at a rate varying between a dozen or so and, in Boo's last desperate round of cost cutting, several hundred. How a business with little to sell ever took on several hundred in the first place is in itself an interesting question.

The problem arises simply because no business can possibly know how many and what type of people it needs before it starts trading. The problem is further compounded by the way in which Internet firms change their shape and business focus in the early years (see Netscape example, Chapter 4, p. 40). So, for Internet entrepreneurs, firing will become as important a task as hiring, and one in which they will need equal expertise.

Any short-run cash flow gains from firing can be promptly lost in loss of output from the remaining demoralized and shell-shocked staff. To get the best result, firing needs to be managed carefully. Following these guidelines will help get cost savings without too much drop in performance.

Successful Firing

Be Legal

How you go about dismissing someone is almost as important in law as your reasons for doing so. Redundancy is usually safe territory, but if you are getting rid of non-performing staff it is safest to meet formally with the person concerned, to explain fully, to give the employee the fullest possible chance to state his or her case, to keep agreed notes of the meetings, and to give at least two written warnings with full reasons. Give the proper period of formal notice, when it finally comes to terminating the employment.

Be Considerate

No matter what the circumstances, all employees are entitled to a high level of consideration and compassion, and the benefit to the company of treating dismissed employees well is that it maintains morale and your image as a responsible employer. It avoids making unnecessary enemies and causing unavoidable stress and pain to departing employees. The Internet world is incestuous – the person you fire today may be in the firm acquiring you tomorrow.

Be Prepared

Decide the best time and place. Don't fire on a Friday – the dismissed employee needs time to adjust before facing his or her family. If possible, choose neutral ground for the task – a private place, quiet and free from interruptions. Rehearse the interview if necessary, and decide in advance how to direct the individual after termination.

Be Quick

Once the decision to let someone go has been made, get on with it, otherwise word of impending action might reach the employee's colleagues, causing them to shun him or her, or the team involved.

Be Honest

Explain the clear, specific and precise reason for the dismissal, without being brutal, preferably backed up by documentary evidence. Many employees cannot believe that they are being fired and will look for any sign of uncertainty as an indication that the job is still negotiable. If the reasons are held back, it may cause unnecessary worry and loss of self-esteem.

Be Objective

The emotional manager will either plunge in too quickly, without sensitivity, trying to get the whole thing over and done with, or hedge about, failing to make the point and leaving the employee unsure about the situation. Defusing an emotional situation is one of the most immediate goals of a termination from the company's point of view, and one of the main reasons why terminations go disastrously wrong is the emotional state of the manager as well as of the employee.

The initial interview should last no longer than 15 minutes. No point in going into a great deal of detail at this stage – the person may be in a state of shock and unable to take in much of the conversation. Give him or her a chance to respond, though, and make a subsequent appointment to discuss details of severance pay, and perhaps references.

Be Open

Tell everyone in the company the reason for the firing, explain what will happen next and reassure those remaining that they have a future with the firm. Bring your VC to this meeting to lend support to the plan. Use the managing change process to ensure this process is effectively managed

These are the 20 questions most commonly asked by the employee being dismissed – make sure you have your answers ready:

1. Why me?
2. Are the terms negotiable?
3. Do I have the right to appeal?

4. I intend to take the matter further.
5. What about my car?
6. What about my life cover and health care?
7. What about my pension?
8. Why wasn't I given prior warning?
9. What help will you give me to find a new job?
10. Are there any alternative jobs I could do, even at a lower grade?
11. Can I apply for, or will you consider me for, any future vacancies?
12. Can I work my notice?
13. Who's going to do my job?
14. I think this is totally unfair, especially given my service and ability!
15. Am I the only one affected?
16. Can I return to my office?
17. What have my colleagues been told?
18. Can I tell my staff?
19. Who will supply me with a reference?
20. When does this come into effect?

Action Checklist: Jettisoning Passengers

❏ What non-core activities are you still undertaking and why?
❏ What are the running costs associated with each of these activities?
❏ Who might be interested in acquiring them and how much might they pay?
❏ List the IP that you currently own the rights to.
❏ What IP is not being used, or could be used in a non-competing industry or sector?
❏ How much is that IP worth and to whom?
❏ Review the output of every member of your staff, using absolute and relative measures if possible, e.g. salesperson X brings in $200 000 net contribution after costs. This is 90% of the best-performing salesperson's results and 120% of the average.
❏ Using the results above, rank your list of people to cull, worst performers first.
❏ Use the guidelines above to plan for firing staff.
❏ How much extra 'fuel' will all the above activities generate, and is that enough to keep you going until profits kick in? If not, read on.

Pumping in More Fuel   20

It is unlikely that anything resembling serious growth can be injected without eventually taking in more cash from outside. The processes discussed earlier will at best provide enough headway to steer a course, rather than being left entirely to the mercy of the elements. But on their own, 'economy' measures will rarely suffice.

If you are under-geared and asset-rich the banks may help, but as neither of those are terms that describe many E-businesses, that is unlikely. In any event, banks, however much window dressing is applied to their corporate literature, do not lend money. They convert one form of asset, usually an illiquid one such as buildings, inventories and receivables, into the more liquid asset, cash, at a hefty discount. In the absence of such security, banks will look to the owners for personal guarantees. For a review of sources of new debt for entrepreneureal ventures, see Barrow (1995).

More likely routes to fresh funds (Figure 20.1) are family and friends, corporate venturing, business angels, venture capital firms (perhaps not the one you are already using!), other E-businesses in the value chain, mezzanine finance or an IPO.

The process can be viewed as being similar to a rocket being fired into space. Several stages of finance (fuel) are required to get to cash flow break-even (orbit). Then more money is needed to move on and become truly profitable. All businesses go through much the same process. But for Internet companies, much more fuel seems to be needed to get into orbit, due in part to profligate waste and in part to mismanagement and unrealistic end goals.

Family and Friends

Those close to you can often lend you money or invest in your business. This helps you avoid the problem of pleading your case to outsiders and enduring extra paperwork and bureaucratic delays. Help from friends, relatives and business associates can be especially

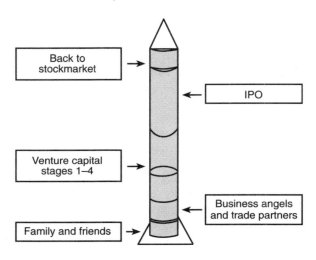

Figure 20.1 Financing Internet firms

valuable if you've been through bankruptcy or had other credit problems that would make borrowing from a commercial lender difficult or impossible. Their involvement brings a range of extra potential benefits, costs and risks, that are not a feature of most other types of finance. You need to decide if these are acceptable.

Some advantages of raising money from people you know well are that you may get easier terms, may be able to delay paying back money until you're more established, and may be given more flexibility if you get into a jam. But once the loan or investment terms are agreed to, you have the same legal obligations as you would with any other source of finance.

In addition, raising money from relatives and friends can have a major disadvantage. If your business does poorly and those close to you end up losing money, you may well damage a good personal relationship. So in dealing with friends, relatives and business associates, be extra careful not only to establish clearly the terms of the deal and put it in writing, but also to make an extra effort to explain the risks. In short, it's your job to make sure your helpful friend or relative won't suffer a true hardship if you're unable to meet your financial commitments. Don't accept money from people who can't afford to risk it.

air2web.com

Founded in 1999 by Sanjoy Malik, air2web.com raised $1.5 million in first-round financing from friends and advisory board members. They develop software and services to connect businesses and consumers to the Internet via mobile 'phones, pagers and hand-held devices. Their customers are content providers in sports, entertainment and financial services. They compete with Saraide.com, 724 Solutions and Wireless Knowledge. Now with 22 employees, the company is set to raise a second round of finance, this time $10–15 million.

Ten things to remember about raising money from family and friends:

1. Do agree proper terms for the loan or investment.
2. Do put the agreement in writing and, if it involves a share transaction or guarantee, have a legal agreement drawn up.
3. Do make an extra effort to explain the risks of the business and the possible downside implications to their money.
4. Do make sure, when raising money from parents, that other siblings are compensated in some way, perhaps via a will.
5. Do make sure you want to run a family business before raising money from them. It will not be the same as running your own business.
6. Don't borrow from people on fixed incomes.
7. Don't borrow from people who can't afford to lose money.
8. Don't make the possible rewards sound more attractive than you would, say, to any other investor.
9. Don't offer jobs in your business to anyone providing money unless he or she is the best person for the job.
10. Don't change the normal pattern of social contact with family and friends after they have put up the money.

Business Angels

One likely first source of equity or risk capital will be a private individual, with his or her own funds and perhaps some knowledge of your type of business. In return for a share in the business, he or she will put in money at his or her own risk. These angels often have their own agendas and operate through managed networks. Angel networks operate throughout the world. In some cases these networks operate on the Internet. In the UK and the USA there are hundreds of networks, with tens of thousands of business angels prepared to put up several billion pounds each year into new or small businesses.

Garage.com

Garage.com is one Internet-based angel network. Guy Kawasaki, former 'chief evangelist' of Apple computers, started the service in 1998.

Garage.com filters business plans vigorously and then sends the best to prospective angels. This encourages e-mail exchanges between angels and companies seeking finance, and raises some interesting challenges to the traditional angel model. For example, angels are characterized as 'invisible' people who value their privacy, yet on the Garage.com website there are a series of named would-be investors. Moreover, some of them are not merely wealthy individuals but are Presidents, Chairmen and former CEOs in major corporations, such as Compaq Computers Corp. Although they are seeking to invest as individuals, it is clear from their willingness to be named that they are looking to encourage companies that may have need of their extensive industry experience to approach them. The time and effort needed to close a deal could also be considerably reduced by such a service, although the extent to which such a service can completely replace face-to-face discussions is also debatable.

Garage.com seeks to raise $1–4 million – amounts that are too small for traditional venture capital firms. Not just anyone can be an investor – potential angels must meet strict US Securities' and Exchange Commission (SEC) guidelines as accredited investors and have a net worth of at least $1 000 000, as well as demonstrating experience in start-ups. Other websites, such as Seedstage.com and offroadcapital.com, also act as portals to angel groups. In the UK and mainland Europe, the British and European Venture Capital associations, respectively, provide a link to the growing band of angels.

Business angels are more likely to invest in early-stage investments, where relatively small amounts of money are needed in areas close to their home base. They operate very quickly, often making decisions in a few days, based on little hard data after only a few meetings with the person seeking finance.

Ten things you need to know about business angels:

1. 40% Suffer partial or complete loss of their investment.
2. 50% Don't conduct research into prospective investments.
3. 55% Don't take up personal references, compared with only 6% of venture capital providers in general.
4. 90% Have worked in a small firm or owned their own business.
5. Business angels meet owners five times on average before investing, compared with venture capital providers in general who require 10 meetings.
6. In business angel investment 10% is for less than £10 000 and 45% is for over £50 000.
7. Most business angels invest close to home. Up to 50 miles is usual, with 200 miles as the limit.
8. Angels rarely invest abroad. Only 2% have made overseas investments.

9. Angels often flock together. Syndicated deals make up more than a quarter of all deals, where two or more angels band together to invest.
10. Angels are up to five times more likely to invest in start-ups and early-stage investments than venture capital providers in general.

One Business Angel

Thirty-five year-old Martin Lowenstein formerly invested exclusively in the stockmarket. But lured by the prospect of stunning returns, he branched out to private ventures. His aim is to keep up to 15% of his assets in start-ups. He spread the word to his accountant, lawyer and friends that he was interested in new investment opportunities.

Mr Lowenstein prefers investing in later-stage deals, but concedes that most companies raising their second or third rounds have no interest in his money. Most opportunities for an investor his size are in the seed round, but that's also where the most risk lies. His first private investment turned out to be a dud. He put $25 000 in a company that was building an on-line database of actors and actresses for the entertainment industry. He lost the lot. Later he invested another $25 000 in Mediaplex, an on-line advertising outfit. Mr Lowenstein got a piece of the company's penultimate financing round. Six months later, Mediaplex went public and his $25 000 investment ballooned to $300 000.

Venture Capital

Venture capital (VC) providers are investing other people's money, often from pension funds. They have a different agenda to that of business angels and are more likely to be interested in investing more money for a larger stake.

VC is a means of financing the start-up, development, expansion or purchase of a company. The venture capitalist acquires an agreed proportion of the share capital (equity) of the company in return for providing the requisite funding. VC firms often work in conjunction with other providers of finance in putting together a total funding package for a business. VC has its origins in the late eighteenth century, when entrepreneurs found wealthy individuals to back their projects. Now VC is a global business, with over 600 active VCs in the USA and a further 200 or so across Europe and Asia.

The funds being invested by venture capital providers have exploded in the past 5 years (Figure 20.2). In the first quarter of 2000, over $22.7 billion went into start-ups in the USA alone. But just because there is a lot of money about, it doesn't mean it's easy to get. One VC, Accel Partners in the USA, went on record to say they received 25 000 business plans asking for finance last year and invested in only 40.

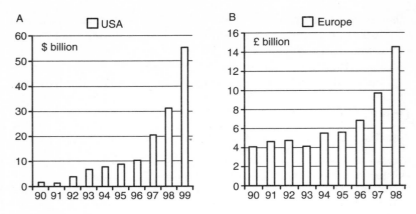

Figure 20.2 Venture capital in (A) the USA and (B) Europe (annual investment). Sources: (A) *Venture Economics*; (B) British Venture Capital Association

Until recently the returns that VCs made were not exactly startling. In the UK the average return on high-tech investments by VCs over the life of the investment was 23%. In the USA the average return across all sectors ranged from a low of 2% in 1990 to a high of 44% in 1995. But in 1999 something startling happened. According to *Venture Economics*, US VC firms made a 147% return. That was brought about mostly by their Internet investments turning into IPOs in less than 3 years after investments were made. This compared with the 7 years that it took before, with the exit route more likely to be a trade sale on a much lower multiple. Turning this nominal return back into cash is another thing again.

Not all VCs are equally as good at picking winners. According to the Yale Endowment Fund, the returns they made ranged from the bottom quartile, making less than 5%, to the top quartile, making over 25% over the 10 years to 1997.

Getting money from VCs is expensive, time-consuming and hard work. Having said that, it is possible to get a quick decision. One short-lived Internet start-up in the UK, Clickmango.com, succeeded in raising £3 million from Atlas Ventures in just 8 days. Such was the enthusiasm for the natural health products website venture, that an earlier meeting with another VC resulted in an offer of £1 million in just 40 minutes.

But usually the due diligence process, which involves a thorough examination of both the business and its owners, takes several weeks if not longer. Past financial performance, the director's track record and the business plan are all subjected to detailed scrutiny, usually by accountants and lawyers. Directors are then required to 'warrant' that they have provided *all* relevant information, under pain of financial penalties. The cost of this process, rarely less than a big five figure sum and often running into six, will have to be borne by the firm raising the money, but will be paid out of the money raised, if that is any consolation.

Most of the companies appearing as cases in this book will have raised at least one round of VC money, if not more. One company, appropriately named eCredit, founded by Venkat Srinisvasan, raised five rounds of VC finance between February 1999 and May 2000. J.P. Morgan Capital, Draper International, CitiCorp, Hambrecht & Quist, Hewlett-Packard and Gateway were amongst the firms who chipped in $58 million. Based in Dedham, Massachusetts, the firm provides credit approval on-line, speeding up the whole payment process between buyers and sellers.

Needless to say, to get venture capital you need a great business plan (see Chapter 4 to get some ideas).

Corporate Venturers

Alongside the venture capital firms are 200 or so other businesses who have a hand in the risk capital business, without it necessarily being their main line of business. For the most part, these are firms with an interest in the Internet who want an inside track to new developments. Their own R&D operations have slowed down and become less and less entrepreneurial as they have grown bigger. So they need to look outside for new inspiration.

Even successful firms such as IBM, Cisco, Microsoft and Hewlett-Packard invest hundreds of millions of dollars each year in scores of Internet businesses. Sometimes, if the company looks a particularly good fit, they buy the whole business out. Apple, after years of confusing its customers with multiple product lines, has produced a clear strategy based on three ranges; the consumer-level iMac, the professional-level G4 and the laptop PowerBook lines. However, to keep its eye on other developments whilst keeping its management team focused on the core business, it has a $12 million stake in Akamai Technologies, the firm whose software tries to keep the Web running smoothly even under unusual traffic demands.

As mentioned earlier, almost everyone you do business with could be in the market for a bit of Internet equity in return for goods, if not cash. So this is a rich area to tap for funds to re-launch a stalling business, if all that is holding you back is cash.

IPO (Initial Public Offering)

For the really big cash injection and access to hundreds if not
thousands of new shareholders, one of the burgeoning number
of stockmarkets is the place to head. And the beauty of the Internet
IPO, until recently at any rate, is that no profits are required, and
even sales are optional (see Table 20.1). It almost appears that the
larger the valuation placed on the business, the less sales are needed
pre-float!

There are two possible types of stockmarkets on which to gain a
public listing. A full listing on the London Stock Exchange, the New
York Stock Exchange or any other major country's exchange calls
for a track record of making substantial profits with decent seven-
figure sums being made in the year you plan to 'float', as this process
is known. A full listing also calls for a large proportion of the
company's shares being put up for sale at the outset.

However, if an IPO appeals, the US market may be the best place
to float. The NASDAQ is the powerhouse of the IPO machine. Once
a stodgy exchange at the corner of Broad and Wall, NASDAQ has
begun launching NASDAQ Europe and NASDAQ Japan and has
forged a partnership with Softbank, the giant of Internet investment. The value placed on new companies on a NASDAQ market is
between three and five times that of UK and European markets
(Table 20.2).

Company	IPO date	Value ($ millions)	Sales 3 months pre-float ($)	Value as multiple of sales ($)
Stamps.co	Jun 1999	454	Nil	Infinite
Netpliance	Mar 2000	1 333	26 000	51 283
b2bstores.com	Feb 2000	65	2 200	29 729
CyberCash	Feb 1996	251	22 000	11 413
CareInsite	Jun 1999	2 153	213 000	10 110
Ventro	Jul 1999	810	184 000	4 177
DSL.net	Oct 1999	509	210 000	2 425
PartsBase.com	Mar 2000	180	362 000	443
Envision Development	Sep 1999	61	388 000	130
Frontline Communications	May 1998	14	321 700	42

Source: company filings

Table 20.1 Valuations of selected IPOs

Market	Number of stocks	Flotation cost (£ millions)	Entry requirements	Minimum market capitalization (£ millions)	Comparable price: earnings ratios (p:e's)
Alternative Investment Market (AIM)	350	0.5	Low	None	1
London Stock Exchange	2 500	1+	High	1+	1
techMARK	200	0.75+	High	50+	× 3
New York Stock Exchange	2 600	7	Very high	12+	× 2
NASDAQ	5 500	6	Very high	10+	× 5

Source: exchange details

Table 20.2 Where to float – and why it matters

Junior markets, such as London's Alternative Investment Market (AIM) or the Nouveau Marché in Paris, are a much more attractive proposition for entrepreneurs seeking equity capital. Formed in the mid–late 1990s specifically to provide risk capital for new rather than established ventures, these markets have an altogether more relaxed atmosphere.

The AIM market is the largest junior market in Europe. Over 300 firms are listed and some £2 billion of new equity capital has been raised. AIM is particularly attractive to any dynamic company of any size, age or business sector that has rapid growth in mind. The smallest firm on AIM entered at under £1 million capitalization and the largest at over £330 million. The formalities are minimal, but the costs of entry are high and you must have a nominated adviser, such as a major accountancy firm, stockbroker or banker.

Internet-based direct public offerings (DPOs) are a relatively new US phenomenon, which has the potential to change the face of financing for small firms. These involve small companies offering their stock direct to would-be investors over the Internet. There are two ways of doing this: one is to use a service; the other is for firms to use their own websites to go direct to the public. There are already some Internet-based listing services for DPOs in the USA. The Access to Capital Electronic Network (ACE-NET) was set up in 1997 by the federal Small Business Administration as a public–private partnership to lower the legal barriers for small businesses needing financing of up to $5 million. The filing form satisfies federal and many States' securities regulations, with 37 states recognizing it, and is relatively cheap at only $450 for an annual listing. The offering document can be completed on-line and can be changed in real time, allowing the entrepreneur the flexibility to modify the offer. Only accredited investors (who have over $1 million to spend) can invest.

Direct Stock Market is a similar, private service that was set up in 1993 and where a listing costs $2000–4000 for a 90 day listing. Firms have to file their own paperwork off-line with the states in which they wish their listing to be registered (unlike the ACE-NET service). It is clear that potential investors from Europe can not participate in companies listed under such schemes. It is almost certain that regulations mean that these Internet services can not sell securities in non-US firms. However, this does not prevent European entrepreneurs from creating a US company to exploit the fundraising potential of such services. What the US difficulties in establishing this sort of service have amply demonstrated is the need for regulation at a federal level, rather than at state level, if the service is to be successful. This suggests that were such a service to be established in Europe, it would be appropriate to regulate it at the European level in order to offer similar sums of money and geographic spread.

US Firms may also decide to go direct and battle their way through various state legislation hoops. The upside for firms is that this method overcomes barriers of geography and information, and that small investors are unlikely to carry out due diligence or download prospectuses. DPOs allow small investors access to genuine possibilities without paying fees to either a matchmaking service or a venture capital firm, and allow much smaller investments (from $500 upwards). The downside of Internet DPOs is that they are time-consuming and high-risk for the angel (or micro-angel), and it is difficult to distinguish between genuine companies and fraudsters. For the firm, there are a raft of different state legislations in operation to protect investors from scams, which can seriously disrupt the offer process. In the USA, 83 individuals have already been charged with Internet securities fraud, 26 for entirely fictional deals.

The killer might be that the multiples are lower on Internet exchanges, so the valuation placed on the firm is low. However, in a crisis this might matter less than not being able to survive.

Timescale for Execution of an IPO

An IPO used to take about 6 months to execute; now it is routinely being done in 13 weeks. Although it may vary from exchange to exchange, the timetable looks broadly as follows.

Week 1

Pick underwriters to take your company to market. This involves listening to a dozen or more bankers telling you why they are number one in doing your type of IPO. At the rate of three a day, this can be a wearying experience, listening to depressingly similar presentations. The bankers will all have done successful IPOs before, probably by the dozen (Figure 20.3), so you will probably be looking more for empathy than technical competence. At the end of the week you need to have chosen a lead and probably a couple of co-managers, to help spread the good word about your great business to the share-buying community.

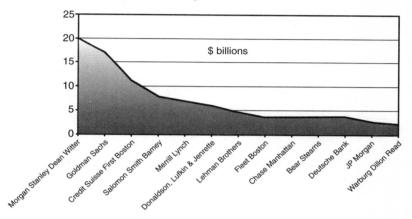

Figure 20.3 Lead-managed technology IPOs in the USA 12 months to January 2000. Source: Thompson financial security data

Week 2

The lead manager begins drafting the company's prospectus. This involves sucking you, your management team and your accountants dry of background information. Your CFO will be involved full-time in this process, so better get some financial back-up in place to deal with routine matters.

Week 3

You and your bankers collaborate on the prospectus. By now, fairly junior staff will be handling the process. The stars you met on week one's presentations have moved on to sell the next deal. This process can involve several 8 hour days with people from your law, banking and accounting firms, going through the documentation line-by-line. This involves a delicate balance between outlining the risks whilst simultaneously describing the business and the investment prospects in a way that will appeal. You can see how other companies have gone about this process by looking at their filings on the Securities and Exchange Commission (SEC) website. In the end, this due diligence process should have flushed out any worries and concerns about you or your business.

Week 4

The lead manager files the registration document, known in the USA as an S1, with the SEC, or its equivalent in what ever country you plan to list.

Weeks 5–8

The lead bankers and you and your team prepare the road show presentation and wait for the SEC to digest your documents.

Week 9

The SEC responds with 20 pages of nitpicking questions. 'What do you mean by "on-line response times?" ' and 'Can you provide evidence that your client X is one of the largest drinks manufacturers in Spain?'. There may well be a second round of questions a few weeks later, but by now you will have got the measure of how to reply.

Probity is important in this whole process. What is required is transparency, the Nevada of the share-dealing community. World Online's float on the Amsterdam Exchanges (AEX) in the spring of 2000 is a salutary warning on disclosure. The company was at the time Europe's largest Internet service provider. They generated an enormous amount of interest among Dutch private investors, the company's home base, with 150 000 subscribing in the March IPO at a price of €43. Within 6 weeks the price was down to €14.80. The reason given for the slump in price was that World Online's chairman, Nina Brink, had disposed of some of her shares to a US private equity fund, Baystar Capital, in December 1999, 3 months before the float. The price she sold at was €6.04 and Baystar sold in the first few days of trading at over €30. Brink was accused of making allegedly misleading statements during the offer period, and was forced to resign on 13 April 2000. Unhappy shareholders are taking legal advice, but the company's bankers claim there was no wrong-doing.

Week 10

The lead manager plans the road show. You go to the bank and sell the company to their institutional sales force. They then get to work with their clients to persuade them to subscribe for your stock. Everyone is bound by what are known as 'the Rules'. Rule 174 of the Securities Act governs the 'Quiet Period', which extends from due diligence to 25 days after the IPO. Over this period, the company must be careful about not hyping the stock or doing anything that would lead to speculation about your firm's performance in the press. Rule 135 explains exactly what you can and cannot say to the press. It's generally best to say nothing. If one of your competitors is doing an IPO, their Quiet Period is a good time to hit at them in the press, or to go out and buy a business you know they might want. They are in effect in limbo and can't retaliate.

This is where the institutional sales team come into their own. Via an ancient ritual of winks, nudges, passive verbs, rhetorical questions and comparisons, they get their story across. The lead bank's sales team can be a mighty force indeed. Goldman Sachs, for example, has some 400 front-line salespeople in their IPO team, and that can result in a very big message reaching a lot of potential investors.

Weeks 11–12

A glorified travel agent in the bank fixes up a punishing schedule, known as the 'road show'. This is the reverse of week 1, when people were selling to you. Now you are selling the stock to institutional investors. This could involve as many as 80 meetings across three continents in 13 days. A lot can be said at road show meetings, but the only document that can be handed out is the S1 prospectus. Anything else could be a violation of Section 5 of the Securities Act.

Commitments start to come in from the institutions. 'I'll take 250 000, but only if it's priced below $20. At $25 I'll only take 100 000'. The bank's syndicate manager has to make sense of this anticipated demand to come up with an IPO price.

Week 13

The day of the IPO. Assuming that the NASDAQ has not gone into one of its habitual nose-dives, the bank's market-maker figures out the highest price someone will sell and someone will buy at and sets a price, usually above the opening price and the price at which the institutions have bought at. If the NASDAQ has plunged and you have to pull the IPO, it's like slipping down a long snake back to the bottom of the snakes and ladders board. You may get another crack at it in 6 months, or perhaps never. One entrepreneur likened doing his IPO to childbirth. Painful, glorious, but not to be done again.

Your company is now public, the bank collects 7% of the proceeds, your employees are rich and you now have the funds and credibility to get back on with growing the business. If the market-maker has got the price too high and the shares plunge quickly, it will leave a sour taste in everyone's mouth. The pre-float share-holders can't realize their gain for months after the float, and having a paper profit slashed in half, as for example with Lastminute.com's float, will not endear you to the staff.

The institutions will be sitting on a loss, and while they are grown-up enough to take it on the chin, they will be very wary when you come back for more money. It is usually best to set the price at a rate that will see the shares rising in the weeks and months following a float. That makes for better press coverage too, which inevitably impacts favourably on customers, suppliers and potential employees.

Action Checklist: Pumping in More Fuel

❑ Review your family and friends, and friends of family and friends, to see who could put up some cash for a stake in your business.

❑ Contact business angel networks and go to some meetings to see the level of interest in your proposition.

❑ Review potential corporate venturing partners.

❑ Look up their accounts to see who else they have stakes in.

❑ Talk with your VC, if you have one, about the prospects for further stages of finance.

❑ Review other VC options. Find out which VCs are doing deals in your sector.

❑ Consider an IPO. Talk informally to a couple of entrepreneurs who have been through the hoop.

❑ If you think an IPO is possible, review the various exchanges you could list on.

❑ Work up a draft S1 filing to use as a basis for talking with possible lead bankers.

❑ Get a list of prospective IPO advisers and start your beauty parade.

Part V

Abandon Ship

After having done everything possible to breathe some life into your faltering venture, without success, it may be time to abandon ship. If the receivers are at the door, then it's too late to do much about it. But if you can keep the pumps, described in earlier chapters, going and keep the water below the level of the deck, you may have time to sell the business and start again. Why waste all that valuable experience? As one nameless business proprietor is reputed to have said to an employee after a particularly expensive mistake: 'No, I won't accept your resignation, after all I have just spent $5 million on your training'.

But hanging on too long can have other serious consequences for the directors of cash strapped Internet companies. Directors have a legal duty to protect creditors by not squandering resources in a futile attempt to keep trading. If they get this judgement wrong, then they are guilty of 'wrongful trading'. Someone found guilty of wrongful trading can be disqualified from serving as a company director for 15 years, fined and perhaps be required to pay towards company assets after the point at which they should have ceased to trade. Knowing when that point has arrived is not easy to decide on, and if your older wiser non-executive directors are busy on the boards of 20 other firms, they may not be able to keep tabs on your particular situation.

Knowing when to Quit

The signs of terminal decline are usually evident before the cash runs out. In an Internet business, with few profit warning signs available as profits are not being made, more intangible indicators have to be used. One such set of indicators is included in the A-score technique (A is shorthand for 'at risk') for predicting company failure, which was developed by John Argenti (1983), a British author and researcher. He referred to a survey which concluded that 93% of company failures result from managerial incompetence: the remaining 77% are accounted for by neglect, fraud and disaster. The survey results may hold few surprises for analysts, but Internet business owners often underestimate the importance of the effects of their actions and decisions on the survival of their company, compared with the importance of external factors, such as changing investor sentiment.

Argenti examined the management characteristics and resulting company defects which are likely to lead to failure. He allocated scores to a number of 'defects', 'mistakes' and 'symptoms', which are weighted in accordance with the importance of their contribution to the failure process (Table 21.1). When tested using a number of conspicuous failures, including Data Magnetics, Sinclair Research and Rolls Royce, the A-score proved a reliable predictive tool.

Defects

The first group of defects is concerned with problems in management structure. The 'autocrat' in Table 21.1 refers to a dominating personality, an individual who may take decisions without heeding the advice or wishes of colleagues or advisers. Many entrepreneurs, not just those in Internet business, believe in a sort of divine right endowed by virtue of being the founder. Although it may be difficult to draw a distinction between an autocrat and a strong leader, the former is likely to feature in a business that has reached the size

	Score
Defects	
Autocrat leader	8
Chairman and chief executive are one and the same	4
Passive board	4
Unbalanced skills	2
Weak finance director	5
Poor management depth	3
No budgetary control	3
No cashflow plans	3
No costing system	3
Poor response to change	8
Maximum sub-total for defects	43
Pass mark for defects	10
Mistakes	
High gearing	15
Less than 6 months' cash reserves	15
Big project	15
Maximum sub-total for mistakes	45
Pass mark for mistakes	15
Symptoms	
Financial signs	4
Creative accounting	4
Non-financial signs	3
Terminal signs	1
Maximum sub-total for symptoms	12
Maximum total overall	100
Pass mark overall	25

Source: adapted and updated from Argenti (1983)

Table 21.1   Defects, mistakes, symptoms and their scores

where it would be more effectively run by a team than by an individual.

'Chairman and chief executive' describes a situation in which one individual fulfils the roles of both chairman and chief executive. Here there is once more a danger that the decision-making process will be dominated by the views of only that individual.

A 'passive board' is a situation, which can easily arise, where other members of the board have a particular interest in specific areas of the business only, or that they are representatives of lending institutions who take little active role in the management of the business. Boo.com's board, as we have already seen, communicated rarely and held board meetings on mobile phone conference calls.

Similarly, unbalanced skills are most likely to be visible in a business where an abundance of technologic whiz kids are in power. The skills refer not only to those of the directors, but also to those in senior management who could play a significant role in business decisions. Argenti quotes as a common scenario the engineering company where most of the board, including the autocratic chief executive, are engineers. The same scenario is visible in many Internet start-ups. The changes of decisions initiated by the chief executive being challenged are thus reduced dramatically.

A 'weak finance director', or a finance function which is not represented at board level, presents a similar problem. Whether accountancy information and business performance are good or bad, these matters do require informed discussion by the board. And in Internet firms shareholder confidence is rapidly eroded by the absence of a CFO. Management depth can undoubtedly affect the operation of a business. A highly effective board of directors cannot necessarily run a successful business without support from managers, team leaders, supervisors and so on. And in Internet firms the top team are often distracted by having to attend to the needs of VCs and institution investors.

The second group of defects is concerned with accounting information. Budgetary control, cashflow forecasts and costing systems all provide the information required to monitor business performance effectively. While it may be clear without this type of information that problems exist within the business, it will be far more difficult to determine where the problem originated and therefore what action should be taken. A lack of accounting information is also likely to be a result of poor management.

Finally in the group of defects is 'poor response to change'. This might refer to changes in market requirements, in the economy, in technology or in other factors that adversely affect the business. For example, a business which expends considerable resources developing a high-tech product, but which does not monitor the products developed by its competitors, can find itself overtaken and lose its niche in the market. A well-managed business will not only be aware of the dangers of change, but will also be able to respond positively and quickly.

Mistakes

'High gearing', low cash reserves and the 'big project' are all discussed in earlier chapters, and all three can be significant factors in business decline. Again, it can be argued that in a well-managed business, the resulting problems should be recognized at a sufficiently early stage for some remedial action – or at least damage limitation – to be undertaken.

Symptoms

'Financial signs' are among the more obvious indicators of decline in a business. Accounts, assuming they present a fair picture, and ratio analysis should reveal the problem areas if these have not already become evident.

However, if creative accounting has taken place, these signs will be less obvious. There are many techniques for distorting a business's trading results or balance sheet position, but the most significant point here is that trouble has been taken to present a misleading set of accounts. The motivation behind creative accounting may not be overtly fraudulent in the mind of the preparer of the accounts or the business owner, but may be felt to be justified in order to keep the business afloat. Internet companies who crow about 'profits before special on-time charges', or 'profits excluding special write-offs', or 'profits on this part of the business' should be treated with some caution.

'Non-financial signs' of decline may become obvious only on a piecemeal basis and can cover a whole variety of factors. These may range from a deliberate reduction in stock levels or unexpected redundancies to the increasingly shabby appearance of offices.

'Terminal signs' of failure tend to occur very shortly before the collapse of a business. Increasing numbers of creditors are threatening legal action, the bank manager is constantly seeking assurances that the overdraft limit will not be breached again, bailiffs are at the door to collect arrears of VAT, creditors refuse to supply any further goods – the list goes on. When these events are occurring with increasing frequency and in increasing number, collapse may be inevitable.

The allocation and interpretation of scores is a straightforward exercise. Either the full score or nil should be allocated for each category; no intermediate scores are permitted. Scores should be allocated only if there is confidence that items are 'clearly visible in the suspect company'. The overall pass mark is 25, and any company achieving a greater score is considered to exhibit so many of the signs that frequently precede failure that serious concern is advised.

A company that scores above the pass mark in any individual category should also be regarded with circumspection. If, for example, it scores less than 10 for defects but more than 15 for mistakes, this might indicate that, while the management team is fundamentally competent, it is taking risks with the future of the company, either knowingly or otherwise.

To demonstrate how A-score analysis is applied, the failed company Boo.com is analysed in Table 21.2. It should be stressed that the scores are subject to the benefits of hindsight but also subject to an inability to observe first-hand the company members as they were, and for this reason they should be regarded largely as illustrative. However, the analysis does provide an insight into how scores might be allocated.

	Boo.com
Defects	
Autocrat leader	–
Chairman and chief executive are one and the same	–
Passive Board	4
Unbalanced skills	–
Weak Finance Director	5
Poor management depth	–
No budgetary control	3
No cashflow plans	–
No costing system	–
Poor response to change	–
Sub-total for defects	12
Mistakes	
High gearing	–
Less than 6 months cash reserves	15
Big project	15
Sub-total for mistakes	30
Symptoms	
Financial signs	–
Creative accounting	4
Non-financial signs	3
Terminal signs	–
Sub-total for symptoms	7
Total overall	49

Table 21.2 Boo.com – what went wrong

Boo.com had no CFO for much of its life, its costs were clearly out of control and the board appeared to be non-functioning. Cash reserves were low, and whilst there was no direct evidence of creative accounting, the founders resorted to presenting selective evidence on sales growth using data which put a more favourable interpretation on achievements than perhaps was warranted (see the Boo.com case study, Chapter 1).

What is interesting is to see that even if Boo's founders had the cash they were so urgently seeking (and berating their backers for not stumping up), the A-score would only have given them a rating of 34. That would still have spelled near-certain death.

A look at your own, or any other business in which you have an interest using this technique may win back a few valuable weeks in which to take avoiding action.

Selling Up   22

Getting the best value for your business involves getting the best corporate finance advice to maximize the price, in the minimum amount of time. Without an auction or controlled auction you could be short-changed by as much as 50%. Sweetheart deals, the favourite strategy for those acquiring E-businesses, where you sell out to someone you know or do business with, are almost always lousy deals for the seller. Having got your price, how can you be sure you will get your money? Warranties, missed earn-outs and bad tax advice could take 70% of that headline price out of your pocket.

These are the pointers to make sure you get the best result in selling up:

1. Although selling a financially troubled business may seem like a long shot, selling an operating business, even one that's in trouble, almost always brings more money than closing it down and selling off the assets. This is particularly true for E-businesses in the first few years, when they have no assets anyway. Before you give up and conclude that no-one will buy your business, consider that people buy businesses, even businesses with financial problems, for all sorts of reasons, including:

    *   The buyer may have a similar business and, by combining the two, operate more efficiently than you can. Many Internet firms could get closer to cash-flow break-even with just 20% more sales, now.
    *   The buyer may be extremely anxious to take over one or more of your business assets – its location, key employees, or domain name, or IP.
    *   The buyer may have better access to needed financing than you do, and therefore be able to stay the course until your good business idea ultimately proves itself.
    *   The buyer may have greater expertise in your business than you do, and see a way to turn a profit by changing how the business is run.

- The buyer may conclude that it's cheaper to buy your business and turn it around than to start a similar business from scratch.

Netimperative.com

When Netimperative, the on-line news service, collapsed, it was rescued within days by a consortium led by the CEO of Bright Station, formerly known as Dialog. Together with AIM, listed Internet business group, and StockHouse Media Corporation, the international financial data company, they raised £1 million and created a special-purpose vehicle to take over the business and assets of the troubled Net company. All 37 jobs at the company were saved and not a single person left, although they all had other job offers. Durlacher, the investment house with a 29% stake in Netimperative, declined to put up the £800 000 needed to keep the business afloat. Netimperative was chaired by Albert Scardino, husband of Pearson chief executive Marjorie Scardino, had net assets of £10 000 and monthly sales of £10 000–15 000 against overheads of £150 000.

2. Don't get into a sweetheart deal with a buyer who claims to be able to act quickly, if you can just keep the corporate finance people out of the deal. In one recent deal, the prospective purchaser offered £7 million for the business and insisted on a lock-out deal, with no other purchasers being involved. But when the business went to auction, they ended up paying £16 million. The purchaser had just pulled an IPO and was desperate to revamp the image of the business and keep their key managers busy.

3. Do beauty parades with corporate finance and lawyers. See at least three of each, preferably on the same day. Not only is time of the essence, you will remember their good and bad points better.

4. Find advisors the right size for your deal – no point in getting the best guys in town to sell a £20 million business. After they have sold you the deal, the partners will vanish and leave you with the office boys. Find a firm that specializes in your size of deal.

5. Everything to do with selling up is negotiable. The corporate finance advisors will want up-front payments and high results-related rewards. You can get everything done on contingency and pay a smaller percentage, the more the business is sold for.

6. Nail down everything with the corporate finance people and get your contract with them vetted by your legal advisors. Otherwise, clauses will slip through. For example, if there is a time clause, you could end up having to sell at a lower price or pay their bill in full when the 6-months search time is up.

7. During the due diligence process done by the acquirer, get every skeleton out of every cupboard. Otherwise, the warranties will come back to haunt you. You could be pursued years later to compensate for any liability not declared.

8. The corporate finance team bring experience, credibility and hopefully a couple of prospective buyers to the table. Two buyers makes for an auction, and auctions make for better prices.

9. Go through the 'term sheet', as the offer to buy document is called, very carefully, line-by-line. The price will only be the headline figure in a fairly complex document. That price may be dependent on customers and key staff remaining with the firm, or certain projects under development being completed on time and to cost.

10. Whatever the logic behind the offer price, multiple of sales, and so on, it is just a yardstick to make people feel comfortable. Price is just the figure people will pay at a given moment for a given business. If you have done an IPO, you will certainly know that.

11. Your share of the business is unlikely to be much, but it will be a lot less if you don't get good tax advice. Owners can end up paying between nothing and 51% tax on any gain (remember that the gain will be calculated on the price of the share options, which may have been granted at very favourable prices).

12. The price you agree to sell at will not be paid. The auction process pushes the price up, but the purchaser can win much of that back again, using two techniques. Once a deal is struck, the purchasers will have a period of exclusivity, during which they can carry out due diligence. As this is going to set them back hundreds of thousands of dollars, they insist that the company is offered to no-one else until that process is completed. They will ask for 8–12 weeks; you will seek to settle for 3 weeks. They will use every trick in the book to extend the exclusivity period – our CFO is on holiday, the board doesn't meet for 3 months, are usual ploys. The aim is to string the negotiations out long enough for any other prospective bidder to have lost interest in you and gone elsewhere. If they succeed, they have effectively destroyed the auction and turned it into a one-horse race.

   The second technique used to lower the offer price is the due diligence process. Here the purchasers seek to say that what you are selling is not quite what they thought they were

buying. The way round this is to have a rigorously prepared
sales memorandum, the document used to describe your
business to prospective purchasers. The more accurately this
reflects the realities of your business, the less room the buyers
have to wriggle on price. In any event, they will end up paying
10–20% less than the price you agreed, so you had better build
that into your thinking from the start.

13.   If you can break the business into parts, separating off, say, the
intellectual property, you may be able to wring some additional
value from the sale. Early entrants to the Internet business
may have interesting domain names that no longer reflect what
they do anyway. There are many examples of big money spent
to secure a name that is crucial to a business. In November 1999,
a California investment company called eCompanies purchased business.com for $7.5 million (£5 million) from Marc
Ostrofsky, a Houston businessman. Bank of America bought
loans.com for $3 million, and BrainwareMedia paid $8 million
for *www.mp3audiobooks.com* to a Boston resident. In the UK, the
owner of the domain name e-buy.com reputedly turned down
an offer of £4.4 million for that name. These figures make the
£¼ million or so paid for Boo.com's site software pale into
insignificance.

Starting all over Again   23

Now you've done it all. Started up, run it and got out. You may even have some real money, rather than all that quasi-cash you've been burning for years (months!). Whatever else, you have an invaluable asset. E-experience. Now the world is your oyster. You could start the same business again, using a different name, of course. It's fairly unlikely the restrictions placed on you by those buying your old firm will be enforceable anywhere, yet alone in your cyber-office domiciled in the Caribbean. Or you could take your old business model and adapt it to a new sector, following the Jim Clarke route to billions. You could start up in an E-incubators, or better still start an incubator yourself. Or if work sounds unappealing and you just want to keep your eye in, why not become an E-business angel? All these options of afterlife, and a few more besides, are explored. Here are some case examples of the afterlives of E-entrepreneurs.

Igabriel

Charlie Muirhead founded Orchestream.com in 1997. At 24 he raised $40 million in three rounds of financing from Deutsche Bank, Reuters, Atlas Ventures, Amadeus Capital Partners, Esther Dyson and Intel.

His company develops and licenses software to Internet service providers and corporate networks that lets administrators provision special service in real-time across an entire network. In 2000 he handed over the reins of the company to seasoned executives led by Ashley Ward, so that he could concentrate on his next venture.

At first glance, Charlie Muirhead's latest venture is a radical departure from his roots as a computer engineer jerry-rigging quality of service for the Internet. But Igabriel, a consortium of big-name international entrepreneurs and investors that will invest in start-ups, is a natural next step.

Launched this spring, Igabriel assembles well-known, seasoned businesspeople into a single social circle that can offer entrepreneurs something mere money can't buy: their collective experience and decades'-worth of business contacts. Mr Muirhead even speaks of the venture in the data-networking terms of his previous company. Like the Internet's underlying design, Igabriel's partners will use a 'best effort' approach to open doors for their start-ups. Among those who've signed on are pundit

Esther Dyson and John Taysom, who by day serves as the managing director of the Reuters Greenhouse Fund. The company will commercialize its own business ideas as well as fund the business plans of others.

In so doing, it will have to compete with the massive number of new European incubators and venture capitalists that have flooded the global tech market with money, raising the ante that established players must pay to play. Igabriel capitalizes on the partners' contacts, rather than on their cash.

One selling point is that Igabriel lets entrepreneurs avoid the 'cookie-cutter' approach for which some EcoNets are criticized. Whereas larger, public companies like CMGI and the Internet Capital Group (NASDAQ, CMGI, ICGE) must take a majority stake in their start-ups – to comply with a US securities law that bars publicly-traded companies from being mere investment vehicles – and often impose strategies and partnerships upon those firms, Mr Muirhead states that Igabriel will remain private, take smaller stakes and give entrepreneurs more independence.

itrustYou.com

Five years ago, E-preneur Simon Kirkpatrick was sitting on a desert island, contemplating retirement. A few years short of his 40th birthday, Kirkpatrick could afford to live it up a bit. He had made an undisclosed nest-egg from the acquisition of his IT communications company, Clarion Training, by a subsidiary of MCI WorldCom, and was contracted to 'rest' for a while from the industry which had made him.

Yet even the tropical glories of Tres Palmeras, a tiny oasis off the coast of Venezuela, was not enough to lure Kirkpatrick into happy idleness. 'I suppose a part of my trouble in life is that my brain is always coming up with new ideas', he says. 'Even when I was sitting on a desert island, I was still wondering why somebody hadn't done something I'd thought of'.

Instead, Kirkpatrick logged on to the Internet and started using the medium as a tool for his restless mind. The result is a website, itrustYou.com, with a concept that he predicts will help revolutionize E-commerce in less than a year. It's called 'escrow'. It's not a novel idea: in the USA, escrow is as 'common as coffee', says Kirkpatrick, but Europe is just waking up to its potential as E-commerce becomes a serious threat to high-street shopping.

Escrow works by introducing a third party into the transaction between buyer and seller. The commodity could be anything – a car, a Beanie Baby or a holiday. An escrow provider simply holds the payment for the item until the customer is completely satisfied with the goods. Only then is the money released. For satisfying both the customer and the seller, itrustYou.com gets 6% of the item's value.

Current forecasts suggest that, within two years, 10 per cent of all online auction-house transactions around the world will go through escrow. That means £50 billion-worth of person-to-person business. For an idea neatly summed up by one bystander as 'a frozen account, released after a series of trigger events', Kirkpatrick has hit the jackpot. He joins that elite band of E-preneurs who succeed simply by coming up with a concept that will never stretch the limits of the Internet. Its apparent beauty is that it solves the Internet safety puzzle: how to protect consumers from fraud or customer dissatisfaction when they are buying something they cannot see.

Some on-line auction houses have a dubious reputation. About 87% of recorded Internet fraud originates from them. But itrustYou.com gives auction houses, as well as any trader, a value-added safety valve in a burgeoning market. Both *Exchange & Mart*'s classified on-line site and European auction house eBay offer itrustYou.com's service exclusively to their customers.

Who Wants to Be a Venture Capitalist?

An example of an E-entrepreneur turned business angel is Josh Newman. Mr Newman is a 20 year-old Yale student who, in between studying for exams, assembled a $10 million venture fund called Paradigm Blue to invest in what he calls dorm-room start-ups.

Despite little experience, little in the way of industry contacts and not much of the poise that is typically associated with successful venture capitalists, Mr Newman believes that his career ambitions are perfectly reasonable. He asserts that the major VC firms, like Benchmark Capital and Kleiner, Perkins, Caulfield and Byers, are not combing the nation's campuses looking for the next big dot-com: 'That leaves the door wide open for someone like me'. Mr Newman's fund will invest exclusively in student-run businesses. It will also provide a host of value-added services, such as teaching young entrepreneurs how to juggle classes and a start-up schedule without flunking out. The Paradigm Blue fund will infuse young companies with anywhere from $200 000 to £450 000 apiece.

Mr Newman is a former entrepreneur who founded a database consulting company called Sharkbyte Technology Consulting in his freshman year at Yale. That kind of operational experience makes him far more credible to other entrepreneurs, as well as potential investors in his fund. Mr Newman raised about $6 million to invest in dot-com start-ups.

Redbus

Back in 1979, Cliff Stanford found accountancy too boring, so he started a software house in his boiler room in London's Finchley. In 1992, Stanford launched Demon Internet at a time when only 'techies' used the Internet. The business started with 200 customers, and his business plan projected up to 4000.

Within 6 years Demon had amassed 250 000 paying users, and Stanford sold out in 1998 to Scottish Telecom for £66 million. Stanford's share of this prize was £30 million – enough to retire on.

But Stanford was not the retiring type, and at 43 felt he had more to do. He worked out that £15 million would provide everything he was ever likely to need. This left him £15 million to invest in making his life interesting and full of new challenges. Stanford decided to become an 'adventure capitalist', backing high-tech businesses – but not necessarily dot-coms. Redbus was reversed into a small shell company with a London stock quote in March 2000. The issue price was 110 p and by June 2000 it had risen to 202 p, almost as much of a gain as the rest of the Internet economy was experiencing as a loss.

Redbus has invested £8.5 million in 10 companies. One of these is a 1.5% stake in 365 Corporation (whose case study is given in Chapter 7, p. 67).

References

Alberts, W.A. and Varaiya, N.P. (1989). Assessing the profitablity of growth by acquisition. *International Journal of Industrial Organization*, **7**, 133–149.

Anslinger, P.L. and Copeland, T.E. (1996). Growth through acquisitions: a fresh look. *Harvard Business Review*, **Jan-Feb**, 126–135.

Argenti, J. (1983). Predicting corporate failure. *Accountants' Digest*, **138**.

Asquith, P., Bruner, R. and Mullins, D. (1983). The gains to bidding firms from mergers. *Journal of Financial Economics*, **11**, 121–140.

Barnard, C. (1938). *The Functions of the Executive*. Harvard University Press: Cambridge, MA.

Barrow, C. (1995). *The Complete Small Business Guide*. BBC Consumer Publishing: London.

Barrow, C., Brown, R. and Clarke, C. (1997). Are entrepreneurs the real barrier to growth? Working Paper, Cranfield University School of Management, March.

Barrow, C. (1998a). The creation of value for shareholders: do mergers and acquisitions deliver? Working Paper, Cranfield University School of Management, October.

Barrow, C. (1998b). The barriers to growth that small and medium enterprises face. Working Paper, Cranfield University School of Management, November.

Barrow, C. (1998c). *The Essence of Small Business*. Prentice Hall Europe: Harlow.

Barrow, C. (1998d). *Financial Management for the Small Business*. Kogan Page: London.

Barrow, C. (1999). UK SME plc: a review of the financial performance of small firms in the United Kingdom, 1994–1999. Working Paper, Cranfield University School of Management, October.

Barrow, C. and Brown, R. (1997). *Principles of Small Business*. International Thomson Business Press: London.

Barrow, C. and Creagh, M. (1997). Taking people seriously: do European SMEs treat human resource management as a vital part of their competitive strategy? Working Paper, Cranfield University School of Management, November.

Barrow, C., Brown, R. and Barrow, P. (1998). *The Business Plan Workbook*. Kogan Page: London.

Barrow, C., Brown, R. and Clarke, E. (1995). *The Business Growth Handbook*. Kogan Page: London.

Barrow, C., Leleux, B., Paliard, R. and St-Cyr, L. (1999). Valuing high performance companies. Working Paper, Cranfield University School of Management, November.

Belbin, M. (1984). *Management Teams: Why They Succeed or Fail*. Butter-worth–Heinemann: Oxford.

Bradley, M., Desai, K. and Kim, E.H. (1988). Synergistic gains from corporate acquisitions and their division between the stockholders of target and acquiring firms. *Journal of Financial Economics*, **21**, 3–40.

Carper, W.B. (1990). Corporate acquisitions and shareholder wealth: a review and exploratory analysis. *Journal of Management*, **16**(4), 807–823.

Churchill, N.C. and Lewis, V.L. (1983). The five stages of small business growth. *Harvard Business Review*, **6**(3), 30–40.

Cotter, J.F., Shivdasani, A. and Zenner, M. (1997). Do independent directors enhance target shareholder wealth during tender offers? *Journal of Financial Economics*, **43**, 195–218.

Datta, D.K., Pinches, G.E. and Narayanan, V.K. (1992). Factors influencing wealth creation from mergers and acquisitions: a meta-analysis. *Strategic Management Journal*, **13**, 67–84.

Dodd, P. and Ruback, R. (1978). Tender offers and stockholder returns, an empirical analysis. *Journal of Financial Economics*, **5**, 351–374.

Drucker, P. (1954). *The Practice of Management*. Harper & Row: New York.

Eberling, H.W. and Doorley, T.L. (1983). A strategic approach to acquisitions. *Journal of Business Strategy*, **3**(3), 44–45.

Fayol, H. (1916). *Administration, Industrielle et Général* (first published in English as *General and Industrial Management*. Pitman: London, 1949).

Firth, M. (1980). Takeovers, shareholder returns and the theory of the firm. *Quarterly Journal of Economics*, **94**, 235–260.

Firth, M. (1979). The profitability of takeovers and mergers. *Economic Journal*, **89**, 316–328.

Follett, M.P. (1941). In Fox, Elliot, Urwick and Lyndall (eds), *Dynamic Administration*. Harper and Row: New York.

Franks, J. and Harris, R. (1989). Shareholder wealth effect of corporate takeovers: the UK experience, 1955–85. *Journal of Financial Economics*, **23**, 225–250.

Gibbs, P. (1997). European mergers of equals: ingredients for success. Morgan Guaranty Trust: New York.

Gould, M., Campbell, A. and Alexander, M. (1994). *Corporate Level Strategy*. Wiley: New York.

Gregory, D. and Westheider, O. (1992). The effect on shareholder wealth of German firms announcing acquisitions in the United States. Working Paper, University of Georgia, March.

Greiner, L.E. (1972). Evolution and revolution as organizations grow. *Harvard Business Review*, **50**(4), 37–44.

Halpern, P. (1973). Empirical estimates of the amount and distribution of gains to companies in mergers. *Journal of Business*, **66**, 554–575.

Halpern, P. (1983). Corporate acquisitions: a theory of special case? A review of event studies applied to acquisitions. *Journal of Finance*, **38**(2), 297–317.

Hertzberg, F. (with Mausner, B. and Snyderman, B.) (1959). *The Motivation to Work*. Wiley: New York.

Hogarty, T.F. (1970). Conglomerate mergers and acquisitions: operational analyses. *St John's Law Review*, **44**, 317–327.

Jarrell, G.A. and Poulsen, A.B. (1989). The returns to acquiring firms in tender offers: evidence from three decades. *Financial Management*, **18**, 12–19.

Jensen, M.C. and Ruback, R. (1983). The market for corporate control: the scientific evidence. *Journal of Financial Economics*, **11**, 5–50.

Kotler, P. (1994). *Marketing Management: Analysis, Planning, Implementation and Control*, 8th Edn. Prentice Hall: Englewood Cliffs, NJ.

Loderer, C. and Martin, K. (1990). Corporate acquisitions by listed firms: the experience of a comprehensive sample. *Financial Management*, **19** (Winter), 17–33.

Lubatkin, M. (1983). Mergers and the performance of the acquiring firm. *Academy of Management Review*, **8**, 215–218.

Malatesta, P.H. (1983). The wealth effect of merger activity and the objective functions of emerging firms. *Journal of Financial Economics*, **11**, 155–181.

Maslow, A. (1954). *Motivation and Personality*. Harper & Row: New York.

McGregor, D. (1960). *The Human Side of Enterprise*. McGraw-Hill: New York.

Mendelker, G. (1974). Risk and return. The case of merging firms. *Journal of Finance and Economics*, **1**, 303–335.

Modahl, M. (2000). *Now or Never*. Orion Business Books: London, p. xxiii.

Pettway, R.H., Sicherman, N.W. and Yamada, M. (1990). Japanese mergers: relative size corporate collectivism and shareholder wealth. In *Pacific Basin Capital Markets Research*, Vol. 1. Elsevier: Amsterdam, pp. 181–202.

Porter, M.E. (1987). From competitive advantage to corporate strategy. *Harvard Business Review*, **65**(3), 43–59.

Ravenscraft, D.J. and Scherer, F.M. (1989). The profitability of mergers. *International Journal of Industrial Organization*, **7**, 101–116.

Robinson, J. (2000). *Sunday Business*, London, 14 May, p. 15.

Roll, R. (1986). The hubris hypothesis of corporate takeovers. *Journal of Business*, **59**, 197–216.

Shaffer, S.T. (2000). *Red Herring*, San Francisco, **79** (June), 506.

Taylor, F.W. (1911). *The Principles of Scientific Management*. Harper & Row: New York.

Tellis, G.J. and Golder, P.N. (1996). First to market, first to fail? Real causes of enduring market leadership. *Sloan Management Review*, **37**(2, Winter), 65–76.

Weidenbaum, M.L. and Vogt, S. (1987). Takeovers and stockholders: winners and losers. *California Management Review*, **29**(4), 157–168.

Weidenbaum, M.L. and Vogt, S. (1988). Murray L. Weidenbaum and Stephen Vogt respond. *California Management Review*, **30**(3), 149–151.

Wilson, C.J. (2000). *Red Herring*, San Francisco, **78**(May), 82.

Index of Cases, Examples and Companies